JONATHAN WORDSWORTH

Ancestral Voices

Revolution and Romanticism
1789–1834

# JONATHAN WORDSWORTH

# Ancestral Voices

*Fifty books from the
Romantic period*

Woodstock Books
*London and New York*
1991

First published 1991 by
Woodstock Books
Spelsbury House, Spelsbury, Oxford OX7 3JR
and
Woodstock Books
Wordsworth Trust America
Department of English, City College
Convent Ave and 138th St, New York, N.Y. 10031

The three lines from *Esthetique du mal* by Wallace Stevens on page 7 are
quoted from *The collected poems of Wallace Stevens*, published in New York by
Alfred A. Knopf Inc and in London by Messrs Faber and Faber

British Library Cataloguing in Publication Data
Ancestral voices: fifty books from the romantic period.
  1. Europe
I. Wordsworth, Jonathan
808.80033
ISBN 1–85477–084–5

Library of Congress Cataloging-in-Publication Data
Ancestral voices: fifty books from the Romantic period / [edited by]
  Jonathan Wordsworth.
     p.   cm. – (Revolution and romanticism, 1789–1834)
  Includes bibliographical references (p.  ) and index.
  ISBN 1–85477–084–5 : $55.00
    1. Books and reading—Great Britain—History—19th century.
2. Books and reading—Great Britain—History—18th century.
3. Bibliography—Best books—Romanticism.  4. Romanticism—
—Bibliography.  I. Wordsworth, Jonathan.  II. Series.
Z1003.5.G7A54  1991
028′.9′0841——dc20      91–365 CIP

Typeset by Gloucester Typesetting Services
Printed and bound in Great Britain by
Smith Settle, Otley, West Yorkshire LS21 3JP

*

# Preface

The essays printed in this volume were written originally as introductions to Woodstock facsimiles in the 1988–9 and 1989–90 series of *Revolution and Romanticism, 1789–1834*. They have been revised, and in many cases considerably lengthened, to present a chronological survey of the Romantic period through a discussion of fifty outstanding books. *Ancestral voices* may be read cover to cover, browsed in at will, used as a reference-work, or read selectively through the index. Scholarly apparatus has been kept to a minimum. Page and line references are to Woodstock facsimiles (with the pagination of the original editions), and (except in the case of standard novels) to other original volumes and editions of the period. Letters, reviews and magazine articles, are identified by date. A small number of works and modern scholarly editions, identified in the text by abbreviations, are listed on pages xi–xii. I should like to record my gratitude to James Price for help of many kinds; not least, for making the index. Henry Wordsworth has word-processed and re-word-processed the many essays, doing a great deal of skilful copy-editing *en route*. I am grateful to Janice Patten for making me aware of the importance of Joanna Baillie, and to John Kerrigan, who first showed me the passage in her tragedy, *Monfort*, that is the literary source of Wordsworth's *There was a boy*.

J.W.

v

*Henrico —*
*filio caro, adiutori daedalo,*
*amico praecellenti*
*d.d.d. J.W.*

*

# Contents

# Contents

# Contents

# Contents

*

# Abbreviations

| | |
|---|---|
| *Autobiography* | Hunt, Leigh: *Autobiography*, 1850. References are to the 2-volume New York edition of 1903. |
| Blessington | Lovell, Ernest J., jr., ed.: *Lady Blessington's conversations of Lord Byron*, Princeton 1969. |
| Butler and Todd | Butler, Marilyn and Todd, Janet, eds.: *The works of Mary Wollstonecraft*, 7 vols, London 1989. |
| Chapman | Chapman, R. W., ed.: *Novels of Jane Austen*, 5 vols, Oxford 1923. |
| Howe | Howe, P. P., ed.: *The works of William Hazlitt*, 21 vols, London 1930–4. |
| *Lakes tour* | Gilpin, William: *Observations relative chiefly to picturesque beauty made in the year 1772 on several parts of England, especially the mountains and lakes*, London 1786. |
| Lockhart | Lockhart, J. G., ed.: *Poetical works of Sir Walter Scott, bart.*, 11 vols, Edinburgh 1833–4. |
| *Memoir* | Coleridge, Hartley: *Poems, with a memoir by his brother* [Derwent Coleridge], London 1851. |
| Morley | Morley, Edith J., ed.: *Henry Crabb Robinson on books and their writers*, London 1938. |
| Patton | Patton, Lewis, ed.: *Coleridge: The watchman*, Princeton and London 1970. |

## Abbreviations

Patton and Mann    Patton, Lewis and Mann, Peter, eds.: *Coleridge: Lectures 1795 on politics and religion*, Princeton and London 1971.

Prothero    Prothero, R. E., ed.: *The works of Lord Byron: letters and journals*, 6 vols, London 1898–1901.

*Recollections*    Clarke, Mary and Charles Cowden: *Recollections of writers*, London 1878.

Sandford    Sandford, M. E. P.: *Thomas Poole and his friends*, London 1888.

*Wye tour*    Gilpin, William: *Observations on the river Wye and several parts of south Wales &c relative chiefly to picturesque beauty made in the summer of the year 1770.* London 1782.

\*

## Introduction

It is the nature of Romanticism that its promptings are distinct, individual, at odds with the standards of the day. Like the ancestral voices that Kubla hears 'from far', they have the power to disquiet, belonging to a realm of consciousness that is unexplained and inexplicable. In Wordsworth's brilliantly careful phrasing, the Romantic imagination is

> a forming hand, at times
> Rebellious, acting in a devious mood,
> A local spirit of its own, at war
> With general tendency . . .

'An auxiliar light', he continues, exemplifying the workings of the power that is partly his to control, and partly not,

> Came from my mind, which on the setting sun
> Bestowed new splendour; the melodious birds,
> The gentle breezes, fountains that ran on
> Murmuring so sweetly in themselves, obeyed
> A like dominion, and the midnight storm
> Grew darker in the presence of my eye.
>                   (1799 *Prelude* ii, ll. 412–22)

If the major Augustans may be said to characterize their period, sharing to a large extent the values and assumptions of their audience, and receiving from the first due recognition, the Romantics bestride theirs, conferring the bounty of their perceptions upon an age that is not especially grateful.

To us Romantic dominance seems an established fact. At the time, it was not even a possibility. There were no Romantics. No one had heard of the word or the concept. *Lyrical ballads* (1798) was recognized by Hazlitt and De Quincey as a new voice in English poetry, but few

I

others noticed a change. As late as 1820, and the publication of Keats's *Lamia* and the Odes, the figures now commonly thought of as members of a Romantic movement were regarded as entirely disparate. Keats belonged to the Cockney School (meaning that he was a follower of Hunt), Wordsworth and Coleridge were Lakers (a term of abuse used first by Jeffrey in the *Edinburgh*), Shelley was little known, Blake unheard of, Byron a law unto himself. Nor, of course, would the major Romantics have regarded themselves as a group. Apart from wide differences over the style and subject-matter of poetry, they belonged to different social classes. Byron was a peer of the realm, and haughty with it. Shelley was a fellow aristocrat, the elder son of a Whig baronet with important political connections. Though not very eligible by the standards of her heroines, Wordsworth and Coleridge would have been accepted by Jane Austen as gentlemen. Keats would not. Blake was a true cockney, the son of a London haberdasher. To understand what the age was really like we have to ask, not only what the Romantics do and do not have in common, but what is their relation to contemporaries who were often more successful (had more readers), and who must therefore in a sense be more representative.

To see a period in terms of its books – books that made an impact at the time – is to become aware of trends, values, achievements, interconnections and disparities, that are normally obscured. Literary history smoothes things out, dealing typically in authors and movements, not individual books. Literary scholarship breaks up the separate volumes that created a writer's reputation, merging their content into conveniently arranged modern editions (often with an indiscriminate printing of late texts under early dates). The fifty books discussed below cover the half century that we have come to think of as the Romantic period, beginning a little before the French Revolution of 1789, and ending just after the English Reform Bill (in which nothing like enough was reformed) of 1832. Many of the books discussed are not Romantic in any sense of the word, but all contribute to a fuller awareness of the age as it was. First comes Thomas West's *Guide to the lakes*, the book that taught Wordsworth at Hawkshead Grammar School in the 1780s how to see the landscape that was to be central to his poetry. Last is the *Poems* of Hartley Coleridge, poet son of poet father, in whose tones of wistful sadness we hear the beginnings of the Victorian era. Every book is regarded as having its own integrity and special qualities – qualities present from the first, not those emphasized or detected by succeeding generations.

The Revolution, which seems in more or less definable ways to prompt all the great Romantics, acts most obviously as a stimulus to the 1790s. There is an extraordinary concentration of impressive books: political books, chiefly, in the first half of the decade, centring on reaction to Burke's *Reflections on the Revolution in France* (November 1790); literary ones in the second half, as the energies released by political discussion find new form in the work of Southey, Coleridge, Wordsworth, and numerous minor writers. Events in the first ten years of the new century provide no comparable stimulus: threats of invasion in 1798 and 1803 make it almost impossible to hold a pro-French position, and radical thinking is still too closely bound up with the Revolution to thrive on its own. The end of the French War, however – first in April 1814, then (after Napoleon's escape from Elba) at Waterloo in June 1815 – is the prelude to another decade of astonishing books. Wordsworth and Coleridge publish major collections (*Poems* 1815, *Sibylline leaves* 1817); the second-generation Romantic poets come into their own (though only Byron is recognized at the time), then die in succession at the height of their powers – Keats from tuberculosis in 1822, Shelley by drowning in 1823, Byron from malaria and excessive bleeding in 1825.

To the minor poet, Helen Maria Williams, author of *Letters written in France* (1790), the Revolution was 'the triumph of human kind . . . man asserting the noblest privileges of his nature'. Witnessing the Fête de la Fédération in Paris on 14 July 1790, she wrote, 'it required but the common feelings of humanity to become in that moment a citizen of the world' (p. 14). In a more detached way, the Revolution had at first been welcomed in England too. *Letters written in France*, however, makes it clear that opinion had swung against the French before Burke came into print in November with his alarmist talk of 'plots, massacres, assassinations'. 'I am told', Williams writes on her return from Paris the previous month,

that every day witnesses a conspiracy; that every town is the scene of a massacre; that every street is blackened with a gallows, and every highway deluged with blood. (p. 217)

Not content with *Reflections*, Burke spent Christmas 1790 composing

3

a second violent attack on revolutionary France. *Letter to a member of the National Assembly* was none the less influential for descending to a level of crazy obsession. French policy, we are told, is decided by 'litigious attornies and Jew brokers, and set in action by shameless women of the lowest condition, by keepers of hotels, taverns, and brothels' (p. 3). Rousseau is now the focus of Burke's attack. Not the *Social contract*, as one might expect, but *Eloisa* (*La nouvelle Héloïse*), with its deep and abiding passion, and profoundly moral example of the good life. The 'false sympathies' of *Eloisa*, Burke would have his readers believe, have been used by the Assembly 'to subvert those principles of domestic trust and fidelity, which form the discipline of social life'.

Of the many replies to Burke – all written before Robespierre and the Terror gave to his denunciations an air of prophecy – Mackintosh's *Vindiciae gallicae* is at once the most cogently argued and best informed. Events in France have been 'malignantly and systematically exaggerated' (p. 170); Burke's commentary on the English Revolution of 1688 shows 'the heroism of paradox' (p. 302), his belief in tradition is nonsensical:

It is not because we *have* been free, but because we have a right to be free, that we ought to demand freedom. Justice and liberty have neither birth nor race, youth nor age. (p. 306)

Though its humanitarianism is entirely genuine, *Vindiciae gallicae* seems a little abstract beside Dyer's *Complaints of the poor people of England* (1793). Mackintosh respects the poor, defends their rights, wishes them to have proper representation: Dyer knows how they live, what they are paid, what they suffer. The son of a Thames boatman, he has bettered himself through education (as a charity-boy at Christ's Hospital), and education is the political remedy he proposes. The poor 'have no time for the improvement of mind'; an enlightened policy would lessen their number 'by putting them into the condition of raising themselves' (p. 163). It was very much the policy advocated in France by the Girondins, 'the twenty-two' as Citeness Roland calls them in her *Appeal to impartial posterity* (1795). Writing in prison in the months that led up to her execution on 8 November 1793, Roland offers a shrewd and moving account of idealism giving way to ruthless (though not entirely unprincipled) ambition. 'That Robespierre', she writes when Brissot and her husband are falsely accused early in October, 'whom

4

once I thought an honest man, is a very atrocious being. How he lies to his own conscience! How he delights in blood!' (i. p. 181). While establishing his power, and seemingly working for the same ends as the Girondins, Robespierre had many times eaten at her table.

Idealism in England did not go to the guillotine. The Terror and later French imperialism led to some dramatic recantations (Mackintosh's being the most famous), but radicals for the most part moved quietly out of politics. Citizen Thelwall, bravest and most effective of the London Corresponding Society's orators, retreated to a farm in Wales, published *Poems chiefly written in retirement* (1801), and found a new career as elocutionist. Coleridge, despite his fervent political lecturing of 1795, and his *Poems on various subjects* (1796), took to denying that he had ever been a jacobin. Few were publicly confronted with the past, but Southey was unlucky. As the radical author of *Poems* (1797), he had been attacked again and again by tory parodists in *The Anti-jacobin*. As the Poet Laureate of 1817, and a tory himself, he was unable to prevent his undergraduate play, *Wat Tyler*, from being pirated by radical publishers. The post-war scene was in many ways parallel to that in 1794 when the play had been composed. Once again Habeas corpus had been suspended, bread prices were high, there was political unrest and talk of an English revolution. Working-class movements, effectively suppressed by Pitt with the Two Bills of 1795, were reappearing to counter the introduction of new machinery and loss of jobs. Southey's play, described in the House of Commons as 'the most seditious book ever written', was perfectly in tune:

> Ye are all equal; nature made ye so.
> Equality is your birth-right . . .
>                    (p. 31)

Two years later would come the Massacre of Peterloo, when a peaceful meeting, organized in St Peter's Fields, Manchester, to demand employment and suffrage, was broken up by mounted troops. A child was trodden to death, ten more people were killed and five to six hundred wounded. In the most powerful and statesmanlike of Romantic political poems, *The masque of anarchy* (written 1819, published 1832), Shelley greeted the event with a call for passive resistance:

> Rise, like lions after slumber,
> In unvanquishable number,

> Shake your chains to earth like dew,
> Which in sleep had fall'n on you . . .
>
> And if then the tyrants dare,
> Let them ride among you there;
> Slash, and stab, and maim, and hew;
> What they like, that let them do.
>
> (sts. xxxviii, lxxxiv)

As a nineteen-year-old, Shelley had expressed magnificent indignation in *Queen Mab* (1813), but the poetry had existed on rather a lofty plane. For all its allegoric form, *The masque* has a practical message. Not even Hazlitt, great commentator on his time in *Political essays* (1819) as in *The spirit of the age* (1825), seems to have understood as Shelley came to do the strength of an 'unvanquishable number'. Perhaps he was too much a fighter himself to conceive of victory through passivity. 'I have', he wrote,

a hatred of tyranny, and a contempt for its tools; and this feeling I have expressed as often and as strongly as I could. I cannot sit down quietly under the claims of bare-faced power. (*Political essays*, p. vii)

With the failure of the Revolution and its exalted hopes for mankind, it was easier to denounce 'bare-faced power' than to define a viable alternative. By Hazlitt's day the attempt to do so had almost ceased. Earlier there had been many and various utopian schemes. Appearing in February 1793, just after the execution of Louis XVI and the French declaration of war, Godwin's *Political justice* offered a vision of human happiness depending on man's innate rationality. Three years later, after the breakdown of his scheme to found a commune of twelve men and twelve women on the banks of the Susquehanna, Coleridge countered with *Religious musings* (*Poems*, 1796), the Unitarian opposite to Godwinian rationalism. Less philosophically inclined, Helen Maria Williams found comfort in prison during the Terror making a translation of Bernardin de St-Pierre's *Paul and Virginia*, an idyll of childhood and innocent love, set in the far-away island of Mauritius. It was the sense of idealism betrayed, and irreplaceable, that gave a special fascination at this period to Schiller's *Robbers* (translated 1792). Pure as are his motives, sublime as are his final acts, Charles de Moor has nothing to put in the place of the order against which he rebels. As the play ends we are roused by the grandeur of the human spirit, but forced in the same moment to confront its impotence.

Faced by this emptiness in its extreme form – the cause lost, her friends dead or condemned – Citizeness Roland, before her execution, addresses the 'supreme being, soul of the universe'. No drama has a more impressive denouement, no statement of faith is more brave, honest and intelligent:

thou in whose existence I believe, because I must needs emanate from something better than what I see around me, I am about to be reunited with thy essence! (ii. p. 113)

In her beautifully measured and dignified utterance, Roland takes us close to the spirit of Romanticism. Hers (to quote Wallace Stevens despite the gap of 150 years), is

> the yes of the realist spoken because he must
> Say yes, spoken because under every no
> Lay a passion for yes that had never been broken.
> (*Esthetique du mal*, pt. viii)

*for Blake .*

The Romantic impulse seems very often to be a 'passion for yes' in the face of an overwhelming no – a quest for the 'something better' that is guaranteed, not by a stable, comforting, all-embracing system, but by the presence of good (or power, or potential) within the self.

Working in a world that is almost entirely private – or perhaps one should say, refracting the public world in a uniquely personal way – Blake writes powerful Romantic poems throughout the 1790s. Perhaps it is significant that his one failure is the quasi-historical *French revolution* (1790). The authentic voice of Romanticism, though prompted at this moment by political disappointment, requires a distancing from events, a generating in tranquility of imaginative resources. Despite the Terror, and later discouragements (French wars of conquest after Robespierre's death in July 1794, refusal of peace offers in spring 1796), France persists as an ideal among British radicals for a surprisingly long time. It is notable that Wordsworth and Coleridge write their first great poetry in 1797–8, the period of *Lyrical ballads* and of the final blow to political hope, the French invasion of republican Switzerland (March 1798). No doubt there were other factors in their coming of age, but energies that have been given to politics (and to political poetry that never achieved the highest imaginative levels) are now suddenly freed. Their work may still, on occasion, take account of social conditions, but it is the product of untrammeled imagination.

# Introduction

Literary history seldom has time for the individual book. Those that are given prominence are almost inevitably given too much, seen in a blaze of hindsight that distorts their relation to the period at which they were written. On its appearance in September 1798, *Lyrical ballads* was not the many-times-reprinted book that we know. It was an anonymous volume of powerful but eccentric poems, written by an author (no reviewer deduced that the work was a collaboration) whose views on poetry were somewhat jacobinical, and who understandably wished to conceal his name. Published in the previous month, Coleridge's *Fears in solitude* quarto (containing *France, an ode*, as well as the original version of *Frost at midnight*) has been almost completely ignored; yet for an understanding of the period, it too is of immense importance. It is well known that *Frost at midnight* inspired the writing of *Tintern abbey*, but few critics have sought out the text that Wordsworth actually knew – a text in which Coleridge's musing over the 'stranger' on the grate at Nether Stowey is ascribed, not to egotism or fancy, but to a vital, imaginative, Wordsworthian, 'living spirit in our frame / That loves not to behold a lifeless thing' (ll. 21–2).

1798 was, as it happens, a remarkable year for new publications. Before the appearance of the *Fears in solitude* volume and *Lyrical ballads*, different aspects of Romanticism had been revealed by Monk Lewis's gothic play, *The castle spectre* (later a source for *Frankenstein*), Godwin's *Memoirs of the author of A vindication of the rights of woman*, Joanna Baillie's *Series of plays* (an influence both on the prose Advertisement to *Lyrical ballads*, and on Wordsworth's *There was a boy*). To the same year belong Plumptre's *Lakers*, Lloyd's *Edmund Oliver* (with its sidelights on Coleridge), and the Inchbald translation of Kotzebue's *Lovers' vows* (to be the focal point of *Mansfield Park*). Aside from the question of links and influences, context is interesting in itself: *The castle spectre* is the outstanding success at a time when Wordsworth and Coleridge have just had plays turned down by Covent Garden; *The lakers* emerges as a satire of Gilpin and the picturesque in the year of *Tintern abbey* and Wordsworth's most subtle exploring of modes of perception.

No critic or historian would think to group such books, but for the reader of 1798 they were what was coming out – what people were talking about. They have the connectiveness of the moment. Of special interest are the unexplained similarities that seem to show the spirit of the age at work. In January 1798 Godwin wrote of Wollstonecraft (of whose religious intuitions he disapproved) in terms that to an extra-ordinary degree anticipate *Tintern abbey* and the original text of *Frost at midnight*:

> She found an inexpressible delight in the beauties of nature, and in the splendid reveries of the imagination. But nature itself, she thought, would be no better than a vast blank, if the mind of the observer did not supply it with an animating soul. When she walked amidst the wonders of nature, she was accustomed to converse with her God. (pp. 33–4)

With a change of pronoun, Godwin's comments on his wife might be taken for an account of Wordsworth. Living through the same hopes and disappointments, Wollstonecraft and Wordsworth had perhaps more in common than has been supposed. Each, it seems, moved from early work rooted in the thinking of the day (*Original stories*, 1787; *An evening walk*, 1793), through a phase of political idealism occasioned by the Revolution, into a Romantic valuing of imagination, nature and God. It is a pattern that must have been followed by many lesser figures of the 1790s. *Tintern abbey* came to be the central Romantic poem, not for its personal Wordsworthian associations, but because it gave form to instincts and aspirations that readers recognized as their own.

If there is a year that is as important to the second-generation Romantics as 1798 is to the first, it is probably 1817. *Wat Tyler* acts (against the wishes of the author) as a reminder of the revolutionary period and the political values that underlie Romanticism. *Sibylline leaves* brings together poetry that Coleridge had scattered in newspapers and inaccessible volumes, making available his prophetic message for the first time in twenty years. The Shelleys' anonymous *History of a six weeks' tour* is Mary's first venture into print, as well as the first publication of *Mont Blanc*. As important, it provides in Shelley's two Geneva letters an account of his and Byron's companionship on the Lake in the summer of 1816. Shelley reads Rousseau's *Eloisa* (apparently in French), writes his letters, and 'doses' Byron with Wordsworth; Byron works on the Wordsworthian third canto of *Childe Harold*; together they experience near shipwreck and the camaraderie of danger. To complete the pattern of 1817 publication, there is Keats's first volume of poems, with *I stood tiptoe* and *Sleep and poetry* and the great sonnet, *On first looking into Chapman's Homer*.

Taking stock of the literary scene in *The feast of the poets* (1814), Leigh Hunt had summoned to the table of Apollo, Southey (Poet

Laureate), Scott (best-seller), Moore and Campbell (Regency success-stories), grudgingly conceding in his notes the importance of Words-worth, but refusing to see lasting quality in Byron's popular eastern tales. Three years later it would have been still harder to send out the invitations. Apollo's four original guests might all have been unseated. With the 1815 *Poems* in print, Wordsworth could not have been denied a place. Coleridge's claims were suddenly evident. The great Byron of *Don Juan*, *Sardanapalus* and *Cain* (1819), was still to come, but his slim *Poems* 1816 offered both the lyricism of 'There be none of Beauty's daughters' and the defiant grandeur of *Napoleon's farewell*:

> Farewell to the Land, where the gloom of my Glory
> Arose and o'ershadowed the earth with her name –
> She abandons me now, – but the page of her story,
> The brightest or blackest, is filled with my fame.
>
> (ll. 1–4)

*Mont Blanc*, meanwhile, might be introduced in the *Six weeks' tour* as 'an undisciplined overflowing of the Soul', but was nonetheless Shelley's first indisputably great poem. And Keats, though still in the spring of 1817 a medical student at Guy's Hospital, had written already the numinous lines on 'looking into' Homer:

> Then felt I like some watcher of the skies
>     When a new planet swims into his ken;
> Or like stout Cortez when with eagle eye
>     He star'd at the Pacific – and all his men
> Look'd at each other with a wild surmise –
>     Silent, upon a peak in Darien.
>
> (ll. 9–14)

We associate the 'wild surmise' of Keats with a special kind of truth – a truth that cannot be other than 'wild' because it catches the sudden expansion of an imaginative thought. Tame it down, render it actuality rather than 'surmise', and it becomes, like the rainbow in *Lamia* (1820), an item 'In the dull catalogue of common things' (ii, 233). But how is truth to be defined and evaluated when it has parted company with fact? Is William Gilbert's inspired, though crazy, *Hurricane*, which sold a handful of copies in 1796, to be regarded as of greater importance than Samuel Rogers's *Pleasures of memory* (1792), which has few claims to imagination, but went through eleven editions by 1800? Is it comforting, or disconcerting, to find alongside Blake's profound comments on his art in the *Descriptive catalogue* (1809) a discussion of the 'minute articulation' of spirits with whom he has talked:

A Spirit and a Vision are not, as the modern philosophy supposes, a cloudy vapour or a nothing: they are organized and minutely articulated beyond all that the mortal and perishing nature can produce. (p. 37)

When Wordsworth tells Crabb Robinson that 'by the imagination the mere fact is exhibited as connected with that infinity without which there is no poetry' (Morley i, p. 191), we feel that we know what he means. Infinity is out there, a state of being (whether transcendental, or not) above and beyond the self. Dealing in the aspiring human mind, Romantic poetry reaches out towards it – whatever it may be. When Blake shows a personal knowledge of the infinite, we are less at ease. Imaginative truth, in which we participate as an act of faith (a more than willing suspension of disbelief), has slid uncomfortably into delusion. In order to trust Blake as author of the *Songs of experience*, we find ourselves treating as myth the spirit-world which to him was fact.

Keats's vision has its ambiguities, but is far closer to our own. Returning from a flight of imagination into the world of the Nightingale ('Already with thee; tender is the night . . .'), the poet asks memorably, 'Was it a vision, or a waking-dream?' (truth, or fantasy). Again the question seems to be, how come that this departure from actuality is not felt to be delusion? What kind of truth can it represent? *Ode on a Grecian urn* offers an equation of truth with beauty, but does so in a context in which the Urn, with its 'brede of marble men', seems a 'Cold Pastoral', a denial of life: 'Bold Lover, never, never canst thou kiss, / Though winning near the goal' (ll. 17–18). Art (in the shape of the Urn, or the timeless sound of the Nightingale's song) offers a vision in which truth and beauty are enshrined as permanence. Life offers them as validated by mortality:

> Now more than ever seems it rich to die,
> To cease upon the midnight with no pain,
> > While thou art pouring forth thy soul abroad
> > In such an ecstasy!
> > > (*Nightingale*, 55–8)

In the acceptance of death the poet achieves the fulness of life, thereby (paradoxically) conferring permanence upon his art.

If Keats's 1820 volume is the high-point of second-generation

# Introduction

Romantic poetry, De Quincey's *Confessions of an English opium-eater* (1822) is no less remarkable for the passionate intensity of its prose. Vision in his case begins with the horrors of the opium-dream:

> I was stared at, hooted at, grinned at, chattered at . . . I was buried, for a thousand years, in stone coffins, with mummies and sphinxes, in narrow chambers at the heart of eternal pyramids. I was kissed, with cancerous kisses, by crocodiles . . . (p. 170)

Emerging (at least temporarily) from his years of horror, De Quincey is able to draw from his experience unique intuitions into the mind and its workings:

> Of this, at least, I feel assured, that there is no such thing as *forgetting* possible to the mind; a thousand accidents may, and will interpose a veil between our present consciousness and the secret inscriptions on the mind; accidents of the same sort will also rend away this veil; but alike, whether veiled or unveiled, the inscription remains for ever . . . (p. 160)

For De Quincey, as for Wordsworth, childhood is the source of understanding; continuities are all-important. Like his fellow opium-eater, Coleridge, he has read the unpublished *Prelude* (in manuscript till Wordsworth's death in 1850), but he is far from being merely a disciple.

In his fragmentary *Suspiria de profundis*, written in the 1840s, De Quincey takes the spirit of Romanticism on into a new age. Events had been gathering fast, however, even at the time of *Confessions*. That Hazlitt should receive the news of Byron's death at Missolonghi while writing *The spirit of the age* (1825) has a sad appropriateness. Keats had died in 1822, Shelley, a year later. Wordsworth was spent. Of his fallen idol, Coleridge, Hazlitt comments with ungenerous accuracy: 'All that he has done of moment, he had done twenty years ago: since then, he may be said to have lived on the sound of his own voice' (p. 64). It was time for an assessment. The sound of Hazlitt's own voice comes through all the time as he writes, speaking an impeccable prose, balanced in its cadence and astonishingly often right in its judgments. Wordsworth's genius, we are told, is 'a pure emanation of the Spirit of the Age.' 'Had he lived', Hazlitt continues (in words that are less often quoted), 'in any other period of the world, he would never have been heard of' (p. 231). Though he does not see it as such, Hazlitt is uniquely sensitive to the Romantic impulse. Wordsworth 'sees nothing loftier than human hopes; nothing deeper than the human heart' (pp. 231–2). His poetry

partakes of, and is carried along with, the revolutionary movement of [the] age: the political changes of the day were the model on which he formed and con-ducted his poetical experiments. (p. 233)

Five years after *The spirit of the age* Hazlitt himself was dead, and Tennyson's first major volume, *Poems chiefly lyrical*, was in print. The old order was giving place to the new. Scott died in 1832. In the same year Hunt finally thought it safe to publish Shelley's *Masque of anarchy*, and the whigs carried through their prudent Reform Bill. Browning's *Pauline* and Hartley's Coleridge's sad *Poems* ('For I have lost the race I never ran') appeared in '33. Next year came the deaths of both Hartley's father and Lamb. Moved to great poetry for the very last time, Words-worth was conscious of marking in his *Extempore effusion* the end of an era. It is the death of Hogg, the Ettrick Shepherd, that sets him writing in November 1835, but he mourns the friends, hopes, values of a life-time:

> The mighty Minstrel breathes no longer,
> 'Mid mouldering ruins low he lies;
> And death upon the braes of Yarrow,
> Has closed the Shepherd-poet's eyes:
>
> Nor has the rolling year twice measured,
> From sign to sign, its steadfast course,
> Since every mortal power of Coleridge
> Was frozen at its marvellous source;
>
> The rapt One, of the godlike forehead,
> The heaven-eyed creature sleeps in earth:
> And Lamb, the frolic and the gentle,
> Has vanished from his lonely hearth.
>
> Like clouds that rake the mountain-summits,
> Or waves that own no curbing hand,
> How fast has brother followed brother,
> From sunshine to the sunless land!

# THOMAS WEST

---

# A guide to the lakes
### in Cumberland, Westmorland and Lancashire
### 1784 (1778)

'My morning walks were early', Wordsworth writes of his days at
Hawkshead Grammar School, by Esthwaite Water,

> oft before the hours of school,
> I travelled round our little lake, five miles
> Of pleasant wandering . . .
> > among the hills I sate
> Alone upon some jutting eminence
> At the first hour of morning, when the vale
> Lay quiet in an utter solitude.
> > (1799 *Prelude* ii, ll. 378–81, 391–4)

Even if we do not know that the lines are from *The Prelude*, the value
they set on quietness and solitude places them as Romantic poetry.
They declare themselves as the preface to imaginative experience:

> Oft in those moments such a holy calm
> Did overspread my soul that I forgot
> The agency of sight, and what I saw
> Appeared like something in myself, a dream,
> A prospect in my mind.
> > (1799 *Prelude* ii, ll. 396–401)

Thomas West would not have understood. He was a connoisseur of
natural beauty, but in an earlier mode. No one (except perhaps his
younger contemporary, William Gilpin) had thought more deeply
about 'prospects', but they were not of the mind. West's great contribution was to seek out and describe the 'stations' (viewpoints) from which
a prospect of the different lakes might be 'taken' to best advantage. His
readers are told in detail what to see, and where to go to do it. Eight

'stations' are selected on Derwentwater, five on Windermere, four on Coniston, four on Bassenthwaite; others on the minor lakes are less formally described. Coniston, Station III:

After crossing the common, where grows a picturesque yew tree on the right hand, and a small peninsula rushes into the lake on the left, crowned with a single tree, enter the grove and pass a gate and bridge that crosses a small rivulet. – Look for a fragment of dark coloured rock on the margin of the water, and near it will be found the best stand for the artist to take the finest view . . . (p. 50)

It is all very matter-of-fact. Yet Wordsworth read West's *Guide to the lakes* as a boy at Hawkshead; as an undergraduate he borrowed from it in his first major publication, the picturesque *Evening walk* (1793); as an established writer he composed a sequel, in his own *Description of the scenery of the lakes* (1822). West was immensely influential. No other work tells us as much about how landscape was viewed at the outset of the Romantic period. A year after the appearance of his book in 1778, West himself died. The *Guide* was taken over by William Cockin, a Kendal schoolmaster, who added an appendix of ten separate items (eleven, in the revised third edition of 1784). Included are Brown's *Description of the vale and lake of Keswick*, the *Journal* of Gray's 1769 tour, and poetry by Dalton and Cumberland. The *Guide* thus becomes a compendium of writing about the Lakes in the early period of the Picturesque, before Gilpin emerged into print with his *Tours of The Wye* (1782) and *Mountains and lakes of Cumberland and Westmoreland* (1786). Pride of place among the appended items is given to Brown's *Description*, issued as a pamphlet in 1767, but written in the form of a letter to Lord Lyttelton as early as 1753. Like Gilpin, whom he knew well, Brown was a Cumbrian, whose eye had been trained by mountain scenery, but who nevertheless thought of landscape in terms of painting. Of Derwentwater he writes memorably, 'The full perfection'

consists of three circumstances, *beauty, horror,* and *immensity* . . . to give you a complete idea of these three perfections . . . would require the united powers of *Claude, Salvator* [*Rosa*] and [*Gaspard*] *Poussin.* The first should throw his delicate sunshine over the cultivated vales, the scattered cots, the groves, the lake, and wooded islands. The second should dash out the horror of the rugged cliffs, the steeps, the hanging woods, and foaming waterfalls; while the grand pencil of *Poussin* should crown the whole with the majesty of the impending mountains. (pp. 192–3)

The three great Continental seventeenth-century landscape-painters (whose work had been the inspiration of British artists in Rome since the 1740s) are invoked to confer status upon native English scenery. It is taken for granted that Nature is picturesque, and that travellers (whether or not they are equipped with Claude-glasses) will wish to form what they see into pictures. Similarly, West's readers are directed, not to the spot where they will gain most immediate pleasure, but to 'the best stand for the artist to take the finest view'. Many professional draughtsmen did indeed 'take' the views from his convenient stations, but the artists whom West was chiefly addressing were summer visitors, young ladies especially, who had had drawing lessons, and whose pencils were their cameras. Even as a boy, we are led to believe, Wordsworth had been more inward. In moments of exceptional responsiveness he had felt a blurring of inner and outer, experienced the landscape before him as a creation of the inner eye 'Which is the bliss of solitude'. Yet he too (as we know from *Tintern abbey*) was a storer-up of particular views. He didn't paint or draw, but as a young man, under the influence of West, he could write in the Alps:

Ten thousand times in the course of this tour have I regretted the inability of my memory to retain a more strong impression of the beautiful forms before me, and again and again in quitting a fortunate station have I returned to it with the most eager avidity, with the hope of bearing away a more lively picture.

'At this moment', he continues,

when many of these landscapes are floating before my mind, I feel a high [enjoyment] in reflecting that perhaps scarce a day of my life will pass [in] which I shall not derive some happiness from these images. (14 September 1790)

It was only gradually that Wordsworth came to value the transforming power of imagination above the memory's ability to retain unchanged 'the picture of the mind'. When he did so, he explained the process to himself in terms that form an extension of West's picturesque observation of detail. Under the heading of '*accidental* beauties', West had noted that though 'the ruling tints' of landscape are permanent,

the green and gold of the meadow and vale, and the brown and purple of the mountain, the silver grey of the rock, and the azure hue of the cloud-topt pike, are frequently varied in appearance, by an intermixture of reflection from wandering clouds, or other bodies, or a sudden stream of sunshine that harmonizes all the parts anew. (p. 11)

At the time of *Lyrical ballads*, Coleridge records in 1817, he and Wordsworth perceived an analogy between the human imagination and 'The sudden charm which accidents of light and shade, which moonlight or sunset, diffused over a known and familiar landscape' (*Biographia literaria* ii, p. 1). West was a man of his time. He crossed no borders. Yet as the predecessor of Romantic attitudes and responses he enables us to define more sharply the new ways of thinking.

It was chiefly Gray's *Journal* (published by Mason in 1775, and third among Cockin's appendices) that brought the tourists to the Lake District, making Londoners and southerners aware of the beauties, horrors and immensities, to be found in the distant north. Gray took the horrors very seriously. Few would now hush their voices walking beneath a lake-district crag for fear of starting an avalanche, or see at Lodore rocks 'deep-cloven perpendicularly by the rains, hanging loose and nodding forwards . . . just starting from their base in shivers' (p. 202). Correspondingly, he found the beauties reassuring. Grasmere impressed him especially:

The bosom of the mountains spreading here into a broad bason discovers in the midst *Grasmere Water* . . . from the shore, a low promontory pushes itself far into the water, and on it stands a white village with the parish church rising in the midst of it . . . Not a single red tile, no gentleman's flaring house, or garden walls, break in upon the repose of this little unsuspected paradise. (p. 209)

It was Gray who decided Cockin's choice of Grasmere as his frontis-piece. And almost certainly it was the *Guide* that drew Wordsworth the schoolboy to his sighting of the promised land where one day he would live: 'Once on the brow of yonder hill I stopped', he recalls in the open lines of *Home at Grasmere*:

> At sight of this seclusion, I forgot
> My haste – for hasty had my footsteps been,
> As boyish my pursuits – and sighing said,
> 'What happy fortune were it here to live,
> And (if a thought of dying, if a thought
> Of mortal separation could come in
> With paradise before me) here to die!'
> (ll. 6–12)

The opening up of the Lakes was a rapid process, and sometimes took forms that would startle the twentieth century. On Ullswater in the 1770s – the time of Wordsworth's moonlight row in the stolen shep-herd's boat – vessels were kept by the Duke of Portland 'provided with six brass cannon, mounted on swivels' for the purpose of stirring the mountain-echoes. There were regattas, mock-battles, new and stylish buildings. Cockin takes leave in a footnote not merely to disagree with West's censure of building on the islands of Windermere, but to suggest 'a bridge from shore to shore', and even a city. Windermere 'might then become a rival to the celebrated lake of Geneva' (p. 61). By the end of the century West's *Guide* had gone through seven editions, and Wordsworth (in the guise of the vicar of one of the remotest parishes in the district) could open a poem, 'These tourists, Heaven preserve us!' Yet the paradisal quality remained. In December 1799 Wordsworth and his sister Dorothy returned to live permanently in the Lakes, soon to be followed by Coleridge and Southey. In his review of Southey's *Thalaba* Jeffrey would lump the three poets together, deriding their work and their perceived faults (poetic and political jacobinism) under the heading of 'the Lake School'. In truth connections between the Lake District and Romanticism in its first generation went far deeper. To Wordsworth in 1800 it seemed that Gray's 'little unsuspected paradise' of Grasmere could offer a whole new way of life to those who had eyes to see and love to give:

> Beauty, whose living home is the green earth . . .
> Pitches her tents before me as I move,
> My hourly neighbour. Paradise and groves
> Elysian, blessed islands in the deep,
> Of choice seclusion – wherefore need they be
> A history, or but a dream, when minds
> Once wedded to this outward frame of things
> In love, find these the growth of common day.
> (Prospectus to *The recluse*, ll. 30–40)

2

# WILLIAM CROWE

# Lewesdon hill
## 1788


Recommending *Lewesdon Hill* to his readers, with a snappy Latin tag
('Quod qui non legit, legat, Qui legit, relegat'), Coleridge in *The
watchman* for 2 April 1796 quotes in full an address written by Crowe
as Public Orator at Oxford in 1793. Though intended to be spoken at
the installation of the Chancellor, Crowe's lines are a passionate attack
on war – and thus on the Government. Ignoring the 'Widow's tears,
the friendless Orphan's cry', those who have stirred the fury of war
'stand at safe distance':

> They in the pomp and pride of victory,
> Rejoicing o'er the desolated Earth,
> As at an altar wet with human blood,
> Sing their mad hymns of triumph, hymns to God
> O'er the destruction of his gracious works! –
> Hymns to the Father o'er his slaughter'd Sons!

War on France had been declared in February; with two short breaks,
it would last until Waterloo in June 1815. This is among the first of the
protest-poems. Though there is no obvious connection, Crowe resembles in his imagery the Wordsworth of *Salisbury plain* (also 1793).
His indignation is no less impressive that Coleridge's in *Fears in solitude*
(1798), or Shelley's in *Queen Mab* (1813). As one might expect the
authorities at Oxford suppressed the poem. It was published, however,
by the *European magazine* in June 1795, and in radical circles contributed
very much to Crowe's reputation.

*Lewesdon hill* is pre-war, and pre-Revolution. It is, as Wordsworth
said, an 'excellent loco-descriptive poem'. Its original audience would
have placed it at once as the most recent in a sequence of hilltop medita-
tions: Denham, *Cooper's hill* (1642); Dyer, *Grongar hill* (1726); Jago,

# Lewesdon hill

*Edge-hill* (1767) – and now, Crowe, *Lewesdon hill* (1788). In a longer view, Crowe takes on a special importance as the link between this Augustan tradition and the Romantic poetry of Coleridge, Wordsworth, Byron, Shelley. He writes as a local resident, who has climbed up Lewesdon (near the coast in West Dorset) as his 'morning exercise'. Wordsworth, who must have done the same climb many times, is amused that he should be so 'expeditious' – 'finishing the whole [poem] on a May-morning before breakfast'.

The comment belongs to 1820, and is found significantly in the Postscript to the *The river Duddon*. Wordsworth goes on to quote the Miltonic ending of *Lewesdon* ('Tomorrow for severer thought . . .'), then tells us, with no apparent connection, that the fourteenth sonnet in the Duddon sequence was written before the rest. At one point in his poem Crowe had traced the course of a river, soon to 'lose itself / In the salt mass of waters' – an 'infant stream' that

> flows along
> Untainted with the commerce of the world,
> Nor passing by the noisy haunts of men . . .
> (ll. 134–8)

The Duddon for Wordsworth is a 'Child of the clouds, remote from every taint / Of sordid industry'; as the series ends, it will merge with the sea. In Sonnet XIV it is specifically 'impelled to leave . . . the haunts of men'. Wordsworth and Dorothy had read Crowe's poem when they were living at Racedown, quite close to Lewesdon, in 1795–7. Linked to this first settled period in their adult lives, it continued to have special associations.

For Coleridge, Crowe ranked with Bowles and Cowper as a poet who 'combined natural thoughts with natural diction . . . reconciled the heart with the head'. *Lewesdon* is named in *Biographia literaria* for its 'genial influence':

> UP to thy summit, LEWESDON, to the brow
> Of yon proud rising, where the lonely thorn
> Bends from the rude South-east, with top cut sheer
> By his keen breath, along the narrow track
> By which the scanty-pastured sheep ascend
> Up to thy furze-clad summit, let me climb;
> My morning exercise; and thence look round
> Upon the variegated scene, of hills,

21

# William Crowe

And woods, and fruitful vales, and villages
Half-hid in tufted orchards, and the sea
Boundless, and studded thick with many a sail.

(ll. 1–11)

In 1796 this opening scene of *Lewesdon* would contribute to one of Coleridge's earliest conversation poems, *Reflections on having left a place of retirement*. Once again, it is a hilltop experience:

But the time, when first
From that low Dell, steep up the stony Mount
I climb'd with perilous toil and reach'd the top,
Oh! what a goodly scene! *Here* the bleak mount,
The bare bleak mountain speckled thin with sheep . . .
The Channel *there*, the Islands and white sails,
Dim coasts, and cloud-like hills, and shoreless Ocean . . .

(ll. 26–37)

Coleridge's language is allegorized, his 'Dim coasts, and cloud-like hills' have a numinous quality that Crowe does not achieve; yet the delightful phrase, 'speckled thin with sheep' is certainly a metamorphosis of 'studded thick with many a sail'.

The 'variegated scene' of *Lewesdon* (Crowe drew the phrase from a passage in Cowper's *Task* that was to be the source of *Frost at midnight*) seems to have been in Wordsworth's mind as well, when in July 1798 he created the landscape of *Tintern abbey*. Crowe's evocative, slightly languid, 'hills / And woods, and fruitful vales, and villages / Half-hid in tufted orchards' reappear as:

These plots of cottage-ground, these orchard-tufts
Which at this season, with their unripe fruits,
Among the woods and copses lose themselves . . .

(ll. 11–13)

The great spiritual poetry of *Tintern*, however, belongs to the world of Romanticism that Crowe from his still-Augustan hilltop merely glimpsed. 'Above the noise', Crowe had written,

and stir of yonder fields
Uplifted, on this height I feel the mind
Expand itself in wider liberty.

(ll. 68–70)

But he could go no further. At the end of his poem he would refer conventionally to 'these thoughts / That lift th' expanded heart above this

22

spot / To heavenly musing'. The early Coleridge of *Reflections*, though writing clumsily enough, was able to cross the border into the fully imaginative experience of oneness with the God in Nature:

> It seem'd like Omnipresence! God, methought,
> Had built him there a Temple: the whole World
> Seem'd *imag'd* in its vast circumference:
> No *wish* profan'd my overwhelméd heart.
> Blest hour! It was a luxury, – to be!
>
> (ll. 38–42)

The way ahead was clear to Coleridge's *This lime-tree bower my prison* and *Frost at midnight*, Wordsworth's *Tintern abbey*, Simplon Pass and Climbing of Snowdon, Byron's *Childe Harold* Canto Three, Shelley's *Mont Blanc* and *Adonais*. Half these poems are literally associated with hilltops; all, in symbolic terms (relating, of course, to Christian allegory, as in the 'Stony Mount' and 'perilous toil', of Coleridge's *Reflections*), ascend the heights of human experience to lose individual consciousness in a merging with the Godhead. As Byron was to put it in *Childe Harold*,

> I live not in myself, but I become
> Portion of that around me; and to me
> High mountains are a feeling . . .
>
> (Canto III, st. 72)

If Crowe in 1788 could not himself quite see the promised land, his poem was of importance to those who did.

# 3

## HELEN MARIA WILLIAMS

---

# Letters written in France

### *in the summer of 1790*
### 1790

Helen Maria Williams, a successful minor poet, aged twenty-eight, reached Paris with her sister on 13 July 1790, returning alone to England early in September. Her *Letters from France* offers an unrivalled picture of what it was like to be caught up in the first enthusiasm of the French Revolution. By chance, Wordsworth landed at Calais on the day that Williams arrived in Paris. Neither poet claims to have selected the day – perhaps neither was yet sufficiently interested by politics to have done so – but it was the eve of the first anniversary of the fall of the Bastille, 14 July 1789. Looking back in *The prelude*, Wordsworth wrote memorably:

> 'Twas a time when Europe was rejoiced,
> France standing on the top of golden hours,
> And human nature seeming born again.
> Bound, as I said, for the Alps, it was our lot
> To land at Calais on the very eve
> Of that great federal day; and there we saw,
> In a mean city and among a few,
> How bright a face is worn when joy of one
> Is joy of tens of millions.
> (1805 *Prelude* vi, ll. 352–60)

Celebrations of 'that great federal day' took place all over France. Wordsworth saw them in the 'mean' coastal city of Calais, Williams in Paris at the Champs de Mars. Here on the 14th the King took an oath of allegiance to the new Constitution which had deprived him of his absolute powers. He never intended to keep it, and the political situation was more complicated than Williams assumed, but her second

Letter takes us to a moment when the ideals of the Revolution – Liberty, Equality, Fraternity – seemed to be in reach:

It was the triumph of human kind; it was man asserting the noblest privileges of his nature; and it required but the common feelings of humanity to become in that moment a citizen of the world. For myself, I acknowledge that my heart caught with enthusiasm the general sympathy; my eyes were filled with tears; and I shall never forget the sensations of that day, 'while memory holds her seat in my bosom.' (p. 14)

Like Wordsworth, Williams was to see the hopefulness turn to violence and despair. Her later *Sketch of the politics of France* covers the Reign of Terror, beginning with her own arrest as Robespierre takes power in June 1793. *Letters from France*, however, is published as well as written in 1790. We are offered a picture that is unqualified by hindsight. Williams notes the gaiety of Paris, the details of the new electoral system, the (usually) patriotic reactions of nobles who have lost their titles, the considerable part played by women in the Revolution. When shown 'La Lanterne' – the lamp-post on which the first 'victims of popular fury' had been hanged – she is not unmoved, but reflects, as Wordsworth will do the following year in his *Letter to the Bishop of Llandaff*, that 'the liberty of twenty-four millions of people' is bound to have a cost.

Williams was unusually well placed to comment on the progress of the Revolution. Her sister had married a Frenchman, and since 1788 she herself had increasingly lived in France. Even before this, her responses had been prepared by her friendship in London with Madame du Fossé, a young Frenchwoman who taught her the language and had suffered under the *ancien régime* 'the dark iniquity of *lettres de cachet*'. As the result of their marriage, M. du Fossé had been thrown into prison by his own father, while she and their child experienced extremes of poverty in exile. Told in the last section of *Letters from France*, the story so moved Wordsworth that he used it in *Vaudracour and Julia*, the tale of thwarted love in *Prelude* Book IX that evokes, and disguises, his own relationship with Annette Vallon.

Caught up as she was in the enthusiasm of the moment, Williams was not an undiscerning witness. 'Our capital subject of debate in this Assembly', she comments 'is, who shall speak first; for all seem more inclined to talk than to listen' (p. 44). Madame Roland will note the same tendency as she awaits execution after the fall of the speech-making Girondins in 1793; Williams in 1790 is still in a position to reflect:

of how little consequence is this impetuosity in debate, if the decrees which are passed are wise and beneficial, and the new constitution arises, like the beauty and order of nature, from the confusion of mingled elements! (p. 45)

Among the members of the National Assembly, Williams is drawn to Mirabeau, not as orator, but as 'the professed friend . . . of the African race' (p. 48). In France as in England proposals to abolish the slave trade have been shelved. Anxiety makes itself felt, together with a certain political shrewdness, as Williams 'trusts' that 'an English House of Commons will never persist in thinking, that what is morally wrong, can be politically right' (pp. 48–9). They will, she knows; but even this painful admission cannot undermine her belief in a final triumph. To her, as to Wordsworth, it seemed that 'a spirit was abroad, / Which could not be withstood' (1850 *Prelude* ix, ll. 521–2). If the English

abide by this system of inhumanity, they will only retard, but will not finally prevent the abolition of slavery. The Africans have not long to suffer, or their oppressors to triumph. Europe is hastening towards a period too enlightened for perpetuation of such monstrous abuses. The mists of ignorance and error are rolling fast away, and the benign beams of philosophy are spreading their lustre over the nations. (p. 49)

The strain on Williams's patriotism is increased when, after two months in Paris, she returns to London. Her account of English responses in autumn 1790 to the still peaceful and constitutional Revolution is of especial interest. It is traditionally assumed that Edmund Burke's denunciation of the French reversed the trend of British sympathy, but *Reflections on the Revolution in France* did not appear until November. Meanwhile, it seems, Williams on her return encountered a consensus of hostile views and precisely the same irresponsible talk of plots and massacres:

Every visitor brings me intelligence from France, full of dismay and horror. I hear of nothing but crimes, assassinations, torture, and death. I am told that every day witnesses a conspiracy; that every town is the scene of a massacre; that every street is blackened with a gallows, and every highway deluged with blood. I hear these things, and repeat to myself, Is this the picture of France? Are these the images of that universal joy, which called tears into my eyes . . . (p. 217)

Finally Williams's book is as important in revealing the attitudes of her countrymen as those of the French. Burke it would seem was preaching to the converted. Williams, however, was not to be daunted. 'Must I be told', she demands,

that my mind is perverted, that I am become dead to all sensations of sympathy, because I do not weep with those who have lost a part of their superfluities, rather than rejoice that the oppressed are protected, that the wronged are redressed, that the captive is set at liberty, and that the poor have bread? (p. 218)

# EDMUND BURKE

---

## Letter to a member of the National Assembly
*(A letter from Mr Burke to a member of the National Assembly; in answer to some objections to his book on French affairs)*
1791

'I feel as a man', Burke wrote to the Comtesse de Montrand on 25 January 1791,

for what humanity suffers; and I feel, as an Englishman, great dread and apprehension from the contagious nature of those abominable principles, and vile manners, which threaten the worst and most degrading barbarism to every adjacent Country.

Six days earlier he had signed and dated his *Letter to a member of the National Assembly*, addressed not (as used to be thought) to the 'very young gentleman at Paris' whose ingenuous questions had prompted *Reflections on the Revolution in France*, but to the adult and experienced French nobleman, De Menonville. *Reflections* had appeared on 1 November 1790. On the 17th De Menonville, who was a Major General and deputy of the extreme right, had written to Burke praising his book, but raising certain objections. Burke's feeling for humanity might be rather selective, but his 'dread and apprehension' were passionately felt. Given the chance to denounce again the 'abominable principles' of the French, he produced over Christmas a new polemic that extends the thinking of *Reflections*, and centres in an attack on Rousseau.

Burke was an outsider exalting and protecting the English tradition that had enabled him to make good. Though not especially successful in his political career, he had the rare distinction of being famous at three different points in his life, for three different reasons. Born in Ireland in 1729, he came to London in 1750 intending to become a barrister, but was never called to the Bar. Instead he published in 1756 his *Philosophical inquiry into the origin of our ideas of the sublime and beautiful*, a work that was to have a profound effect for the rest of the century on poetry, painting, aesthetics, the history of taste. In the '70s he emerged as the great political orator and apologist for American freedom:

When this child of ours wishes to assimilate to the parent, and to reflect with a true filial resemblance the beauteous countenance of British liberty, are we to [refuse them]? . . . If this be the case, ask yourselves this question, will they be content in such a state of slavery? If not, look to the consequences. Reflect how you are to govern a people, who think they ought to be free, and think they are not (*Speech on American taxation*, 19 April 1774).

Then, as a man of sixty-one, Burke offered to the world his reflections on revolutionary France.

Fame this time did not come at once. As a whig politician, Burke had never been entrusted with Cabinet office. In 1790, with his party in Opposition, he was an isolated and unpopular figure, much involved in Indian affairs and the impeachment of Warren Hastings. At first his views on the Revolution were shared by few. His friend and ally, Fox, was an ardent French supporter: 'How much the greatest event that ever happened in the history of the world, and how much the best!' Even Pitt, later the implacable enemy of France, assumed to begin with that her 'convulsions' would 'culminate in general harmony and regular order'. 'She will enjoy', he concluded, 'just that kind of harmony which I venerate'. Among those least prepared for *Reflections* was De Pont ('the very young gentleman at Paris'). On receiving his copy, he wrote to Burke saying that had he known the outcome he would never have asked his opinion.

Burke's talk of 'plots, massacres, assassinations' in 1790 sounds less extraordinary to us than it should. We hear the words in terms of Robespierre and the Reign of Terror – either forgetting that they were written two years earlier, when the Revolution was still in a peaceful and constitutional phase, or regarding them as some curious form of prophecy, justified in retrospect. In truth they embody the writer's personal terror. The American Revolution had not been a revolution at all, merely an awkward parting with the now grown-up child. The American leaders were like as two pins to the English gentlemen who sat in the House of Commons, discussing their fate. It had not been

# Edmund Burke

difficult to plead that they should have comparable freedom. The French, on the other hand, were asking for something dangerously like democracy. Liberty, in their very different case, meant the overthrow of a God-ordained social structure. 'I am unalterably persuaded', Burke wrote impressively in the *Letter to a member of the National Assembly*:

that the attempt to oppress, degrade, impoverish, confiscate, and extinguish the original gentlemen, and landed property of an whole nation, cannot be justified under any form it may assume.

Who, one might ask, was making such an attempt? Burke answers without hesitation. French policy had been

guided by the prudence of litigious attornies and Jew brokers, and set in action by shameless women of the lowest condition, by keepers of hotels, taverns, and brothels, by pert apprentices, by clerks, shop-boys, hair-dressers, fidlers, and dancers on the stage . . . (p. 3)

The conjunction of 'original gentlemen' and 'landed property' is of immense importance. Sitting before his fire at Beaconsfield (the too-large estate for which he had impoverished himself), Burke sees land and inheritance as sustaining the gentry who are themselves the nation's most important property. In them are vested the nation's tradition and the nation's standards. Without them there would be anarchy. Where *Reflections* has as its point of departure the satiric account of Price's sermon of November 1789, and as its centrepiece the account of insults offered to Marie Antoinette ('the age of chivalry is gone . . . the glory of Europe is extinguished for ever'), the *Letter* is remarkable above all for its attack on Rousseau:

Him they study; him they meditate; him they turn over in all the time they can spare from the laborious mischief of the day, or the debauches of the night. Rousseau is their canon of holy writ . . . (pp. 31–2)

There is much sarcasm over the *Confessions*, and the callous attitude of Rousseau to his children – 'The bear loves, licks, and forms her young; but bears are not philosophers (p. 35).' It is *Eloisa* (*La nouvelle Héloïse*), however, that has rendered 'the females of the first families in France' a prey to dancing-masters and valets de chambre. 'The great object' of the rulers in the Assembly

is to destroy the gentlemen of France . . . To destroy that order, they vitiate the whole community . . . by the false sympathies of this Nouvelle Eloïse they endeavour to subvert those principles of domestic trust and fidelity, which form the discipline of social life. (pp. 42–3)

The vehemence comes to seem crazy. In case we think it for that reason harmless, it is well to remember that Burke was an actor in the events of his day. *Reflections* was presented to the French royal family, and widely read in France; the *Letter* was published first in Paris. No writer did more to polarise opinion.

Nor was Burke without a vindictive side. 'The hell-hounds of war', he predicts with satisfaction, 'will be uncoupled and unmuzzled':

if ever a foreign prince enters into France, he must enter it as into a country of assassins. The mode of civilized war will not be practised: nor are the French who act on the present system entitled to expect it. (p. 45)

The 'present system' was a sincere attempt – hampered by a weak and treacherous king (eulogized by Burke) – to give the bulk of the citizens of France a better life.

# 5

## JAMES MACKINTOSH

---

# Vindiciae gallicae

*Defence of the French Revolution and its English admirers against the accusations of the Right Hon. Edmund Burke; including some strictures on the late production of Mons. de Calonne*

1791

Few turncoats have made their recantation as public as James Mackintosh. Not only did he in 1799 'abhor, abjure and forever renounce' the French Revolution, which he had so skilfully defended in *Vindiciae gallicae*, 1791, he denounced it as a 'conspiracy against God and man, the greatest scourge of the world, and the chief stain upon human annals' (to George Moore, 6 January 1800). William Godwin, who in 1793 had been helped by him to formulate the radical ideals of *Political justice*, complained at the time of the 1799 lectures on *The law of nature and of nations* that he was being treated as a 'highwayman or an assassin'. Hazlitt has made famous Godwin's rueful departure from the Hall at Lincoln's Inn, driven out by 'an exulting taunt' from Mackintosh about the 'chimera' of human perfectibility:

The havoc was amazing, the desolation was complete . . . Poor Godwin, who had come, in the *bonhommie* and candour of his nature, to hear what new light had broken in upon his old friend, was obliged to quit the field, and slunk away . . . (*Spirit of the age*, p. 216)

Not surprisingly this drama of renunciation has distracted attention from Mackintosh's original views. If he turned his back so quickly on the Revolution, surely he must have been hasty when in 1791, he joined in the pamphlet-war that followed Burke's *Reflections on the Revolution in France*? Yet *Vindiciae gallicae* was one of the most delayed and considered replies, as well as one of the ablest. Burke came out in November 1790; Mary Wollstonecraft was in print within a month;

32

Part One of Tom Paine's *Rights of man* appeared in March 1791;
Mackintosh did not appear till June.

*Vindiciae gallicae* is well argued, well balanced, well researched:

All the Governments that now exist in the world, (except the United States of
America) have been fortuitously formed. They are the produce of chance, not the
work of art. They have been altered, impaired, improved and destroyed by
accidental circumstances, beyond the foresight or controul of wisdom. (p. 115)

In place of Wollstonecraft's passionate indignation, and the political
know-how of Paine (who had been through the American Revolution,
and was soon to become a member of the French Legislative Assembly),
Mackintosh offers a scholarly assessment of Burke's position, with a
judicious account of his distortion of French politics. His own information (though to some extent overtaken by events before publication) is
detailed and impressive. He is convincing in his discussion of motive
and clear-sighted in his analysis of argument. Burke emerges by comparison as devious and highly emotional.

Confronted by tales of plots and massacres in France, Mackintosh, as
barrister, offers the jury a single crushing piece of evidence:

No series of events in history have probably been more widely, malignantly, and
systematically exaggerated than the French commotions. An enraged, numerous
and opulent body of exiles, dispersed over Europe, have . . . filled the public ear
with a perpetual buz of the crimes and horrors that were acting in France. Instead
of entering on minute scrutiny . . . let us content ourselves with opposing one
general fact to this host of falsehoods. *No commercial house of importance has failed in
France since the Revolution!* (pp. 170-1)

By contrast the case has to be argued in detail against Burke's view of
the 'complete abdication and surrender of all natural rights . . . made
by man in entering into Society'. In the face of Burke's sophistries
about the English Revolution of 1688, Mackintosh sides firmly with
Price:

To contend that the deposition of a King for the abuse of his powers did not
establish a principle in favour of the like deposition, when the like abuse should
again occur, is certainly one of the most arduous enterprizes that ever the heroism
of paradox encountered. (pp. 301-2)

His own view of the matter is entirely clear:

The Revolution of 1688 . . . established, by a memorable precedent, the right of
the people of England to revoke abused power, to frame the Government, and
bestow the Crown. (p. 294)

# James Mackintosh

Mackintosh's prose is less rhetorical than Burke's, but has its own characteristic power:

The massacres of war, and the murders committed by the sword of justice, are disguised by the solemnities which invest them. But the wild justice of the people has a naked and undisguised horror. Its slightest exertion awakens all our indignation . . . (p. 174)

Awakens, that is, the indignation on which Burke had so shamelessly played! Again and again in *Vindiciae gallicae* one hears the tones of genuine humanitarian concern:

If penal statutes hang over our Catholic brethren, if test acts outrage our Protestant fellow-citizens, if the remains of feudal tyranny are still suffered to exist in Scotland, if the press is fettered, if our right to trial by jury is abridged . . . the reason of all these oppressions is the same. No branch of the Legislature represents the people. Men are oppressed, because they have no share in their own government. (p. 341)

Of all people it seems to have been Burke who persuaded Mackintosh to turn his back on these deeply felt, and impressively argued, positions. By the time of his visit to Beaconsfield, however, at the end of 1796, Mackintosh was ready to be persuaded. The Reign of Terror had not only shocked him as deeply as it shocked other British radicals, it convinced him – quite illogically – that he had been wrong. None of his arguments were impugned by the course of events, but emotionally he felt betrayed. He was by nature circumspect; he had stepped out of line, and wished once more to be accepted. To visit the dying Burke in these circumstances was a gesture of surrender.

# 6

# MARY WOLLSTONECRAFT

## Original stories from real life
*with conversations calculated to regulate the affections, and form
the mind to truth and goodness*
1791 (1788)

Joseph Johnson's 1791 reissue of *Original stories*, with new plates by
Blake, coincided with the rise of Wollstonecraft as a political writer.
Her *Vindication of the rights of men* had been first of the many replies to
Burke's *Reflections on the Revolution in France*, appearing within a month
in December 1790. Now she was at work on the famous second
*Vindication* – of the *Rights of woman* (published 1792). In such a context,
the 1788 *Original stories*, with its pervading moral emphasis, might
seem out of place. But in fact Wollstonecraft's values had changed very
little. The education for which she argues so passionately in *The rights
of woman* is designed to create God-fearing wives and mothers, not
political activists. Her new partnership with Blake is of considerable
importance. After his long apprenticeship to the engraver, James
Basire, Blake had become an accomplished (if rather old-fashioned)
craftsman, producing for Johnson book-illustrations from the designs
of Stothard and others. Alongside this commercial engraving he had
etched and illuminated *The songs of innocence* and *Thel* in 1789, and *The
marriage of heaven and hell* in 1790.

Like the *Songs of innocence*, *Original stories* is intended for the moral
improvement of children. In the words of the title page, the conversations it contains are 'calculated to regulate the affections, and form the
mind to truth and goodness'. Wollstonecraft had all the right qualifications. Five years' experience of running a school had been followed
in 1786–7 by a time in the uncomfortable role of governess to an
aristocratic family. Both *Thoughts on the education of daughters* (1787) and

her autobiographical novel, *Mary: a fiction* (1788), show her preoccupation with training the mind to cope rationally with suffering and injustice. As the location of her school she had chosen Newington Green, an outlying village north of London, and home of Richard Price. It is arguable that Price – aside from Priestley, the leading dissenter of his day – was the greatest intellectual influence on her life. She did not concern herself with his theology (faith was for her largely instinctual), but adopted from him the dissenter's proud and positive attitudes to exclusion. Denied the vote, barred from the Universities and public life, dissenters occupied a position in society close to that of the would-be independent woman. Far from being put down, however, they formed in the 1780s an intellectual elite.

'Few are the modes of earning a subsistence', Wollstonecraft comments in *Thoughts on the education of daughters*, 'and those very humiliating'. She is thinking of the experience of women in her own position, educated, unmarried and without money. To be the 'humble companion of some rich old cousin' is to be betwixt and between, 'above the servants, yet considered by them as a spy, and ever reminded of her inferiority when in conversation with the superiors'. Seen in this light, the single woman's two alternatives are no less degrading:

A teacher at a school is only a kind of upper servant, who has more work than the menial ones.

[Life as] A governess to young ladies is equally disagreeable . . . The children treat [one] with disrespect, and often with insolence. In the mean time life glides away, and the spirits with it . . . (Butler and Todd, ii, p. 25)

Wollstonecraft's answer to this, and to the frequently worse subservience of marriage, is that women must 'be taught to think'. 'Thinking', she adds, 'is a severe exercise' – and she means it. At this early stage of her career we are offered no political solutions, just obedience to the will of God. 'Adversity is mercifully sent us to force us to think':

A sensible, delicate woman, who by some strange accident, or mistake, is joined to a fool or brute, must be wretched beyond all names of wretchedness, if her views are confined to the present scene. Of what importance, then, is intellectual improvement, when our comfort here, and happiness hereafter, depends upon it. (Butler and Todd, ii, pp. 32–3)

*Original stories* belongs to a long-established tradition. The volume may surprise us two hundred years later with its moral earnestness, but by the standards of Thomas Day's *Sandford and Merton*, or Hannah More's *Cheap repository tracts*, its piety is not excessive. Godwin in his *Memoirs of the author of A vindication of the rights of woman* chooses to play down Wollstonecraft's faith (reporting with pleasure that she never referred to religion on her deathbed). But, for her, reason is a God-given faculty that leads the individual to virtue, and finally to eternal life. *Original stories* is written on the assumption that teaching is a form of rescue. The author's task is 'to cure those faults by reason, which ought never to have taken root in the infant mind'. Mrs Mason, who tells the stories, is a paragon. Mary and Caroline, who listen, are 'shamefully ignorant'. Having been brought up largely by servants, they possess 'every prejudice that the vulgar casually instill' (one might think Wollstonecraft not entirely without prejudice herself). Mary is fourteen, Caroline twelve. They have 'tolerable capacities', but Mary has 'a turn for ridicule, and Caroline [is] vain of her person'. To the modern reader the girls seem venial in their faults, astonishingly willing to accept correction (after spending her pocket-money on 'paltry orna-ments', Caroline suffers anguish at not being able to give it to the poor), and positively avid in their response to cautionary tales.

Mrs Mason is relentless. Crazy Robin dies in a cave – finally. Before that he has been thrown unjustly into gaol, and lost his wife and two children from putrid fever. The two remaining children join him in his cell, and die there (giving Blake scope for a harrowing plate). Now mad, Robin escapes with his dog, to live on berries in his cave until the dog is shot by 'a young gentleman' whose horse it has barked at. Then he dies too:

Was that the cave? said Mary. They ran to it. Poor Robin! Did you ever hear of any thing so cruel? Yes, answered Mrs. Mason; and as we walk home I will relate an instance of still greater barbarity. (p. 27)

There follows the case of the Bastille prisoner, whose only friend – a spider – is crushed by the gaoler on orders from above.

Blake's illustrations add greatly to the volume. Crazy Robin stands rigid and abstracted above the corpses of his children, laid out upon the strangely short prison-bed as if upon a monument. A dog, woolly and lamb-like, licks his hand unnoticed. The same powerful stylization is present in the frontispiece, where Mary and Caroline lose completely their individuality to fit beneath the outstretched sheltering arms of their Good Angel. *Be calm, my child* has perhaps the most satisfying Blakean composition, and admits a tenderness such as Mrs Mason (in the text) very rarely shows. It has always been held that Wollstonecraft's feminism was an influence on Blake's *Visions of the daughters of Albion* (1793); it looks very much as if there may be an earlier verbal borrowing in *The marriage of heaven and hell*. We read in the Preface to *Original stories of* 'the senses, the first inlets to the heart' ('inlet', 1788). Denouncing 'All Bibles or sacred codes' as the causes of error, the voice of the Devil proclaims in Plate 4 of the *Marriage*:

Man has no body distinct from his Soul for that call'd body is a portion of Soul discerned by the five senses, *the chief inlets of Soul* in this age.

It is difficult to know whether the author of *Original stories* would have been flattered by the borrowing. If she saw her illustrator's original writing she must have thought him a little heterodox. Which is nothing to what Mrs Mason would have felt had she seen in the *Marriage* that 'Prisons are built with stones of Law, Brothels with bricks of Religion'.

# 7

## FRIEDRICH SCHILLER

## The robbers

*translated by A. F. Tytler*

1792 (1780)

'*The Robbers* was the first play I ever read', wrote William Hazlitt in 1820. 'It struck me like a blow . . . Five and twenty years have elapsed since I read the translation . . . but they have not blotted the impression from my mind' (Howe vi, p. 362). Coleridge is more extravagant, but records his impression at the time of reading. 'My God! Southey!' he writes a little after one in the morning on 4 November 1794,

Who is this Schiller? This Convulser of the Heart? Did he write his Tragedy amid the yelling of Fiends? – I should not like to [be] able to describe such Characters – I tremble like an Aspen Leaf – Upon my Soul, I write to you because I am frightened – I had better go to Bed. Why have we ever called Milton sublime? That Count de Moor – horrible Wielder of heart-withering Virtues! Satan is scarcely qualified to attend his Execution as Gallows Chaplain.

Alexander Tytler's many-times-reprinted version of Schiller's *Die Raüber* appeared in 1792, the year in which Schiller was invited by the French National Assembly to become an honorary citizen. Hazlitt seems to have read it in 1795, at the age of seventeen. Two years later it was to be the inspiration both of Wordsworth's powerful, but unperformed, tragedy, *The borderers,* and of Coleridge's *Osorio* (successfully produced, as *Remorse,* 1813). Tytler must in fact have been read by most, if not all, the major Romantics. There would be further translations of Schiller – Coleridge's *Wallenstein,* for instance, in 1800 – but it was through *The robbers* that his unique reputation was established in England. No other play of the period had a comparable impact, or exerted a comparable influence. Written as early as 1780, it embodies what came to be the great themes and aspirations of Romanticism.

# Friedrich Schiller

Schiller was nineteen, and confined in a military academy that he hated. But his thoughts were on liberty, and his mind at least was free:

> To escape from the formalities of a discipline that was odious to my heart, I sought a retreat in the world of ideas and shadowy possibilities, while yet I knew nothing at all of that human world from which I was harshly secluded by iron bars.

De Quincey, in an article for the *Encyclopaedia Britannica* (fourth edition, 1840), singles out Schiller as the greatest of German poets. In doing so, he defends the improbabilities of *The robbers* by a comparison with Shakespeare. A resumé of *Hamlet* or *Macbeth* might well appear similarly extravagant – both dramatists no doubt require the 'willing suspension of disbelief' which, in Coleridge's famous definition, 'constitutes poetic faith'. But the 'shadowy possibilities' of Schiller are not witches or ghosts in armour; they are the attitudes, assumptions and grand dramatic gestures, of the central character. The new elements in the play are idealism, of a kind that confuses and complicates judgment (Brutus might be a parallel), and the presence of the sublime. Unlike Shakespeare's villains (Claudius, Edmund, Iago) and villain-heroes (Richard III, Macbeth), Charles Moor is betrayed into his life of crime. As leader of a peculiarly ruthless robber-band he carries with him an integrity that would have fitted a benefactor of the human race. It could be said of him, as Shelley says of Prometheus, that he is 'exempt from the taints of ambition, envy ... and personal aggrandisement' (Shelley adds 'revenge') that qualify our sympathy for Milton's Satan. In many ways he is the first Satanic hero according to a Romantic definition.

Evil – Iago's, for instance – is fascinating in its own right, but can hardly be sympathetic. Despite the horrors and the bloodshed, Macbeth to a large extent retains our sympathy, because of the all-important fact of having been once a good man. Moor remains a good man throughout. Yet he burns a whole town of women and children in effecting the escape of one of his band. He is, as Coleridge says, a 'horrible Wielder of heart-withering Virtues'. He carries his idealism into the robber's way of life, committing appalling acts of violence from motives of loyalty to the men he has bound himself to lead. Conscience, that tells him all along what he is doing, forces him to go on. In Tytler's words, he 'is hurried on to the perpetration of a series of crimes, which find

from their very magnitude and atrocity, a recommendation to his dis-
tempered mind' (p. xii). The comment brings us close to a definition of
the sublime, but Tytler in fact thinks in terms of Aristotle: the play
'touches equally those great master-springs of Terror and of Pity'
(p. viii). Tacitly we are asked to place *The robbers* next to *Oedipus rex*.
To do so is to be forced to ask in what sense this is a tragedy at all.
Unlike the terrible suicide of Jocasta (or the murders of Cordelia and
Desdemona), Amelia's death brings no pain. For the characters it is a
triumph, for the audience, shocking – and sublime. Moor himself goes
to his fate (prolongèd torture, we infer) with a sense of fulfilment, and
a gesture of compassion:

Good citizen! And am not I too worthy of that name? What law so terrible as
that which I have obeyed? What vengeance or atonement of offence that's like to
mine? – Be my fate fulfilled! – Hard by I have observed a wretch who labours by
the day, an officer – He has eleven children. – To him who shall deliver up the
Robber Moor, a high reward is now proclaimed. – He and his babes shall have it!
(pp. 219–20)

Those who saw *The robbers* as an embodiment of revolutionary ideals
– the French National Assembly among them – saw only what they
wanted to see. Schiller's idealism is political only in the most general
sense. Revolution is punished, the old order upheld. The impact of the
play in England, however, twelve years after its unparalleled success in
Germany, does have a great deal to do with events in France. Alone in
his Paris hotel-room in October 1792, the twenty-two year old Wordsworth suffered pangs of guilt by association as he

> thought of those September Massacres,
> Divided from [him] by a little month,
> And felt and touched them, a substantial dread . . .
> (1805 *Prelude*, x, ll. 64–6)

He had become a 'patriot', given his heart to the people. Now the
Revolution, in which he passionately believed, had turned to bloodshed. Like Moor he felt at once caught up and betrayed. The violence
was, and was not, his own. Subsequent events – the execution of
Louis XVI, the Reign of Terror, the growth of French imperialism –
tested his faith, and that of all British radicals. At the same time they
created an emotional and political climate in which *The robbers* came to
exemplify hopes, promise, idealism, betrayed and yet resilient in defeat.

41

Moor stays true to himself, achieving in the denouement new heights of the sublime. The play offered a triumph of the human spirit at a time when progress, and humanity itself, seemed baffled and suppressed.

'German Tragedy' Hazlitt concludes, with *The robbers* in mind, 'is a good thing. It is a fine hallucination: it is a noble madness':

There is something in the style that hits the temper of men's minds; that, if it does not hold the mirrour up to nature, yet 'shews the very age and body of the time its form and pressure'. It embodies, it sets off and aggrandizes in all the pomp of action, in all the vehemence of hyperbolical declamation, in scenery, in dress, in music, in the glare of the senses, and the glow of sympathy, the extreme opinions which are floating in our time, and which have struck their roots deep and wide below the surface of the public mind. (Howe, vi, p. 360)

If Wordsworth, in a phrase elsewhere used by Hazlitt, is 'a pure emanation of the spirit of the age', *The robbers* is its pure theatrical embodiment.

# 8

## SAMUEL ROGERS

# The pleasures of memory
*a poem in two parts*
1792

In a life of ninety-two years, 1763–1855, Samuel Rogers came to know
the literary and political figures of four generations. He was himself
famous chiefly for *The pleasures of memory* (1792), but there was also a
late success for his travel-poem, *Italy*, printed in 1830 with vignettes by
Turner and Stothard. As a child, Rogers was inspired by the great
radical preacher, Richard Price, and wished himself to become a minister. As a young man he went into the family bank, met Lafayette and
Condorcet in revolutionary Paris, and was Joseph Priestley's host on
the night before he emigrated to America. He also inherited £5,000 a
year. William and Dorothy Wordsworth were living on £100. In his
middle years, Rogers moved in the fashionable London circles of Fox
and Lady Holland. He visited Wordsworth and Coleridge in the Lakes,
and stayed in Italy with Byron and the Shelleys. By nature a gossip, he
gave elegant breakfast-parties at his house in St James's Place, and was
on familiar terms with everyone from Talleyrand to Sir Robert Peel.
Despite being eighty-six at the time, he was offered the Laureateship
when Wordsworth died in April 1850.

Money was a help, but this lifetime of comfortable recognition rested
upon the eight hundred lines of *The pleasures of memory*. Byron, though
he paid Rogers for some tittle-tattle in 1818 with lines of extraordinary
viciousness –

> Eyes of lead-like hue, and gummy;
> Carcase picked out from some mummy . . .
> (*Question and answer*, ll. 7–8)

# Samuel Rogers

– had named him in *English bards and Scotch reviewers* (1809) as the chief
hope of English poetry:

> melodious ROGERS ! rise at last,
> Recall the pleasing memory of the past;
> Arise! let blest remembrance still inspire,
> And strike to wonted tones thy hallowed lyre;
> Restore Apollo to his vacant throne,
> Assert thy country's honour and thine own.
>
> (ll. 803–8)

As Rogers noted wittily in his *Table talk*, Byron liked to be perverse,
and no doubt on this occasion he enjoyed putting down the Lakers.
Yet his admiration for *The pleasures of memory* was genuine.

We tend to think of the age as dominated already by the major
Romantics, but in 1809 the pattern had not emerged. Shelley and Keats
were still at school. Byron was twenty-one, and had written no considerable work. Blake was virtually unknown. Coleridge, though his
lesser poems had gone through three editions, had yet to publish *Kubla
Khan* and *Christabel* (and had printed *The ancient mariner* as an anonymous contribution to *Lyrical ballads*). Wordsworth had decided to
withhold publication of *The prelude*, but was better represented than the
others, with the ballads and *Tintern abbey* gaining support, and *Poems
in two volumes* newly in print. Scott alone, with *The lay of the last
minstrel* (1805), had an established reputation.

The success of Byron's *Childe Harold* in 1810 would sweep aside all
competition; but (except for the *Minstrel*) *The pleasures of memory* was
certainly the best known of recent poems at the time of *English bards
and Scotch reviewers*. It had gone through four editions in 1792, and
eleven by the end of the century. By 1820 sales were in the region of
25,000. Coleridge, Wordsworth, Shelley, Keats, sold in hundreds,
Blake hardly at all; only the great Regency story-tellers – Byron himself, and Scott – achieved a larger readership.

*The pleasures of memory* is, as its title suggests, reflective poetry. In its
preoccupation with the past –

> 'Twas here we chas'd the slipper by its sound;
> And turn'd the blindfold hero round and round.
>
> (pt. I, ll. 35–6)

– it forms a link between the nostalgia of Goldsmith's *Deserted village*
and Wordsworth's sharper awareness of the origins of consciousness.

Rogers is a disciple of David Hartley's *Observations on man* (reprinted 1791), concerned like Wordsworth with

> the curious links
> With which the perishable hours of life
> Are bound together, and the world of thought
> Exists and is sustained.
>
> *(Pedlar,* ll. 78–81)

It is likely in fact that Wordsworth first encountered Hartley's associationist theory of mind through *The pleasures of memory*:

> Lull'd in the countless chambers of the brain,
> Our thoughts are link'd by many a hidden chain.
> Awake but one, and lo, what myriads rise!
>
> (pt. I, ll. 169–71)

Memory is given by Rogers, for the first time in English poetry, both the moral force, and the direct relation to the writer's own creativity, that we see in *The prelude.* 'On her agency depends', he comments in his prose Analysis, 'every effusion of the Fancy, whose boldest effort can only compound or transpose, augment or diminish, the materials she has collected and retained' (p. 29). We are still some way from Coleridge's definitions of imagination in *Biographia literaria,* but the affinities are clear. In the 1790s Rogers's influence had been so strong as to bring out Coleridge's earliest recorded denial of plagiarism (coupled, to his discredit, with an accusation that Rogers himself was a plagiarist).

Perhaps it is the mildness of *The pleasures of memory* that is now chiefly surprising. We expect best-sellers to call attention to themselves. And we expect the Romantic period to turn its back promptly on earlier values, tones, techniques. Rogers is a reminder that there are no convenient demarcations:

> As the stern grandeur of a Gothic tower
> Awes not so deeply in its morning hour
> As when the shades of Time serenely fall
> On every broken arch and ivied wall;
> The tender images we love to trace
> Steal from each year 'a melancholy grace'!
>
> (pt. II, ll. 187–92)

## 9

# WILLIAM WORDSWORTH

---

## An evening walk

*an epistle in verse, addressed to a young lady from
the lakes of the north of England*
1793 (1789)

Appearing in January 1793, *An evening walk* was Wordsworth's first
major published work. Though written chiefly during the Cambridge
summer vacation of 1789, when he was only nineteen, it is an accomplished and professional late-eighteenth-century poem. Couplets are
taut and varied, interest is sustained, as the poet allows his thoughts to
move across the well-known landscape of his boyhood. Like Rogers
(whose *Pleasures of memory* he seems to have read while revising his
poem for the press) Wordsworth saunters 'Memory at [his] side',
anticipating as he does so the great reflective poetry of *Tintern abbey*
and *The prelude*. As in *Tintern abbey*, the poetry is addressed to Wordsworth's 'dearest friend', his only sister, Dorothy, of whom he had seen
very little since their mother's death when he was eight.

It is Dorothy's presence that warrants the personal musings of *An
evening walk*, and associative trains of thought. The verse moves easily
as Wordsworth passes on from the tuneful stream, which, 'Dash'd
down the rough rock, lightly leaps along' (l. 104), to the mock-heroic
cock, monarch of his 'native walks',

> Spur clad his nervous feet, and firm his tread,
> A crest of purple tops his warrior head . . .
> (ll. 115–16)

– from the slate-quarry, with its pigmy workers and echoes of Milton's
Pandemonium,

> These by the pale-blue rocks that ceaseless ring
> Glad from their airy baskets hang and sing . . .
>
> (ll. 133–4)

to the shepherd, working his dog high above him on the fells:

> Waving his hat, the shepherd in the vale
> Directs his winding dog the cliffs to scale,
> That, barking busy, 'mid the glittering rocks,
> Hunts, where he points, the intercepted flocks . . .
>
> (ll. 149–52)

More obviously a set-piece is the comparison of swans on Winder-mere (paired, happy, thriving, a perfect natural family group) and the wretched war-widow who drags herself and her babes through the scorching summer heat, only to die with them homeless in a winter storm:

> No more her breath can thaw their fingers cold,
> Their frozen arms her neck no more can fold . . .
>
> (ll. 265–6)

Wordsworth's lines belong to the tradition of the sentimental episode, seen in Thomson's *Seasons* and most recently in Erasmus Darwin (*The botanic garden*, 1789–91). But already Wordsworth shows the care for the individual that underlies his commitment to the Revolution and infuses the humanitarian poetry of *Lyrical ballads*.

Looking back as an old man, Wordsworth felt proud that descriptions of the Cumbrian landscape in *An evening walk* had not been 'confined to a particular walk or an individual place'. Even at this early stage, his poetry had been imaginative – displayed his 'unwillingness to submit the poetic spirit to the chains of fact and real circumstance'. On the other hand, nothing had been vague or fake. There was, he declared, not an image in the poem which he had not personally observed. Very probably he was telling the truth; to a modern reader, however, *An evening walk* is bound to seem a literary poem. Without being imitative, or showy, the writing is full of pleasurable allusion – to the early Milton of *L'allegro* and *Il penseroso* and *Lycidas*, to Thomson, Gray, Collins, Goldsmith, and many lesser figures of the time. Still more important in establishing the poet's idiom is his relation to the picturesque. He had read Gilpin's *Mountains and lakes of Cumberland*

47

*and Westmoreland*, 1786, while he was still at school, but his introduction to the picturesque had been West's *Guide to the lakes*. It is West (quoting Mason) who is the source of the *Evening walk* description of the Lower Fall at Rydal. His comments on how the fall is to be viewed are extraordinarily detailed:

> Not a little fragment of rock thrown into the bason, not a single stem of brushwood that starts from its craggy sides, but has a picturesque meaning; and the little central current dashing down a cleft of the darkest coloured stone, produces an effect of light and shadow beautiful beyond description. (*Guide to the lakes*, p. 78)

The young Wordsworth is far from merely versifying the prose account, but he has taken his cue, and presents a scene full of 'picturesque meaning':

> Inverted shrubs, and moss of darkest green,
> Cling from the rocks, with pale wood-weeds between;
> Save that, atop, the subtle sunbeams shine,
> On wither'd briars that o'er the craggs recline;
> Sole light admitted here, a small cascade,
> Illumes with sparkling foam the twilight shade.
>
> (ll. 59–64)

Judging from *The prelude*, we think of the poet's early experiences of landscape as fraught with guilt and fear. Nature was transformed by the 'visionary dreariness' of the child's imagination, not the fashionable *chiaroscuro* of the painter. The experiences of adolescence we think of as more quietly imaginative, but still as intensely personal. It may come as a surprise to find him aged nineteen looking at the Lake District with the eyes of a tourist. Yet the picturesque was on the whole a beneficial influence. When Wordsworth later condemned it as 'a strong infection of the age', accusing his former self of merely aesthetic judgments – liking and disliking 'by rules of mimic art, transferred / To things above all art' (1805 *Prelude* xi, ll. 153–6) – he had forgotten the extent to which West and Gilpin had been responsible for training his eye, creating the poet of Nature.

It is, for instance, Gilpin's observation of the River Wye that lies behind the detail in *Tintern abbey* of 'steep and lofty cliffs' that 'connect / The landscape with the quiet of the sky' (ll. 5–8). Smoke from the fires of charcoal-burners, he noted, 'spreading its thin veil over' the hills, 'beautifully breaks their lines, and unites them with the sky' (*Wye tour*, 12). *An evening walk* is not *Tintern abbey*, but the picturesque eye is already sensitive and alert. Already there is a numinous quality to the best writing that is recognizably Wordsworthian:

> The scene is waken'd, yet its peace unbroke,
> By silver'd wreaths of quiet charcoal smoke,
> That, o'er the ruins of the fallen wood,
> Steal down the hills and spread along the flood.
> (ll. 413–16)

'He who works *from imagination*', Gilpin writes in the Preface to the *Lakes tour*, 'will in all probability make a much better landscape, than he who takes it all as it comes' (pp. xxvi–xxvii). It is advice that Wordsworth is happy to take, as the mountains of Lake Windermere respond like Orpheus's listening animals to the enchantment of his evening scene:

> 'Tis restless magic all; at once the bright
> Breaks on the shade, the shade upon the light,
> Fair spirits are abroad; in sportive chase
> Brushing with lucid wands the water's face,
> While music stealing round the glimmering deeps
> Charms the tall circle of th'enchanted steeps.
> (ll. 329–34)

GEORGE DYER

---

# The complaints of the poor
# people of England
## 1793

It is Lamb who creates the Dyer we know – the totally good, lovable, vain, innocent eccentric who stands beside the shelves in Oriel library passive as a book ('I longed to new coat him in russia, and assign him his place', *Oxford in the vacation*), or walks fully clothed out of the front door into the river, and wholly disappears (*Amicus redivivus*). The Dyer of these affectionate portraits is a sort of holy fool, a grown-up and sophisticated version of Wordsworth's Johnny Foy, whose 'life is hidden with God':

> For with G.D., to be absent from the body is sometimes (not to speak profanely) to be present with the Lord. At the very time when, personally encountering thee, he passes on with no recognition – or, being stopped, starts like a thing surprised – at that moment, reader, he is on Mount Tabor, or Parnassus, or co-sphered with Plato, or, with Harrington, framing 'immortal commonwealths' – devising some plan of amelioration to thy country, or thy species . . . (*Oxford in the vacation*)

Mount Tabor is in Galilee, half way between Nazareth and the Jordan. If we bring Dyer's thoughts, and Lamb's flights of fancy, down to earth, they may be said to concern religion, poetry, and utopian politics. By the time Lamb knew him, Dyer was a middle-aged bachelor and no doubt genuinely eccentric. Born in 1755, he had been sent (as Coleridge and Lamb would be, almost a generation later), to the charity-school, Christ's Hospital. His father was a Thames boatman (Lamb's was a head servant at the Inner Temple). After four years at Emmanuel College, Cambridge, Dyer became a schoolmaster; then in the early 1780s he returned to Cambridge as tutor to the children of the Unitarian minister, Robert Robinson (whose *Life* he wrote in 1796). It was through Robinson that Dyer came to know Frend, later to be Coleridge's mentor at Jesus. Frend was among the most articulate Unitarians of the day, 'exhorting' his audience in *Address to the inhabitants of Cambridge* (1788) 'to turn from the false worship of Three Persons, to the worship of the One True God'. 'Consult common sense', he wrote,

Could God lie in the womb of a woman? could God expire on the Cross? could God be buried in the grave? shocking suppositions! ... Search the Scriptures; point out one single passage, in which Jesus Christ declared himself to be God. Point out one, in which the Apostles declared him to be God. (p. 8)

Five years later Frend was to be tried by the University, and dismissed, on the grounds of his seditious and irreligious book, *Peace and union* (1793).

Frend was Priestley's disciple, Dyer (like Coleridge) was Frend's. *Complaints of the poor people of England* is written at the same moment as *Peace and union*. The two works put forward plans for reform, in a political situation where views have been polarised by Burke's attack on the Revolution. Both are overtaken by events, as the execution of Louis XVI (21 January 1793), and the French declaration of war ten days later, make peace and union more than ever unlikely. Frend makes, however, few concessions. His tone could not fail to cause offence to the establishment and the established church:

The ... priest in every age, whether he solemnizes the orgies of Bacchus, or solemnizes the rites of the Eucharist, will, should either his victims or his allowance fail, oppose ... every truth which threatens to undermine his altars, or weaken his sacerdotal authority. (*Peace and union*, p. 41)

Though not conciliatory, Dyer is less assertive. His Unitarianism is an under-presence – a support in all his thinking, but not forced upon his readers.

It is truly as a representative of the poor that Dyer writes. He is giving voice to the complaints which lack of education has denied them the ability to make. His tones are earnest and without condescension:

I have seen the rich man pay with reluctance, what has been earned with hard labour; and insult, when he ought to have relieved. I have seen the poor man, after the toil of the day, return at night to behold nothing but want and wretchedness ... I have heard men plead for keeping slaves in the West Indies, and treating them like beasts, by asking, 'Are they not as well off as many poor people in

# George Dyer

England?' I have been witness to the miseries, and, in many instances, the oppressions of men confined in gaol . . . (pp. 2–3)

Nor is he merely complaining. 'The prosperity of nations', he is prepared to assert, 'depends on the poor. They dig the ore out of the mine, and the stone out of the quarry. They build our houses, work our vessels, and fight our battles' (p. 4). 'I do not see', he concludes at a later point, 'how the force of this rule can be evaded, viz. that the profits of the labourer should bear some proportion to those of the master' (p. 188).

With a quiet vehemence, Dyer contrasts the lives of place-men and office-holders at Court with those of the poor who are taxed to support them. The Duke of Newcastle, 'under the name of auditor of the exchequer, receives 28 or £30,000 a year'. The Duke of Richmond, 'besides the 20 or £24,000 which he receives from coals brought into the river, receives £5,000 a year as master of the ordnance' (p. 37). Dyer's protest is extraordinarily muted. It is, he says,

very hard that poor people should be pinched [taxed] in every thing they eat and wear, so as to be incapable of saving a penny, and kept always poor, always dependent on their oppressors; till they, at length, die in a wretched workhouse. (p. 36)

'In Cambridgeshire, the shepherds' wages are five shillings a week' (£13 a year – before tax). Facts speak for themselves, but for good measure we are given the views of 'a sensible and humane gentleman-farmer' on labourers and the afterlife: 'How comfortable is the doctrine of a future state to these poor fellows, who are little better than slaves in this!' (p. 187).

'The nations of Europe', Dyer writes, 'are in want of some wise and humane plan of NATIONAL EDUCATION: they are also in want of some wise plan of NATIONAL CHARITY' (p. 154). Charity and education had between them given him his privileged position as a member of the professional middle class. He is in no doubt that 'The true policy of nations would be to lessen the number of the poor, by putting them into the condition of raising themselves' (p. 163). They have, as he says, no time 'for the improvement of mind'. Only Dyer could tell the story that follows without condescension:

I once knew a poor man, who had a sickly wife, and nine children. He could only earn a shilling a day, by working on the public roads; and his family lived on bread and water, with a little salt thrown into the water to give it a relish. Yet the honest man used to say, 'Ned shall have a little learning, and Ned shall teach Bet, and Bet Susan, and so on'; and he was willing to stint himself of bread, to pay fourpence a week to a country dame [school-teacher], to have his poor boy taught to read. (p. 48)

In his Conclusion, Dyer addresses himself briefly to possible remedies. He has three graduated plans: legal reform within the present system, universal suffrage within a constitutional monarchy, and the setting up of a full-scale republic. Some of the changes that he advocates have since been achieved: most have not. Many never will be. Yet, for all Lamb's mockery, Dyer seems a very down-to-earth thinker. Closer to Paine than Plato, but with a warmer heart.

## JOSEPH PRIESTLEY

---

# A farewell sermon

*(Letters to the members of the New Jerusalem Church, 1791; and*
*The present state of Europe compared with antient prophecies;*
*a sermon preached at the gravel pit meeting in Hackney)*
1794

To mark the second anniversary of the Fall of the Bastille, a 'Church
and King' mob in Birmingham, with the connivance of the local
magistrates, burned down the house of Joseph Priestley. Friends helped
Priestley himself to escape – in disguise – but his laboratory and library
were destroyed. Banned as a dissenter from the university and from
public office, he was nearing the end of an immensely distinguished
career as physicist, chemist, historian, educationalist, grammarian,
political theorist, philosopher and theologian. Joseph Johnson in his
five-page *Catalogue of books written by Dr Priestley*, issued 1791, could
offer sixty-five titles.

Alongside works that chart the course of Priestley's scientific re-
searches – *The history and present state of electricity* (1767), for instance,
and his major break-through in the discovery of oxygen, *Experiments
and observations on different kinds of air* (1774–86) – are the theological
enquiries that show him as the founder of modern Unitarianism:
*Disquisitions on matter and spirit* (1777), *History of the corruptions of
Christianity* (1782), and many more. Unitarianism, with its emphasis on
a single, all-pervasive God, who as 'the Divine Energy' was clearly
analogous to electricity, is the product of an age in which it was
expected that the riddle of the universe would presently be solved.
Priestley, like his disciple Coleridge in the next generation, saw intellectual enquiries of every kind as having the same underlying purpose.
None of this would have been known to the Birmingham mob, for

whom it was sufficient that Priestley should be a dissenting minister – and therefore, almost by definition, pro-French. At the time when his house and papers are destroyed, Priestley had been working on an address to the Swedenborgians. *Letters to the members of the New Jerusalem Church* was published shortly after his move to London, where in November 1791 he became Morning Preacher at Hackney in succession to Richard Price. The subject was topical because in 1787 the Swedenborgians had separated themselves off into an official 'church' – in defiance of their founder's wishes, and to the disgust of William and Catherine Blake, who walked out of the London conference.

Swedenborgians – addressed throughout as 'My Fellow Christians' – are shown in Priestley's *Letters*, logically and patiently, to be in fact misguided Unitarians. Conveniently laid side by side are two systems of thought that have special significance in any attempt to define the origins of Romanticism. Blake repudiated Swedenborg in his annotations, and parodied his heavenly encounters in *The marriage of heaven and hell*, yet had learned far more from him than he wished to admit. In their blending of prophetic vision and downright practicality the two men were, and are, uncomfortably alike. Priestleyan Unitarianism, meanwhile, is not merely the religion of the early Coleridge, as seen in his contribution to Southey's *Joan of Arc* (1796):

> Glory to Thee, Father of Earth and Heaven!
> All conscious PRESENCE of the Universe!
> Nature's vast Ever-acting ENERGY!
> In Will, in Deed, IMPULSE of All to All . . .
> (ll. 442–5; *Sibylline leaves*, p. 302)

– but, as such, directly inspires the pantheism of *Tintern abbey*, which has come to seem essentially Wordsworthian:

> And I have felt
> A *presence* that disturbs me with the joy
> Of elevated thoughts . . .
> A motion and a spirit, that *impels*
> All thinking things, all objects of all thought,
> And rolls through all things . . .
> (ll. 94–6, 101–3)

Priestley was no less at risk in London than in Birmingham. 'On the 14th of July 1792', he writes in his Preface to *The present state of Europe*

# Joseph Priestley

*compared with antient prophecies* (1794), 'it was taken for granted by many of the neighbours that my house was to come down, just as at Birmingham the year before.' In the event there was no more personal violence. Though the compensation he received was delayed and inadequate, Priestley replaced his apparatus, bought more books, and returned to work. His sons, however, were mistreated and obliged to emigrate; early in 1794 he decided to join them in America. Celebrating Priestley as 'Patriot, and Saint, and Sage', Coleridge commented in *Poems on various subjects* (1796):

> Him from his native land
> Statesmen blood-stain'd and Priests idolatrous,
> By dark lies mad'ning the blind multitude
> Drove with vain hate: calm, pitying he retir'd,
> And mus'd expectant on [the] promis'd years.
>                                   (*Religious musings*, ll. 398–402)

*The present state of Europe*, delivered as a sermon at Hackney on 28 February, was at once Priestley's farewell and a highly important updating of his theological views – an updating that gave chapter and verse for his anticipation of the 'promised years'.

In an age when (to quote Southey, looking back on the Revolution), 'nothing was dreamed of but the regeneration of the human race', the attraction of Unitarianism was that it suited Christian millenarian thinking to contemporary events. Like Cowper and Blake, among others, Priestley accepted the conventional belief that the world would come to an end after six thousand years, and also the traditional date of Creation, established by Archbishop Ussher at 4004 BC. In his 1791 reply to Burke's *Reflections on the Revolution in France*, he saw the American and French Revolutions as the beginning of a 'reign of peace', 'distinctly and repeatedly foretold' by prophets of the Old Testament. It was not a view that could easily be sustained as the war with France became more violent, and as Robespierre gained control in Paris.

Secular radicals, such as Wordsworth, put their faith during the Reign of Terror in the return of moderation, and were meanwhile forced to hope that their own country would be defeated. Priestley went back instead to *Daniel* and the *Book of Revelation*. At the same time he found in Hartley's *Observations on man* (always the inspiration of his theology, and now cited at length in an Appendix) support for a U-turn. 'Great calamities', he concluded,

56

such as the world has never yet experienced, will precede that happy state of things, in which 'the kingdoms of this world will become the kingdom of our Lord Jesus Christ' . . . (p. 2)

It is difficult now to enter into such thinking, but Priestley's sermon was to become the basis of Coleridge's statement of faith in *Religious musings*. And if this grand apocalyptic precursor of *The ancient mariner* is not to our liking, it is well to remember that Wordsworth admired it (and drew upon it), and that Coleridge's fellow Unitarian, Lamb, thought it 'the noblest poem in the language, next after the *Paradise lost*'. 'And even that', Lamb added, 'was not made the vehicle of such grand truths':

> Believe thou, O my soul,
> Life is a vision shadowy of Truth,
> And vice, and anguish, and the wormy grave,
> Shapes of a dream! The veiling clouds retire,
> And lo! the Throne of the redeeming God
> Forth flashing unimaginable day
> Wraps in one blaze earth, heaven, and deepest hell.
> (ll. 421–8)

# 12

# THOMAS CHATTERTON

## The Rowley poems

*(Poems supposed to have been written at Bristol
in the 15th century, by Thomas Rowley)*
1794 (1777)

On 21 September 1819, two days after composing *To autumn* – 'Season
of mists and mellow fruitfulness' – Keats remarks in a letter, 'I always
somehow associate Chatterton with autumn'. To which he adds,
apparently without connection:

He is the purest writer in the English Language. He has no French idiom, or
particles like Chaucer – 'tis English Idiom in English Words. I have given up
HYPERION – there were too many Miltonic inversions in it . . . English ought to
be kept up.

The previous autumn Keats had spent nursing his dying younger
brother Tom. That he should 'somehow associate' the season with early
death is not surprising, and Chatterton had taken arsenic at the age of
seventeen. Chatterton, for Keats's generation, had the aura of myth
that Keats himself was later to achieve, standing for promise, talent,
genius, cut off before its time. One thing that he did not commonly
stand for was purity of language. His poetry was after all a fake,
allegedly 'wroten bie the gode Prieste Thomas Rowley, 1464'.

It may be that Wordsworth would have understood Keats's train of
thought. Worried by Coleridge's dejection and addiction, he had
written in *Resolution and independence* of 'fear that kills . . . And mighty
poets in their misery dead':

> I thought of Chatterton, the marvellous Boy,
> The sleepless Soul who perished in his pride;
> Of Him who walk'd in glory and in joy
> Behind his plough upon the mountain-side . . .
>
> (ll. 43–6)

That Wordsworth was indeed thinking about Chatterton is confirmed by his use of the archaic spenserian stanza of *An excellent balade of charitie*. Behind *Resolution and independence* lies Coleridge's *Monody on the death of Chatterton* (1794), where he too had brooded on the fates of earlier poets. As modern representatives, Chatterton and Burns are linked in Wordsworth's mind, partly because they both died young (Burns, not very), partly by primitivist assumptions about language, such as Keats is tacitly making. Though one wrote in Scots, the other in a bogus medieval English, they are united as working-class writers whose language expressed the feelings of the heart, and seemed a guarantee of Wordsworth's own position.

Apart from Wallis's dramatic painting of his suicide, *Resolution and independence* has proved the most lasting contribution to Chatterton's myth. The myth had been building, however, since 1770, the year of Wordsworth's birth. As with Macpherson's spurious 'translations' of Ossian, controversy had played a big part. Readers were intrigued to know whether the *Balade* and other poems did indeed belong to the middle ages. Could an eighteenth-century Bristol charity-school boy, with no scholarly training, really have forged them? The fraud had been exposed by Tyrwhitt as early as 1777, in *Poems supposed to have been written by Thomas Rowley*; but Sharpe, in his Preface to the 1794 volume, has no wish to close off the discussion. As editor, his 'sole design'

is to furnish the public with a neat Edition of these Poems, which, whether the Author of them may have been ROWLEY, or CHATTERTON, or some third person, (as has been ridiculously supposed) fully entitle him to be ranked in the fourth place among our British Poets.

Chaucer, Spenser, Milton, Chatterton – there were some (as Hazlitt complains in his lecture of 1818) who went still further and talked as if Chatterton was the greatest genius since Shakespeare. Hazlitt is at his most incisive:

He did not show extraordinary powers of genius, but extraordinary precocity. Nor do I believe he would have written better had he lived. He knew this himself, or he would have lived. Great geniuses, like great kings, have too much to think of to kill themselves. (Howe, v, p. 122)

It was scarcely charitable, but brings the discussion down to earth:

As to those who are really capable of admiring Chatterton's genius, or of feeling an interest in his fate, I would only say, that I never heard any one speak of any one of his works as if it were an old well-known favourite, and had become a faith and a religion in his mind. It is his name, his youth, and what he might have lived to have done, that excite our wonder and admiration. (Howe, v, p. 125)

'I was very disappointed by his treatment of Chatterton', was the comment of Keats, after the lecture; but to a large extent Hazlitt must be right. Even Wordsworth, whose admiration is genuine, is forced to emphasize Chatterton's precocity, and sounds a little general in his praise. 'I asked Wordsworth this evening', Crabb Robinson writes in his *Diary* on 14 January 1842,

wherein Chatterton's excellence lay. He said his genius was universal; he excelled in every species of composition, so remarkable an instance of precocious talent being quite unexampled. His prose is excellent, and his powers of picturesque description and satire great.

Interestingly, Coleridge's view was that Chatterton's poems had never been popular. 'The very circumstance', he writes on 17 July 1797 (only three years after publishing the *Monody*), 'which made them so much talked of – their *ancientness* – prevented them from being generally read'.

Chatterton's spelling is certainly a problem. Many are daunted by the Scottish poetry of Burns, and almost no one can now hear the Dorset cadences of Barnes and Hardy, the Lincolnshire of Tennyson. What looks difficult, or different, isn't read. But Chatterton is not dialect. He knows some middle English, and enjoys inventing more ('slughorne', for instance, famously picked up by Browning in *Childe Roland*), but, as Hazlitt astutely points out, the secret of his 'imposture' lies 'in the repetition of a few obsolete words, and the mis-spelling of common ones':

the whole controversy might have been settled . . . from this single circumstance, that the poems read as smooth as any modern poems, if you read them as modern compositions; and that you cannot read them, or make verse of them at all, if you pronounce or accent the words as they were spoken at the time when the poems were pretended to have been written (Howe, v, p. 124)

We no more have to be frightened by Chatterton's ancientness than we are by that of Coleridge's spelling in the original text of *The ancient mariner*. His rhythms are strong and fluent, and as he carries us along we can enjoy the game that he is playing. *The dethe of Syr Charles Bawdin* (recollected by Blake in *The marriage of heaven and hell*) is an excellent example:

> 'Howe oft ynne battaile have I stoode,
>   Whan thousands dy'd arounde;
> Whan smokynge streemes of crimson bloode
>   Imbrew'd the fatten'd grounde:
> Howe dydd I knowe thatt ev'ry darte,
>   That cutte the airie waie,
> Myghte nott fynde passage toe my harte,
>   And close myne eyes for aie?'

(ll. 129–36)

Equally accomplished, and equally accessible, is the Shakespearean *Mynstrelles songe* in *Aella*:

> See! the whyte moone sheenes onne hie;
> Whyterre ys mie true loves shroude;
> Whyterre yanne the mornynge skie,
> Whyterre yanne the evenynge cloude;
>   Mie love ys dedde,
>   Gon to hys deathe-bedde,
>   Al under the wyllowe tree

(ll. 872–8)

As Keats so memorably said, ' 'Tis English Idiom in English Words.'

Chatterton seems to have had a collection of medieval documents, filched by his sexton father from a coffer in St Mary Redcliffe. His spellings (like Dickens's spellings of working-class speech) are there to create an atmosphere, without causing actual difficulty to the reader. Many are in fact perfectly possible in a fifteenth-century scribe. As well as being a distinguished poet and forger, Chatterton was obviously a fascinated linguist. Glossing his improbable coinage, 'glommed', he writes in a footnote to the *Balade*:

Clouded, dejected. A person of some note in the literary world is of opinion, that *glum* and *glom* are modern cant words; and from this circumstance doubts the authenticity of Rowley's Manuscripts. Glum-mong in the Saxon signifies twilight, a dark or dubious light; and the modern *gloomy* is derived from the Saxon *glum*.

It may not prove the authenticity of Rowley's manuscripts, but Chatterton's etymology is largely correct. Like Keats, he believed that 'English ought to be kept up'.

# 13

# JEANNE MARIE ROLAND DE LA PLATIÈRE

## Appeal to impartial posterity

*by citizeness Roland, wife of the minister of the home
department; or, a collection of pieces written by her
during her confinement in the prisons of
the abbey, and St Pélagie*
1795

'You have more courage than many men', one of the commissioners
who is arresting her says to Citizeness Roland, 'you submit to justice
calmly.' 'Justice!' she replies,

Were justice done, I should not now be in your hands: but should an iniquitous
procedure send me to the scaffold, I would mount it with the same firmness and
tranquillity, with which I now go to a prison. (i, p. 22)

*An appeal to impartial posterity* was composed during the writer's five-
months' stay in the prisons of Robespierre's Paris: first in the Abbey,
then at St Pélagie, and finally, in the days before her execution on
8 November 1793, at the Conciergerie. Her courage never fails. There
is no self-pity, no weakness, no bitterness, no useless indignation.
Arrived at the Abbey (scene of appalling butchery during the September Massacres the previous year), she writes to the Assembly, takes
stock, congratulates herself on the copy in her pocket of Thomson's
*Seasons*. Hearing that her fellow Girondins – 'the twenty-two' – have
been impeached, she responds dramatically: 'my country is lost!'
Almost at once, however, she settles into her role as the historian who
will see that they, and especially her husband, are properly reported.

Roland had been sent to Paris in February 1791 to arrange financial
help for the city of Lyons. Since then he had twice held the post of
Minister of the Interior: first, under Lafayette and the plausible but

treacherous Louis XVI (December 1791–June 1792), then, following the deposition of the King (10 August 1792), on an Executive Council with a Girondin majority but largely controlled by Danton. Roland was sincere and limited, and more dependent than he knew on his far more intelligent wife. 'Good God', she recalled saying to him when he fell for the blandishments of the King, 'every time I see you set off for the council with that wonderful confidence, it seems to me that you are about to commit a folly' (ii, p. 12). She wrote his letters, directed his thinking, wielded through him at times considerable power. Her house was a frequent meeting-place for Roland's colleagues; her presence contributed much to whatever cohesion the Girondins could be said to possess. 'Roland *without me*', she wrote

> would not have been a worse minister; his activity, his knowledge, and his probity, were all his own; but *with me* he attracted more attention, because I infused into his writings that mixture of energy and of softness, of authoritative reason, and of seducing sentiment, which are perhaps only to be found in a woman of a clear head and a feeling heart. (ii, p. 18)

Citizeness Roland knew personally almost all the principal figures of the Revolution: not just Brissot and the Gironde, but Lafayette, Dumouriez, Pétion, Paine. She many times entertained those – Danton, Robespierre – who sent her to the guillotine. Writing in prison, she is extraordinarily dispassionate:

> Lewis XVI behaved to his new ministers with the greatest appearance of frankness and good nature. This man was not precisely what he was depicted by those who took a pleasure in vilifying him: he was neither the brutish blockhead, who was held up to the contempt of the people; nor was he the honest, kind, and sensible creature, whom his friends extolled to the skies. Nature had endowed him with ordinary faculties, which would have done very well in an obscure station, but he was depraved by his princely education . . .

To which she adds laconically, 'A common understanding, educated for the throne, and taught dissimulation from the earliest infancy, has a great advantage in dealing with mankind' (ii, p. 8).

It is mankind, rather than any particular class, group or faction, of which she has come to despair. 'The thing which surprised me the most', she writes, 'after my husband's elevation had given me an opportunity of knowing a great number of persons, particularly of those employed in important affairs, was the universal meanness of their minds' (ii, p. 29). The 'twenty-two' are largely (and reasonably) exempted from this judgment, but she is well aware of their faults. Even Brissot, who is 'the best of men: a good husband, an affectionate father, a faithful friend, a virtuous citizen', has 'a sort of levity of mind' that gives her pain:

Sometimes for very vexation I could have boxed the ears of these philosophers, whom I daily learnt to esteem for the honesty of their hearts, and the purity of their intentions: excellent reasoners all, learned politicians in theory; but totally ignorant of the art of leading men ... (i. pp. 55–6)

It was the story of the Revolution. Had the Girondins thrown up a strong leader, they might indeed have brought about the more just society of which they talked. As it was, they went under.

'He cannot believe anyone vicious', Madame Roland remarked of Brissot, 'who speaks to him with an open countenance' (i, p. 53). At first, she herself had been unable to place Robespierre. She disliked his self-love and his reserve, yet believed him to be 'passionately enamoured of liberty', and admired his defence of principle. As she waits for the guillotine, she reflects calmly, 'I esteemed [him] on this account, and I told him so' (i, p. 57): 'At that time Robespierre had to me the semblance of an honest man' (i, p. 56). Later she would define him as 'fiery, jealous, greedy of popularity':

it is very evident, that he labours for himself; and that, in his greedy ambition to pass for the sole deliverer of France, he would remove out of the way all, who have in any manner served their country ... (i. p. 164)

Her final view is expressed on 3 October 1793, after she has seen in the papers Robespierre's false accusations against Roland and Brissot:

That Robespierre, whom once I thought an honest man, is a very atrocious being. How he lies to his own conscience! How he delights in blood! (i. p. 181)

The lies in the press – like the accusations that she herself was forced to answer – are for public consumption. It is interesting that in her view of Robespierre she stresses instead those to his own conscience. However 'atrocious', he remains for her a moral being. It was hardly a time to be generous, but is there perhaps a hint of Coleridge's brilliant reading of 1795:

I rather think that the distant prospect, to which he was travelling, appeared to him grand and beautiful ... If however his first intentions were pure, his subsequent enormities yield us a melancholy proof, that it is not the character of the possessor which directs the power, but the power which shapes and depraves the character of the possessor. (*Addresses to the people*, ii)

True to herself and her beliefs, Citizeness Roland mounted the scaffold with complete 'firmness and tranquillity', showing to the end 'more courage than many men'. Not till the last pages of her immensely moving book do we discover the spiritual basis of her resilience. She addresses herself to God, as she addresses herself to posterity, confident that her appeal must be upheld:

Divinity, supreme being, soul of the universe, principle of every thing great, good, and happy; thou in whose existence I believe, because I must needs emanate from something better than what I see around me, I am about to be reunited with thy essence! (ii. p. 113)

The final scene is given to us by her friend and editor, Bosc, in the words of a fellow-prisoner:

she was neatly dressed in white, and her long black hair flowed loosely to her waist . . . she passed through the wicket with a quick step, bespeaking something like joy; and indicated, by an expressive gesture, that she was condemned to die. She had, for the companion of her misfortune, a man whose fortitude was not equal to her own, but whom she found means to inspire with gaiety, so cheering and so real, that it several times brought a smile upon his face.

At the place of execution, she bowed down before the statue of Liberty, and pronounced these memorable words: *O Liberty, how many crimes are committed in thy name!* (ii. pp. 145–6)

# 14

## J. H. BERNARDIN DE ST-PIERRE

---

# Paul and Virginia

*translated by Helen Maria Williams*
1796 (1787)

Bernardin de Saint-Pierre's *Paul et Virginie*, first published separately in 1789, was a best-seller in many languages. In England alone it went through nine editions by 1814, sixty by 1900. That Helen Maria Williams in Paris should choose to translate it 'amidst the horrors of Robespierre's tyranny' has a certain appropriateness. It is a book about innocence, set in the distant tropical island of Mauritius, far away from politics and ambition. Witnessing the joyous early stages of the French Revolution in the summer of 1790, Williams had believed herself to be sharing in 'the triumph of human kind . . . man asserting the noblest privileges of his nature'. 'The French nation', she declared in *Letters written in France*, 'will inviolably guard, and transmit to posterity, the sacred rights of freedom'. Imprisonment during the Terror, and daily thoughts of the guillotine, led not to disillusionment with the ideals of the Revolution, but to a sickening awareness of man's potential for evil. Bernardin, with his highly romantic version of Rousseau's primitivism, offered a welcome alternative: 'I found', Williams writes in her Preface, 'the most soothing relief in wandering from my own gloomy reflections to those enchanting scenes of the Mauritius.'

Goodness in *Paul and Virginia* is strictly incredible. Returning from a mission to help an escaped female slave, the two children get lost in the jungle. Virginia, 'her feet bleeding with the sharpness of the stony paths', makes herself 'buskins' from 'long leaves of the hart's tongue', provided by beneficent Nature. 'In her eager desire to do good', Bernardin comments, 'she had forgot to put on her shoes' (p. 45). As with the Rousseau of *Émile* and *La nouvelle Héloïse* (*Eloïsa*, see chapter 31 below), a moment's cynicism on our part will destroy the whole fabric. Bernardin's is not the conventional goody-goodiness of Thomas Day's *Sandford and Merton* (1783-9), but his novel is nonetheless a moral fable – and nonetheless to be enjoyed for, not despite, its sentimentality.

Mauritius, where Bernardin spent three years, 1768-71, before returning to Paris and embarking on his long friendship with Rousseau, is presented in *Paul and Virginia* as an island paradise. As in Wordsworth's *Ruined cottage*, however – begun in 1797, a year after the poet bought his copy of Williams's translation – we know from the first that there can be no happy ending. Bernardin's opening sentence speaks of 'the ruins of two small cottages', amid a landscape 'bearing the marks of former cultivation'. It is among these ruins that the old man, who is to become Wordsworth's Pedlar, tells the narrator of the lives of the peasant woman Margaret (forbear of Wordsworth's central figure, and mother of the illegitimate Paul) and her gentle friend, Madame de la Tour (widowed mother of Virginia). As in *The ruined cottage*, desolation in a once fruitful landscape offers its comment on the fragility of an ideal past existence.

The outside world, it seems, cannot finally be escaped. Whatever the virtues of the characters, or the wishes of the reader, political realities intervene. Class may have no relevance in Madame de la Tour's island friendship for Margaret; their children may be brought up as brother and sister, and later encouraged in their wish to be married; but Paris, with its alien values, has the power to intrude, claiming Virginia as its own and parting the lovers. In the denouement it seems for a moment that all may be well, but the cottage-ruins are there at the back of our minds to tell us it cannot be. It may be that this is for the best. Like his follower, Byron, who so crudely shatters the idyll of Juan and Haidée on their comparable isle, Bernardin knows the dangers for the writer who dares to depend upon sentiment. The sweetness, sensuousness, innocence, that give to *Paul and Virginia* its extraordinary appeal, could not have survived fulfillment. Sleepless, and too young to understand her emotions, Virginia bathes at midnight in a rocky pool:

She flung herself into the bason, its coolness re-animated her spirits, and a thousand soothing remembrances presented themselves to her mind. She recollected that in her infancy her mother and Margaret amused themselves by bathing her with Paul in this very spot. That Paul afterwards, reserving this bath for her use only, had dug its bed, covered the bottom with sand, and sown aromatic herbs

# J. H. Bernardin de St-Pierre

round the borders. She saw, reflected through the water upon her naked arms and bosom, the two cocoa-trees which were planted at her birth and that of her brother, and which interwove above her head their green branches and young fruit. She thought of Paul's friendship sweeter than the odours, purer than the waters of the fountain, stronger than the intertwining palm-trees, and she sighed. (pp. 95–6)

Belonging to the same tradition of sensibility, and yearning for the naturalness that she describes, Williams is as free from self-consciousness as Bernardin himself. No modern translator can reproduce for us as she has done the essential qualities of this novel, or show us so clearly why its tender wistfulness held such power over the imagination.

## 15

# GEORGE COLMAN THE YOUNGER

---

# The iron chest
## 1796

'*The Iron Chest*', Hazlitt wrote in 1816, 'is founded on the story of *Caleb Williams*, one of the best novels in the language, and the very best of the modern school'. 'The play itself', he adds, 'is by no means the best play that ever was written, either in ancient or modern times, though really in modern times we do not know of any much better' (Howe, v, p. 342). It is a backhanded compliment from a lover of Shakespeare and the Jacobeans, but one that nonetheless offers George Colman's dramatic version of Godwin's novel as among the best plays of the Romantic period.

Colman himself had no doubts as to its value. The preface that he added to the second edition is an outraged defence of his play, which had run for only four nights when presented by Kemble as actor-manager of Drury Lane, in March 1796:

on the word of an honest man, I have bestowed no small pains on this *Iron Chest*, which I offer you. Inspect it; examine it; you see the maker's name is upon it. I do not say it is perfect . . . but, I trust, you will find that my *Iron Chest* will hold together, that it is tolerably sound, and fit for all the purposes for which it was intended.

Then how came it to fall to pieces, after four days wear? (pp. i–ii)

The play had not been properly rehearsed – even by the very low standards of the day. Kemble, on whom everything depended, was ill, taking opium-pills just before the performance, and probably drunk as well. In the all-important role of Sir Edward Mortimer (Godwin's Falkland) he had 'toil'd on, line after line, in a dull current of un-diversified sound':

Frogs in a marsh, flies in a bottle, wind in a crevice, a preacher in a field, the drone of a bagpipe, all, all yielded to the inimitable, and soporific monotony of Mr KEMBLE. (p. xvii)

In his play, as in his preface, Colman is revealed as a decidedly good writer. Commissioning him to make a dramatic version of Godwin's novel – correctly entitled, *Things as they are: or, the adventures of Caleb Williams* – the proprietor of Drury Lane intended to cash in on the reputation of *Political justice*, 1793, as well as the radical implications of *Caleb* itself (written the following year). *The iron chest* was, however, composed and performed in a time of active Government censorship. Colman reminded his readers in the Advertisement, 'The stage has, now, no business with Politicks: and, should a Dramatick Author endeavour to dabble in them, it is the Lord Chamberlain's office to check his attempts . . .' (p. xxi). His task of creating an unpolitical *Caleb* was not made easier by the fact that it is a novel in which prolonged suspense is followed by long drawn-out pursuit. The process by which Caleb (Wilford) discovers that Falkland (Mortimer) is a murderer is so curtailed in the play as almost to seem perfunctory, and Falkland's later persecution of his secretary – likened by Godwin to the vengeance of an omniscient God – becomes the merest gesture.

'Much of Mr Godwin's story I have omitted', Colman writes, 'much, which I have adopted, I have compress'd; much I have added; and much I have taken the liberty to alter' (p. xxi). A new centre of interest had to be found, and Colman found it above all in the language. Kemble's soporific monotony galled him especially because he had created for Mortimer a blank verse of genuine power. Inevitably it is Shakespearean, but where Wordsworth in *The borderers* (begun the same year) moves in and out of pastiche, usually seeming strongest when he is furthest from his sources in *Lear* and *Othello*, Colman rarely seems imitative. Wordsworth is a poet writing drama, who cannot avoid mimicry because the great images and rhythms throng his mind: Colman is a professional dramatist who (in this aspect) has learned his trade from Shakespeare. Hazlitt is no doubt right to say that his comic minor characters do not enhance, or advance, the main plot as Shakespeare's commonly do, but they are nonetheless skillfully handled. Colman's scenes move well, providing scope for the character-actor, yet sustaining for the reader a sense of variety and interchange. One unexpectedly successful aspect of the play is the frequent use of songs, including duets and choruses. Though retaining its brooding central character, Godwin's novel has become an entertainment.

Comparison with Shakespeare tends to obscure the very nature of this drama. It is not failed tragedy, but a form, characteristic of its age, that deals in heightened emotional states akin to the Gothic and accompanied by a tradition of theatrical gesture which we tend unhelpfully to associate with Victorian melodrama. Half baffled, half amused, by the conventions of the time, we find this the most difficult of all periods of English drama to respond to with imaginative sympathy. Hazlitt, though, who saw Edmund Kean's revival of *The iron chest* in 1815, regarded the last highly theatrical struggles of Mortimer as a 'consummation of the art' and a test of the audience's capacity for fellow-feeling:

The last scene of all – his coming to life again after his swooning at the fatal discovery of his guilt, and the falling back after a ghastly struggle, like a man waked from the tomb, into despair and death in the arms of his mistress, was one of those great consummations of the art . . . (Howe, v, pp. 344–5)

# 16

# SAMUEL TAYLOR COLERIDGE

## Poems on various subjects

### 1796

The importance of Coleridge's *Poems on various subjects*, published in Bristol on 16 April 1976, has not always been recognized. Coleridge was twenty-three. *Kubla Khan* and *The ancient mariner* were still eighteen months away. The poetry is uneven, much of it dating back to under-graduate days. Even the most recent work is horribly stuffed with epithets and Miltonic imitation ('Unshudder'd, unaghasted, he shall view . . .'). In *The Eolian harp* and *Religious musings*, however, this first volume of Coleridge's poems contains the origins of the great philo-sophical poetry of Alfoxden: his own *Lime-Tree bower* and *Frost at midnight*, Wordsworth's *Tintern abbey*, and their joint scheme for *The recluse*.

It is all too easy to make fun of the early Coleridge. In 1795 Charlotte Poole described him wittily as:

a young man of brilliant understanding, great eloquence, desperate fortune, democratick principles, and entirely led away by the feelings of the moment. (Sandford, i, p. 124)

Led away by such feelings, Coleridge as an undergraduate got himself into debt, contemplated suicide (in the manner of Chatterton), and enlisted as a dragoon, under the charming alias, Silas Tomkyn Comber-bache. There was a war on; whether or not one encumbered the back of one's horse, cavalry charges were a dangerous activity. Bought out by his family, Coleridge returned to Cambridge in April 1794. In no time he and Southey were devising a scheme to emigrate to America and set up a commune – *pantisocracy*, the 'rule of all' – on the banks of the Susquehanna. The scheme duly fell through. Coleridge, however, found himself getting married to a woman who would have come with him to Pennsylvania, but whom he would never have chosen under normal circumstances. To make matters worse, he was in love with somebody else.

Yet, looked at in another way, the Cambridge years were not so disastrous. Aside from his prize-winning Greek ode on the slave trade (July 1792), there were to be no academic successes to reward Coleridge's extraordinary learning. In December 1794 he left the University without a degree. But the foundations of his career as a writer and thinker had been laid. William Frend (disciple of Priestley and Fellow of Jesus College, dismissed for seditious writing in May 1792) had passed on to him the Unitarian faith, and matching political principles, that would sustain his greatest poetry. And he had begun to publish. *The fall of Robespierre* was rushed into print with Southey in September 1794, but contains much that is of interest. The *Sonnets on eminent characters*, printed in the *Morning chronicle* at the end of the year, established Coleridge on the London scene as a radical poet, not afraid to celebrate the heroes of revolution (Erskine, La Fayette, Koskiusko, Godwin, Stanhope), or to attack Pitt as the Judas betraying his country.

Even pantisocracy was not so ridiculous. Conditions would no doubt have been harder than Southey supposed –

When Coleridge and I are sawing down a tree we shall discuss metaphysics; criticise poetry when hunting a buffalo, and write sonnets whilst following the plough. (22 August 1794)

– but many did leave for America at this period. Habeas corpus had been suspended, seven leading radicals were in the Tower; there was much to be said for escaping Government repression, and setting up a new life. In doing so they would have followed the example of Priestley, who had emigrated in the spring, and whom Coleridge reverenced as 'Patriot, and Saint, and Sage'.

The early Bristol period, during which Coleridge and Southey attempted to raise money for a cut-price pantisocracy in Wales, was extraordinarily productive. Coleridge wrote an important section (later published as *The destiny of nations*) for Southey's *Joan of Arc*, and built up a reputation as a lecturer on politics and religion. His material was hastily assembled, and (as in *Biographia literaria*) sometimes borrowed verbatim, but there could be no doubting his commitment. 'Undaunted by the storm of popular prejudice', the *Observer* commented in summer 1795, unswayed by magisterial influence, he spoke in public what none had the courage in this City to do before, – he told Men that they have Rights. (Patton and Mann, xxxi)

*Poems on various subjects* was in fact Coleridge's sixth independent publication – the most recent being his valiant periodical, *The watchman*, produced single-handed since the beginning of March, but soon to reach its sad conclusion: 'O Watchman! thou hast watched in vain' (13 May 1796).

The second number of *The watchman* had included a trailer for Coleridge's great new Unitarian poem, *Religious musings*. Given that its subject is the Millennium, and its source the *Book of Revelation*, the excerpt's title – 'The Present State of Society' – comes as a surprise. As a follower of Priestley, Coleridge is drawing on the *Farewell sermon* of February 1794, in which the Revolution and Reign of Terror had been interpreted as fulfilment of biblical prophecy:

> Rest awhile,
> Children of Wretchedness! More groans must rise,
> More blood must steam, or ere your wrongs be full.
> Yet is the day of Retribution nigh:
> The Lamb of God hath open'd the fifth seal:
> And upward rush on swiftest wing of fire
> Th' innumerable multitude of Wrongs
> By man on man inflicted!
>
> (ll. 320–7)

It is an apocalyptic vision. Contemporary suffering – the present state of society – is part of the divine plan.

Irritated by Coleridge's defensiveness, Southey commented in 1809, 'if he was not a Jacobine . . . I wonder who the Devil was'; but it was a strangely theological Jacobinism. Coleridge offers it as his political message that the poor should not rebel, but wait. They are part of 'the vast family of Love', protected by a God who is at once the 'omnipresent Mind' and the 'Lord of unsleeping Love'. Their guarantee of future happiness is Jesus – not as God (second 'person' of the Trinity), but as the *man* who, through love, achieved perfection open to us all. As in *The ancient mariner* (and the original plans for *The recluse*), to share in this love is to be saved from self – saved from being 'the smooth Savage', who roams 'Thro' courts and cities',

> A sordid solitary thing,
> Mid countless brethren with a lonely heart . . .
> Feeling himself, his own low Self the whole,
> When he by sacred sympathy might make
> The whole ONE SELF . . .
> (*Religious musings*, ll. 169–74)

In the more speculative mood of *An Eolian harp* (leading on to *Frost at midnight* and *Tintern abbey*) Coleridge could see the 'sacred sympathy' of love as 'an intellectual Breeze', sweeping across the 'organic harps' of 'animated nature'. The breeze, in this central Unitarian definition, becomes 'At once the Soul of each, and God of all'. As the divine breath, it is also for the poet an image of inspiration. *Poems on various subjects* shows that Coleridge has found already his true theme, started on his quest for a definition of imagination that will explain both man's relation to God, and the poet's to his art.

# 17

GOTTFRIED AUGUSTUS BÜRGER

---

# The chase
## *and* William and Helen
*translated by Walter Scott*
1796 (1774)

Walter Scott was twenty-five, and practising as an advocate, when his two translations from Gottfried Bürger were published anonymously in Edinburgh. *The chase* (*Der wilde Jäger*) would have been new to his readers; by contrast, *William and Helen* was one of no less than five English versions of *Lenore* that appeared in 1796. Coming as it did immediately after the publication of Radcliffe's *Mysteries of Udolpho* and Lewis's *Monk*, the vogue for Bürger's supernatural ballads was largely a spin-off from the popularity of the gothic novel. It was sudden and short-lived, but offers an important way of looking at the period leading up to the publication of Wordsworth and Coleridge's *Lyrical ballads* in September 1798. William Taylor of Norwich had made a translation of *Lenore* early in the 1790s, and allowed it to circulate in manuscript. By March 1796 it was clear that he had imitators, and he printed his text in the new radical *Monthly magazine*, with an introduction designed to place Bürger for an English audience:

His extraordinary powers of language are founded on a rejection of the conventional phraseology of regular poetry, in favour of popular forms of expression, caught by the listening artist from the voice of agitated Nature.

The tones that we hear are those of the 1798 Advertisement, and more famous 1800 Preface, to *Lyrical ballads*. Taylor's sensitive criticism shows how far the decorum of the eighteenth century had in fact been displaced before the influence of Wordsworth and Coleridge came to be felt. With its 'hurrying vigour' and 'impetuous diction', Bürger's poetry created an impression of Romantic spontaneity. Lamb as usual was quick to respond to a new literary development. 'Have you read the ballad called *Leonora* in the second number of the *Monthly magazine*', he asks Coleridge on 5 July 1796, 'if so !!!!!!!!!!!!!!!' There are many exclamation-marks in the Lamb–Coleridge letters, but fourteen is un-surpassed. Scott was less exclamatory, but nonetheless impressed. He had been present at a reading of Taylor's *Leonora* in Edinburgh as early as 1794, and recalls in his *Essays on imitations of the ancient ballad* (1830): 'The wild character of the tale was such as struck the imagination of all who read it' (Lockhart, iv, p. 55).

The problem for Bürger's translators was how to recreate in English the power and strangeness and rapid onward movement of his verse. As Taylor commented in the *Monthly*, 'onomatopoeia is his prevailing figure; the interjection, his favourite part of speech'. To mask the obviousness of these sound effects, Taylor himself had used a pseudo-medieval diction in *Leonora*, at the same time introducing a flavour of the traditional ballad. Coleridge later imitated his technique in *The ancient mariner*, but it could hardly be used in making a second transla-tion of a single poem. Scott had been led to Bürger in the first place through Taylor, and found his presence difficult to ignore. There is an almost Coleridgean deviousness about the way in which the Preface to *William and Helen* implies that the translator has never encountered *Leonora*, yet contrives to acknowledge the borrowing (thanks to the dim recollection of a friend!) of two particularly characteristic lines:

> Tramp! tramp! along the land they rode,
> Splash! splash! along the sea . . .

On the whole Scott copes well in *William and Helen*, but he is notice-ably more at ease in *The chase*, where there is no need to look over his shoulder.

*The ancient mariner* has to be the greatest poem inspired by Bürger, but it is significant that he should be Wordsworth's source in both *The thorn* (1798) and *Hart-leap well* (1800). Writing in Germany at the end of 1798, Wordsworth makes the comment that we should expect from the author of *The ruined cottage* and the Lucy poems. His original letter is lost, but Coleridge quotes it verbatim in writing to Taylor on 25 January 1800:

# Gottfried Augustus Bürger

Bürger is one of those authors whose book I like to have in my hand, but when I have laid the book down I do not think about him. I remember a hurry of pleasure, but I have few distinct forms that people my mind, nor any recollection of delicate or minute feelings which he has either communicated to me, or taught me to recognize.

In neither *The thorn*, nor *Hart-leap well*, is the 'hurry of pleasure' a sufficient explanation of Wordsworth's interest. In Scott's phrase, Bürger's wild tales have 'struck the imagination', but Wordsworth cannot agree with Taylor that they are truly 'caught . . . from the voice of agitated Nature'.

*The thorn* shows Wordsworth transforming a particularly sensational Bürger poem, *Des Pfarrers Tochter von Taubenhain* (Taylor's *Lass of fair wone*), into a monologue in which the horrors are at work solely within the mind. *Hart-leap well* – drawn almost certainly from *The chase* – retains the headlong, hell-bent ride of the original, retains the central moral opposition to be found in Bürger, yet defines the hunter's sacrilege precisely in terms of the 'delicate and minute feelings' that Bürger is felt to lack:

> This beast not unobserved by Nature fell,
> His death was mourned by sympathy divine.
>
> The being that is in the clouds and air,
> That is in the green leaves among the groves,
> Maintains a deep and reverential care
> For them the quiet creatures whom he loves.
>
> (ll. 163–8)

Bürger's vogue was over. Voices at once more imaginative and more sensitive had replaced him. Yet he had been of immense importance to the *Lyrical ballads* experiment. The very name of the volume – with its qualifying of the narrative implication of the ballad by the personal feelings of lyric – suggests how the joint authors had responded to Bürger's stimulus and yet defined themselves against him. Wordsworth was telling less than the truth when he claimed to have laid his book down and ceased to think of him.

# 18

## WILLIAM GILBERT

---

## The hurricane

*a theosophical and western eclogue. To which is subjoined
a solitary effusion in a summer's evening*
1796

Though he was a friend of Coleridge, and twice quoted admiringly by
Wordsworth, William Gilbert is best viewed as a Swedenborgian contemporary of Blake. Sending a copy of *The hurricane* to Thelwall on
17 December 1796, Coleridge described it as 'A strange Poem, written
by an Astrologer here, who *was* a man of fine Genius'. 'Ah me', he continues, 'Madness smote with her hand, and stamped with her feet, and
swore that he should be hers – and hers he is. He is a man of fluent
Eloquence and general knowledge, and gentle in his manners, warm
in his affections; but unfortunately he has received a few rays of supernatural Light through a crack in his upper story.'

Gilbert was born in Antigua *c.* 1760. Little is known about his life,
but after coming to England he trained as a barrister, and spent a year
in a mental asylum. In spring 1796 he arrived in Bristol, where Southey
(who would later call Blake 'a decided madman') referred to him as
'the most insane person I have ever seen at large'. Joseph Cottle, however, was impressed by his conversation, and Coleridge, whatever his
later views, took Gilbert seriously enough in April to print his essay on
trade and war in *The watchman*. Six weeks later, *Fragment by a West
Indian* was included in the journal's final issue (13 May 1796).

*The fragment* consists of passages from three different parts of the still
unpublished *Hurricane*, fitted together to form a brief conversation
poem in the manner of Coleridge's own *Eolian harp* and *Reflections on
having left a place of retirement*:

# William Gilbert

Near where with Tropic heats bright CANCER glows,
And Sun-beams glitter with perennial force;
Girt by the azure wave an Island lies . . .
                              Here, oft at Eve,
When length'ning shadows to the calmy wave
Shot dubious twilight and alluring gloom,
I've sat contemplative – and viewed the breeze
Checquer the water, with far-streaming light
That glistened as with gems: I've sat and thought
That all the hopes attending various man
Were robbers of his rest; I've thought that Love
Was all the sum indulgent Heaven e'er meant
To form our Bliss. I thought so and was blest.

Gilbert's tones and tricks of style ('I've sat contemplative', 'I thought so and was blest') belong to the self-regarding early Coleridge, whose work he had no doubt heard, and seen in manuscript. *The hurricane* is, however, a much odder poem than the *Fragment* would suggest. The crack in the poet's 'upper story', like that in Blake's more distinguished cranium, receives its 'supernatural light' as a refraction of Swedenborg's 'theosophy'. Gilbert's subtitle, 'A Theosophical and Western Eclogue', points also to a bizarre view of the relation between America and Europe. Citing Swedenborg as authority, the Preface claims that 'all Countries have a specific *Mind*, or determinable *principle*'. Much the same could be deduced from Blake (in *America*, for instance) but Gilbert's view depends on a cosmic tit for tat principle: 'a primary Law of Nature, that EVERY ONE MUST FALL INTO THE PIT THAT HE DIGS FOR OTHERS' (p. v). The time has come when America (the West), subjugated in the past by European invaders, will turn the tables:

the question is now settled for ever, and Europe yields to the Influence, Mind and Power of AMERICA, linked in essential principle with AFRICA and ASIA, for ever. (p. vi)

Africa has special importance for Gilbert as the ancient source of energy, and site (he claims) of Eden. To be 'linked in essential principle' with Africa is to be emotionally and imaginatively strong. Gilbert's emphasis on American influence is to some extent a reflection of political fact: the New World had shown the Old the way to revolution, the French Constitution of 1790 was based on the American. At bottom, however, his thinking is a form of primitivism. It is significant that Wordsworth should single out from the Notes Gilbert's discussion of 'the internal man', 'the Man of Mind' (as opposed to 'Mode'), who is 'at once a child and a king'. In its complicated, only-partly-construable, Blakean allegoric narrative, *The hurricane* tells of the defeat of 'Cold Europe's man', and reassertion of primal innocence. The first quarter of the poem is heavily annotated, the remainder hardly at all. Given the arcane significances pointed to in the opening section ('by AMERICAN MERMAIDS ... I mean the intelligence and love of NATURAL or SENSUAL Life among and appropriate to the [native] AMERICANS' (p. 61), it seems unlikely that the story that follows is as simple as it looks, but no help is offered.

Not that Gilbert's prose makes all things plain. His notes are such as Blake might have written had he concerned himself with the reactions of an audience:

By SEA I always mean the external, the body or crust, of the world; I mean also Europe, or still more specifically, England; as having understandings calculated for the Sea or for Physics; and excelling alike in the sciences and the arts by which these two are jointly contemplated. (p. 60)

EUROPE is the *fountain* of *Slavery*; AMERICA the FIELD of FREEDOM: The *Fountain* of it is GOD in *Man*, and FIRE in NATURE. (p. 85)

After all, I well know, that the *natural* man discerneth not the things of the SPIRIT OF GOD; neither indeed can he, for they are spiritually discerned. (p. 99)

'I see in Wordsworth', Blake comments in the margin of *Poems* 1815, 'the natural man rising up against the spiritual man continually, and then he is no poet but a heathen philospher'. Crabb Robinson, who owned the volume, was unable to accept a distinction between the natural and the spiritual; Wordsworth, for all his love of Nature (condemned by Blake), could probably have done so. It was, after all, his view that 'the mind of man becomes / A thousand times more beautiful than the earth / On which he dwells' (1805 *Prelude* xiii, ll. 446–8). The passage from *The hurricane* singled out in his notes to *The excursion* shows a traveller, amid scenes of wild American beauty, responding as a Wordsworthian spiritual being:

He who is placed in the sphere of Nature and of God, might be a mock at Tatter-sall's and Brookes's, and a sneer at St. James's: he would certainly be swallowed alive by the first *Pizarro* that crossed him. – But when he walks along the River of Amazons; when he rests his eye on the unrivalled Andes; when he measures the long and watered Savannah; or contemplates, from a sudden Promontory, the distant, vast Pacific – and feels himself a Freeman in this vast Theatre ... His

exaltation is not less than Imperial . . . He becomes at once a Child and a King . . .
(1814 *Excursion*, pp. 427–8)

'The Reader, I am sure, will thank me for the above Quotation',
Wordsworth concludes, 'which, though from a strange book, is one of
the finest passages of modern English Prose.' One reader who did, it
seems, feel gratitude was Keats. As well as Chapman's *Homer*, we know
that in 1816 he had been looking into Wordsworth's *Excursion*. 'Stout
Cortez', 'silent upon his peak in Darien', surely takes his origin from
Gilbert's unnamed voyager, who contemplates 'from a sudden
Promontory, the distant, vast Pacific'.

# 19

## ROBERT SOUTHEY

━━━━━━━━━━

# Poems

## 1797

It is no wonder that the tory editors of the *Anti-Jacobin* should have singled out Southey's *Poems* 1797 for attack. The volume (published in fact in December 1796) proclaims its radical sympathies from the first. Titles such as *To Mary Wollstonecraft, Poems on the slave trade, The soldier's wife, Botany Bay eclogues, The pauper's funeral*, draw attention to the humanitarian concern which at this period marked out writers of dangerous left-wing political views. But Southey had gone still further, making his jacobinism explicit in a preface to the slave trade poems, and addressing his tea-drinking audience as 'ye who at your ease / Sip the blood-sweeten'd beverage':

> Oh he is worn with toil! the big drops run
> Down his dark cheek; hold – hold thy merciless hand,
> Pale tyrant! for beneath thy hard command
> O'erwearied Nature sinks . . .
>                  gasping he lies
> Arraigning with his looks the patient skies,
> While that inhuman trader lifts on high
> The mangling scourge.
>              *(Sonnet* III, ll. 1–3, 6–9)

On the face of it the 'Inscription' so brilliantly travestied by Canning (or perhaps by Frere) in the first issue of the *Anti-Jacobin* has nothing to do with contemporary politics. Its title, though, hints at an historical parallel that was in everybody's mind: *Inscription for the apartment in Chepstow-Castle where* HENRY MARTEN *the regicide was imprisoned thirty years*. To condone the British execution of Charles I (1649) was to condone the French execution of Louis XVI (1793), and to present oneself as an undeterred republican:

> For thirty years secluded from mankind,
> Here Marten linger'd. Often have these walls
> Echoed his footsteps, as with even tread
> He paced around his prison: not to him
> Did Nature's fair varieties exist;
> He never saw the Sun's delightful beams,
> Save when thro' yon high bars it pour'd a sad
> And broken splendor. Dost thou ask his crime?
> He had rebell'd against the King, and sat
> In judgment on him; for his ardent mind
> Shaped goodliest plans of happiness on earth,
> And peace and liberty . . .
> (*Inscription* IV, ll. 1–12)

The *Anti-jacobin* does not answer Southey, it prints his poem in full and follows it with an appropriately titled travesty, *Inscription for the Door of the Cell in Newgate, where Mrs. Brownrigg, the Prentice-cide, was confined Previous to her Execution*:

> For one long Term, or e'er her Trial came,
> Here Brownrigg linger'd. Often have these cells
> Echoed her blasphemies, as with shrill voice
> She scream'd for fresh Geneva. Not to her
> Did the blithe fields of Tothill, or thy street,
> St Giles, its fair varieties expand;
> Till at the last in slow-drawn cart she went
> To execution. Dost thou ask her crime?
> SHE WHIPP'D TWO FEMALE PRENTICES TO DEATH,
> AND HID THEM IN THE COAL-HOLE . . .
> (*Poetry of the Anti-jacobin*, p. 6)

Southey's earnest tones are captured, his sympathy is debased. His rather effortful heightening of drama – 'Dost thou ask his crime?' – turns all too easily into the bathos of the female prentices and the coal-hole. Marten, by implication, was a common criminal. His 'goodliest plans' for human happiness at the time of the Commonwealth are no more to be taken seriously than those of the modern republican poet.

Yet the fact that *Poems* 1797 was parodied in all but one of the first five issues of the *Anti-jacobin* speaks for itself. As in Jeffrey's famous attack on the Lakers in the first issue of the *Edinburgh review* (October 1802), Southey is given prominence among his contemporaries because to the literary establishment both his political views and his way or writing seemed a threat. To use the term later applied by Hazlitt to

# Poems

Wordsworth, Southey's was 'a levelling muse'. Two years before the Advertisement to *Lyrical ballads* 1798 made its revolutionary claims, he had developed a plain style that was quite as 'experimental' as anything in Wordsworth and Coleridge, and quite as affronting in its social implication. At the same time he responded with great swiftness to contemporary trends. *Mary*, for instance, is written in the metre of Monk Lewis's *Alonzo the brave and the fair Imogine*, and several of Southey's narratives show the blending of the traditional ballad with the German influence of Bürger, that was to be so important for *The ancient mariner* and Wordsworth's *Thorn*. Like the dead crusader of *Lenore*, Donica and Rudiger both prove to be transmorts, able to pass as human with their loved ones, but compelled to return to the grave:

'Oh turn thee – turn thee Rudiger,
    The rising mists behold,
The evening wind is damp and chill,
    The little babe is cold!'

'Now hush thee – hush thee Margaret,
    The mists will do no harm,
And from the wind the little babe
    Lies sheltered on my arm.'

'Oh turn thee – turn thee Rudiger,
    Why onward wilt thou roam?
The moon is up, the night is cold,
    And we are far from home.'
                    (*Rudiger*, ll. 93–104)

Southey was later to borrow material from the Coleridge/Wordsworth ballads (while not very creditably ridiculing them in the *Critical review*), but at the time of *Poems* 1797 it was he who was making the running.

There could be no doubt as to Southey's skills, but Wordsworth seems to have noted by Spring 1797 that they came too easily to him: 'he seldom "feels his burthened breast / Heaving beneath th'incumbent Deity"'. Passing on the judgment to Joseph Cottle in early April, Coleridge adds significantly:

I am fearful that he will begin to rely too much on *story* and *event* in his poems, to the neglect of those *lofty imaginings*, that are peculiar to, and definitive of, the poet.

One looks in vain in Southey for imagination, the power of mind, the sense of the numinous, that distinguish the greater Romantics; yet he

# Robert Southey

was throughout his life an extremely professional and accomplished writer. His early poems especially deserve to be read for the clear humanitarian light which they shed on the period. No other poet was wondering what it felt like to be transported to Botany Bay.

# 20

# MATTHEW GREGORY LEWIS

---

## The castle spectre
*a drama in five acts*
1798

Appearing in summer 1795, *The monk* was an immediate and immense success. In spite of *The castle spectre*, numerous other plays, and a literary career of almost thirty years, the novel's author – Matthew Gregory Lewis – has been known as 'Monk' Lewis ever since. He was educated at Westminster and Christ Church, Oxford, and wrote the novel at the age of twenty. 'I was induced to go on with it,' he commented in May 1794, 'by reading *The mysteries of Udolpho* which is, in my opinion, one of the most interesting books that has ever been published'. *Udolpho* was just out; Lewis had no time to distance himself, yet produced in *The monk* gothicism of a very different kind. Radcliffe is first and foremost a writer of romance. Emily St Aubert is detained by her wicked Italian uncle-by-marriage, Montoni, and separated from her lover. The gothic setting of Castle Udolpho provides a string of mysteries, seemingly supernatural episodes which are painstakingly revealed to have a natural source. Radcliffe is careful to discourage superstitition. If gothicism can ever be morally improving, hers surely is. The chaste heroine wins through and marries her chaste admirer.

To Radcliffe's stock-in-trade of spooky voices, apparent apparitions, secret panels and underground passages, Lewis adds sex, black magic, incest and moral ambiguity. Ambrosio, Abbot of the Capuchins in Madrid, prides himself on his virtue, is seduced by an accomplice of Lucifer, and finally sells his soul. Two years before reading *Udolpho*, Lewis had been introduced in Weimar to 'the celebrated author of *Werter*' (remarking wittily in a letter home of 30 July 1792, 'you must not be surprised if I shoot myself one of these fine mornings'). Lewis admired Goethe, and translated Part One of *Faust* for Byron in 1817. A connection between *Faust* and *The monk*, however, is difficult to prove. Goethe began work on Part One in 1770, but did not publish it till 1808; Lewis meanwhile claims to have drawn his story of diabolic possession from an obscure version of the Faust legend, called *Santon Barisa*.

The fact that Ambrosio's compact with Lucifer comes at the end of *The monk* gives the book an unexpected shape. Only gradually do we become aware that he is possessed. The novice Rosario seems unthreatening in his hero-worship, until the [partial] revelation that he is a woman in disguise. Playing on Ambrosio's devotion to the Virgin, Rosario/Matilda seduces him, then encourages his seduction of Antonia (*via* a wonderfully louche scene of Antonia getting into the bath, viewed in Matilda's magic mirror). Finally, when the Monk has been led on to rape and murder, and sold his soul to cheat the Inquisition, Lucifer reveals Matilda to have been a spirit all along:

Know vain man! that I long have marked you for my prey: I watched the movements of your heart; I saw that you were virtuous from vanity, not principle, and I seized the fit moment of seduction. I observed your blind idolatry of the Madonna's picture. I bade a subordinate but crafty spirit assume a similar form, and you eagerly yielded to the blandishments of Matilda. Your pride was gratified by her flattery; Your lust only needed an opportunity to break forth ... It was I who threw Matilda in your way; It was I who gave you entrance to Antonia's chamber; It was I who caused the dagger to be given you which pierced your sister's bosom ... (ed. Anderson, *World's Classics*, Oxford 1980, p. 440)

Despite the presence of the supernatural (Lewis was advised by all to cut his ghost), *The castle spectre* is in some ways closer to *Udolpho* than it is to *The monk*. We are back in a sub-Shakespearean world of the envious usurping younger brother (Osmond), the guilty soliloquy, the paragon heroine (Angela) and appropriate rescuer (Percy). Hazlitt recalls Wordsworth, who saw the play in Bristol in February 1798, as saying 'it fitted the taste of the audience like a glove' (Howe xvii, 118). The contempt is uneasy. Lewis was a success, Wordsworth a failure. The *Spectre* had run for three months in London (most productions lasted a matter of days), and was said to have brought in £18,000. Wordsworth and Coleridge had both written tragedies for the stage the previous year, and both had been turned down by Covent Garden a day or two before the *Spectre* opened at the Theatre Royal (14 December 1797). Chagrin was to be expected. Wordsworth took refuge in thoughts of 'a great reform . . . in the Stage', and joined Coleridge in disparaging their rival.

Coleridge, it seems, had a copy of the *Spectre* by 20 January 1798. On the 23rd he lists the play's faults for Wordsworth, under the headings of Language, Character, Passion, Sentiment, reserving his skimpy praise for what he terms 'Conduct' (management of plot and situation):

This Play proves how accurately you conjectured concerning *theatric* merit. The merit of *The castle spectre* consists wholly in its *situations* . . . the play is a mere patchwork of plagiarisms – but they are very well worked up, and for stage effect make an excellent whole.

On one point only, Coleridge is generous:

There is a pretty little Ballad-song introduced – and Lewis, I think, has great and peculiar excellence in these compositions. The simplicity and naturalness is his own . . . it is made to subsist in congruity with a language perfectly modern – the language of his own times . . .

Depending for its effect upon situation, rather than a portrayal of the inward workings of the mind, the *Spectre* has merely '*theatric* merit'. On the other hand, as a writer of song, Lewis is capable of the naturalness that will be the hallmark of Coleridge and Wordsworth themselves in *Lyrical ballads* (published the following autumn).

It is a dichotomy that reflects the contemporary scene. Wordsworth's 'great reform . . . in the Stage' would never come, despite the fact that he and Coleridge were soon to achieve a comparable break-through in the sphere of poetry. Theatrical tradition was too strong. Lewis, though capable of powerful simplicity as a novelist, was reduced by the stage to the exaggeration that was the style of the day. He could move a play along, he could be very funny (Motley to Percy, 'whatever you may think of it, my Lord, I shouldn't be at all pleased at waking to-morrow morning, to find myself dead in my bed'; p. 21), but he nowhere creates a character in whose emotions we deeply believe. It is interesting to see his style transmuted by a writer who has shed the conventional gestures. Angela, whom Osmond is trying to seduce, and whose mother he has loved and killed (while trying to kill his brother), embraces her guilty uncle in a dream:

a female form glided along the vault: It was Angela! – She smiled upon me, and beckoned me to advance. I flew towards her; my arms were already unclosed to

89

clasp her – when suddenly her figure changed, her face grew pale, a stream of blood gushed from her bosom! – Hassan, 'twas Evelina!

SAIB *and* HASSAN. Evelina!

OSMOND. Such as when she sank at my feet expiring, while my hand grasped the dagger still crimsoned with her blood! – 'We meet again this night!' murmured her hollow voice. 'Now rush to my arms, but first see what you have made of me! Embrace me, my bridegroom! We must never part again!' While speaking, her form withered away; the flesh fell from her bones; her eyes burst from their sockets . . . her rotting fingers pressed my hand, and my face was covered with her kisses . . . (p. 67)

'I slept indeed', Victor Frankenstein recalls, telling of the hours that followed his creature's awakening,

but I was disturbed by the wildest dreams. I thought that I saw Elizabeth, in the bloom of health, walking in the streets of Ingolstadt. Delighted and surprised, I embraced her; but as I imprinted the first kiss on her lips, they became livid with the hue of death; her features appeared to change, and I thought that I held the corpse of my dead mother in my arms; a shroud enveloped her form, and I saw the grave worms crawling in the folds of the flannel. (*Frankenstein, World's Classics*, Oxford, p. 58)

Gothicism is most successful where most is left to the imagination; the stage tradition of Lewis's time left very little. The major gothic novels survive partly because their authors wrote more suggestively, partly because we invest their work with psychological depths of which they were unaware. In *Frankenstein* Mary Shelley's great pre-Freudian dream takes off from Lewis's clumsiness, not merely refining his graveyard extravagance ('her rotting fingers pressed my hand'), but evoking in a few brilliantly horrific phrases both the central relationships of the book and the course of her story.

# 21

# WILLIAM GODWIN

## Memoirs of Wollstonecraft
### (*Memoirs of the author of A vindication of the rights of woman*)
### 1798

'From my very heart and soul I give you joy', Thomas Holcroft wrote to Godwin and Mary Wollstonecraft on hearing the news of their marriage on 6 April 1797, 'I think you the most extraordinary married pair in existence.' Perhaps they were. As their enemies pointed out with glee, given their published views on the institution of marriage, it was extraordinary that they were married at all. More extraordinary – and closer presumably to Holcroft's meaning – was the fact that two such intellects should be paired.

As the author of *A vindication of the rights of woman* (1792), Wollstonecraft was famous or notorious according to the reader's point of view. Despite its cumbersome title, her recent *Letters written during a short residence in Sweden, Norway and Denmark* (1796) had been well received and widely read. Godwin was probably right in suggesting that 'no female writer [had] ever obtained so great a degree of celebrity throughout Europe' (p. 73). His own reputation at the time of their marriage was still at its height. The huge success of *Political justice* (1793) had been followed a year later by publication of his great obsessional novel, *Caleb Williams*. At the end of 1794 his pamphlet *Cursory strictures* had shown how effective he could be in practical terms, undermining the prosecution case, and turning the course of the Treason Trials against the Government. A revised second edition of *Political justice* had appeared in 1796, and *The enquirer* in February 1797.

Godwin's *Memoirs of the author of A vindication of the rights of woman* is a celebration of this short-lived extraordinary marriage, written immediately after Wollstonecraft's death from septicemia on 10 September 1797. It is also an act of justice to her reputation, a putting of the record straight:

Every benefactor of mankind is more or less influenced by a liberal passion for fame; and survivors only pay a debt due to these benefactors, when they assert and establish on their part, the honour they loved. (p. 2)

In performing this duty Godwin was honest in a way that no biographer had ever been before – let alone a grieving husband. He told the world not only of the tenderness of his own relationship, but of his wife's earlier passions for Fuseli and Gilbert Imlay; he described her suicide attempts (regarded still as sin); he gave the most painful account of her lingering death, ten days after the birth of the future Mary Shelley. Godwin seems to have had no idea of the shock that he would cause. The *Memoirs*, according to the *European magazine* in April 1798, would be

read with disgust by every female who has pretensions to delicacy; with detestation by every one attached to the interests of religion and morality; and with indignation by any one who might feel any regard for the unhappy woman, whose frailties should have been buried in oblivion.

*The Anti-jacobin review*, with its doggerel Spenserians, descended in August 1801 to the level of personal abuse:

William hath penn'd a waggon-load of stuff,
And Mary's life at last he need must write,
Thinking her whoredoms were not known enough,
Till fairly printed off in black and white.
With wondrous glee and pride, this simple wight
Her brothel feats of wantonness sets down . . .

In a sense perhaps Godwin *was* a 'simple wight'. Certainly he had been surprised by the strength of his love. *Political justice*, with its total commitment to reason, had asserted that marriage was a question of property, 'a monopoly, and the worst of monopolies'. Procreation had its necessary place, but no rational man could permit himself to be swayed by emotion – deflected from his duty to the race by his feelings for an individual. Since becoming a success, Godwin had permitted himself to flirt with a number of female admirers, notably Mrs Inchbald, Maria Reveley (later Gisborne) and Amelia Anderson (later Opie), but the feelings that Wollstonecraft brought out in him were entirely new.

They had disliked each other when they met at a dinner-party given for Paine in 1791 (by their publisher, Joseph Johnson). Five years later, as Wollstonecraft emerged from her sad prolonged encounter with Imlay, there was a gradual coming together. Looking back in the *Memoirs*, Godwin describes the acknowledgement of love in tones that would have been wholly impossible to the rationalist philosopher:

There was, as I have already said, no period of throes and resolute explanation attendant on the tale. It was friendship melting into love. Previously to our mutual declaration, each felt half-assured, yet each felt a certain trembling anxiety to have assurance complete.

Mary rested her head upon the shoulder of her lover, hoping to find a heart with which she might safely treasure her world of affection; fearing to commit a mistake, yet, in spite of her melancholy experience, fraught with that generous confidence, which, in a great soul, is never extinguished. I had never loved till now ... (pp. 153–4)

'We did not marry,' the next paragraph begins, trusting to the reader to make a feeling response – 'nothing can be so ridiculous ... as to require the overflowing of the soul to wait upon a ceremony' (p. 154). Godwin's rationalism had always been akin to the Romantic impulse, in that it too was an act of faith in human potential. The 'omnipotence of reason' was to bring about general future happiness. Wollstonecraft's thinking was broadly in line with Godwin's own, but her Romanticism was openly felt. She brought to their relationship a commitment to 'the overflowing of the soul' that places her unexpectedly with Coleridge and Wordsworth. 'Her mind', Godwin wrote,

constitutionally attached itself to the sublime and amiable. She found an inexpressible delight in the beauties of nature, and in the splendid reveries of the imagination. But nature itself, she thought, would be no better than a vast blank, if the mind of the observer did not supply it with an animating soul. When she walked amidst the wonders of nature, she was accustomed to converse with her God. (pp. 33–4)

Godwin's words were published in January 1798, a month before Coleridge wrote *Frost at midnight* and six before Wordsworth's composition of *Tintern abbey*, yet the views they imply are similar in all respects to those that inspired the two poets in the year of *Lyrical ballads*. Coleridge told his brother on 10 March that the aim of his poetry was, 'to elevate the imagination and set the affections in right tune by the beauty of the inanimate impregnated, as with a living soul, by the presence of Life.'

93

# William Godwin

Only the last chapters of the *Memoirs* directly concern the relationship of Godwin and Wollstonecraft. Almost the whole book, though, is what she told him of herself. Facts and dates were checked as far as possible with friends, but Wollstonecraft's relatives refused to help – as did Fuseli – and Godwin had no access to Imlay's papers. Four and a half months after the funeral, the book was in print. Early chapters tell us of Wollstonecraft's unsettled childhood and the death of her mother ('A little patience, and all will be over', p. 28), of her friendship with Fanny Blood ('The grave has closed over a dear friend, the friend of my youth; still she is present with me, and I hear her soft voice warbling as I stray over the heath', p. 47), of her responsibility to her family and determination to establish herself as a writer ('She considered herself as  standing forth in defence of one half of the human species', p. 79). The relationships with Fuseli and Imlay are treated not as folly, but as an expression of the life-force that was within her: 'She was playful, full of confidence, kindness and sympathy' (p. 113). Even the rhythms of Godwin's prose are informed with the tenderness of loss: 'Wherever Mary appeared, admiration attended upon her' (p. 159). Writing has been an act of love, a prolonging of joy.

# 22

# JOANNA BAILLIE

---

## A series of plays

*in which it is attempted to delineate the stronger passions
of the mind. Each passion being the subject of a
tragedy and a comedy*
1798

Joanna Baillie's very readable *Poems* (published in 1790 by Joseph Johnson) attracted no attention; her 1798 volume of plays, however, was noticed at once. Southey, who was to be so harsh about that other anonymous collection of the year – *Lyrical ballads* – commented excitedly to Williams Wynn in a letter of 8 July:

A very good work has passed through my hands, called *A Series of Plays exemplifying the effects of the stronger passions*. The author (whoever he may be) bids fair to become an honour to English literature.

Six months later Southey promised Grosvenor Bedford 'a great pleasure to come' if he had not yet read the plays, adding, 'I would go fifty miles to see the author' (3 January 1799). Had he been given directions for the journey, he would have found to his surprise that the writer of two powerful blank-verse tragedies about two powerful male characters was a woman. Baillie's secret was not widely known until the Kemble production of *Monfort* at Drury Lane in 1800.

At seventy pages, Baillie's Introductory Discourse has the distinction of being longer than the Preface to *Lyrical ballads* (sixty-four, with the 1802 additions); it is also more elegantly written, and very similar in its views. Her quarrel with romance and the novel anticipates Wordsworth's objection to 'idle and extravagant stories in verse': 'they have', she says bluntly, 'represented men and women speaking and acting as men and women never did speak or act' (p. 19). Where Wordsworth and Coleridge, in the 1798 Advertisement, proclaim an experiment with 'the language of conversation in the middle and lower classes of society', she asserts that

those works which most strongly characterize human nature in the middling and lower classes of society, where it is to be discovered by stronger and more un-equivocal marks, will ever be the most popular. (p. 20)

Baillie's statement is in fact doubly Wordsworthian. Her assumption that 'stronger and more unequivocal marks' of human nature are to be found among the lower orders resembles his justification in the Preface for writing about 'humble and rustic life': 'in that condition the essential passions of the heart find a better soil' (1800 *Lyrical ballads*, p. xi).

The thinking behind *Lyrical ballads* and its later Preface depends most obviously on Hugh Blair, whose *Lectures on rhetoric and belles lettres* (1783) Coleridge took out of the Bristol Library in January 1798. Blair, however, is a primitivist. He looks for unfeigned emotion, not in the contemporary British 'middling and lower classes', but among 'the first ages of society'. From a practical point of view it could be said that Burns had made the transition to modern democratic simplicity. But he was not a theorist, and he belonged to the lower social group himself. Wordsworth and Coleridge wished to establish that poets, whatever their class, should write with the spontaneity they associated with unsophisticated people. Two pieces of evidence confirm that in evolving a theory for such writing, they found help in Baillie's Introductory Discourse.

Waiting to be murdered in a rather gothic wood at the end of *Monfort*, Rezenfelt allows his thoughts to go back to boyhood:

> Ha! does the night-bird greet me on my way?
> How much his hooting is in harmony
> With such a scene as this! I like it well.
> Oft when a boy, at the still twilight hour,
> I've leant my back against some knotted oak,
> And loudly mimick'd him, till to my call
> He answer would return, and thro' the gloom
> We friendly converse held.
>
> (p. 378)

It comes as a shock to think of *There was a boy*, of all poems, as having a literary source. Coleridge recognized it at once as quintessentially Wordsworthian: 'had I met these lines running wild in the deserts of Arabia, I should instantly have screamed out "Wordsworth"' (10

December 1798). Given the verbal echoes, however, there can be little doubt that Rezenfelt prompted Wordsworth's memory of hooting to the owls of Windermere:

> There was a Boy, ye knew him well, ye Cliffs
> And Islands of Winander! many a time,
> At evening . . .
> > would he stand alone
> Beneath the trees, or by the glimmering lake,
> And there . . .
> Blew.mimic hootings to the silent owls
> That they might answer him. And they would shout
> Across the wat'ry vale, and shout again,
> Responsive to his call . . .
>
> > *(There was a boy*, ll. 1–13)

*There was a boy* shows that Wordsworth had read Baillie by October 1798; the Advertisement to *Lyrical ballads*, however, with its seeming echo of the Introductory Discourse, was written by early July. Coleridge's deviousness comes to the rescue. In a manuscript note to *Lewti*, ll. 44–7, he writes accusingly, 'This image was borrowed by Miss Bailey in her *Basil*, as the dates of the poems prove' (E. H. Coleridge, i, 255n). The dates do no such thing. A review in the *Analytical* shows that Baillie's *Plays* appeared in, or more probably before, April 1798; *Lewti* was printed in the *Morning post* on the 13th. The lines from which Coleridge drew occur in a description of Victoria in Act I, Scene ii:

> Her robe, and tresses floating on the wind,
> Like some light figure in a morning cloud . . .
>
> > (p. 85)

In his anxiety to accuse someone else of plagiarism, Coleridge (who, be it said, never made clear that *Lewti* is a rewritten early Wordsworth poem) establishes for us that a copy of Baillie was available at Alfoxden at the height of the *Lyrical ballads* period.

Irrespective of links and echoes, Baillie and Wordsworth are kindred spirits. 'Let one simple trait of the human heart', she writes, 'one expression of passion genuine and true to nature, be introduced, and it will stand forth alone in the boldness of reality' (p. 21). With this creed, she proposes to attempt

a series of tragedies, of simpler construction, less embellished with poetical decorations . . . in which the chief object [shall] be to delineate the progress of the higher passions in the human breast . . . (p. 41)

# Joanna Baillie

Each tragedy is to exhibit a particular emotion, and to be paired with a comedy. In a remarkably Wordsworthian phrase, Baillie's concern is for 'passion that is permanent in its nature', yet 'varied in progress' (p. 39). There is, she believes, a neglected source of tragedy in

those strong and fixed passions, which seemingly unprovoked by outward circumstances, will from small beginnings brood within the breast, till all the better dispositions, all the fair gifts of nature, are borne down before them . . . (p. 38)

*Count Basil* and *The tryal* represent love, *Monfort* (as yet without its comic partner) features hate. Though technically accomplished, *Basil* hardly lives up to the Introductory Discourse. For all the talk of 'small beginnings', the hero's love comes on him suddenly, and requires no apparent brooding 'within the breast'. It is entirely one-sided, and too obsessional to seem a 'passion that is permanent in its nature'. Baillie is conscious of having provided the reader 'a stick wherewith to break [her] own pate', but hopes all the same that in her series of comedies 'bustle of plot, brilliancy of dialogue, and even the bold and striking in character, [will] be kept in due subordination to nature' (p. 56). It was a lot to ask. In the event, *The tryal* is lively, pleasurable, bustling, unnatural from first to last.

It is to *Monfort* – unsuccessful at Drury Lane, but nonetheless 'an honour to English literature' – that we should look for the 'passion genuine and true to nature' that singled Baillie out as the major playwright of her day. The hero is moody and magnificent, without being too obviously satanic (or too close to Godwin's Falkland). The verse is powerful. The climax is effective and unstrained. And though the theme of the play is hate, we see in Jane de Monfort a convincing portrayal of love.

# 23

## CHARLES LLOYD

---

# Edmund Oliver
### 1798

> My COLERIDGE! take the wanderer to thy breast,
> The youth who loves thee, and who, faint, would rest
> (Oft rack'd by hopes that frensy and expire)
> In the long sabbath of subdued desire!

Charles Lloyd's emotional lines form the conclusion of an address to Coleridge, printed in *Poems by Coleridge, Lamb and Lloyd*, 1797. 'Too warm by a half', Coleridge has written beneath them in a copy of the *Poems* given to Thomas Hutchinson in 1799: 'Am obliged to C.L. for his wishes, but would rather not!' The sarcasm shows bitterness, but also pain. Coleridge had reacted to Lloyd's *Edmund Oliver*, published in April 1798, as a personal attack. A number of details – the hero's 'love-fit, debaucheries, leaving college, and going into the army' – were clearly based on his own experience. Only Southey, his brother-in-law and erstwhile collaborator, could have provided the information. As Coleridge himself put it, Lloyd's 'infirmities' had 'been made the instruments of another man's darker passions' (18 May 1798). Nor had the process stopped there. What Lloyd was alleging we do not know, but Lamb had surprisingly taken his side, breaking off correspondence (for two years) with the man who was his chief support in a troubled life. Joseph Cottle too seems to have become involved. Lloyd even wrote a crazy letter denouncing Coleridge to Dorothy Wordsworth.

In its early stages the relationship had been very different. Charles Lloyd the banker had arranged for his son to live with Coleridge at Nether Stowey, receiving board, lodging, tuition and companionship, for the sum of £80 a year. Lloyd, who was two years younger than Coleridge, had already shown both talent and instability. Proving too restless for work in the bank, he had sampled the life of a medical student in Edinburgh, then turned poet, producing his *Poems on various subjects* 1795 at the age of twenty. 'Charles Lloyd wins upon me hourly', Coleridge wrote on 24 September 1796, soon after his arrival at Stowey:

his heart is uncommonly pure, his affections delicate, & his benevolence enlivened, but not sicklied, by sensibility . . . His Joy, & gratitude to Heaven for the circumstances of his domestication with me, I can scarcely describe to you – & I believe, that his fixed plans are of being always with me.

Interestingly from the point of view of *Edmund Oliver*, the letter reveals too that Lloyd has received from Coleridge a 'conviction of the truth of Christianity', having been 'if not a Deist, yet quite a Sceptic'.

In March 1797 Lloyd moved to Lichfield for mental treatment in Erasmus Darwin's sanatorium. Though Coleridge had drawn up an exalted scheme for his education, little had been achieved. Lloyd seems, however, to have left without resentment. Friction came in the autumn, after his stay with Southey in August–September. Coleridge was not blameless, foolishly publishing in November the 'Nehemiah Higginbottom' Sonnets ('Pensive at eve on the *hard* world I mus'd . . .), which contained parody of Lloyd's affectations, alongside Lamb's and his own. By this time, however, *Edmund Oliver* had been written. The book's relation to Coleridge is more complex, and more pervasive, than has been supposed. There is no caricature, no evident antagonism. Oliver may go through experiences that belong to Coleridge's past, may even be described at one point in terms that physically resemble him, but he stands in the same relation to Charles Maurice as Lloyd himself stood to Coleridge. 'You taught me to see things in their essence', Oliver writes to Maurice:

you opened to me the beauty of Christianity, shewed to me the necessity of evils we at present labour under, deduced from the character of those evils the sublime system of optimism, convinced me that the mind is governed by definite laws . . . led me on to the grand spectacle of universal final happiness to the whole creation. (i, p. 72)

Maurice, who is the spiritual centre of *Edmund Oliver*, converts the hero – as Coleridge had converted Lloyd – to a belief in Priestleyan Unitarianism. The 'sublime system of optimism', on which the book rests, had been developed by Priestley from Hartley's *Observations on man*, 1749. It depended on the assumption of 'definite', God-given laws of association, that govern the human mind and lead, *of necessity*, to 'the grand spectacle of universal final happiness'. The system had been expounded (to some extent, enacted) in Coleridge's *Religious musings*, published in April 1796, five months before Lloyd came to Stowey. In accepting it as the basis of his thinking, Lloyd showed himself Coleridge's disciple as clearly as Coleridge had shown himself a follower of Hartley and Priestley. There are, however, different influences at work in *Edmund Oliver*. The childhood love between Oliver and Gertrude is reminiscent of Bernardin de St-Pierre's *Paul and Virginia* (translated by Helen Maria Williams, 1796) – and behind Bernardin is Rousseau. In the later, jacobin, relationship of Gertrude and D'Oyley, we feel the presence of Holcroft's *Anna St Ives* (1792). Wordsworth's *Borderers* (completed March 1797) has been a powerful stimulus. And, like *The borderers, Edmund Oliver* seems at times to borrow from Godwin's novel, *Caleb Williams* (1794), while questioning the authority of *Political justice* (1793).

Wordsworth may not himself have read *Edmund Oliver*, but reports on 9 May 1798 that Dorothy 'thinks it contains a great deal, a *very* great deal of excellent matter'. Her one criticism – that it 'bears the marks of a too hasty composition' – is most clearly true of the final pages. The happy marriages of Lloyd's conclusion seem a cross between pantisocracy and Shakespearean comedy. 'Basil, Edmund and I', Maurice writes, 'have taken lands which lie contiguous to each other – we have banished the words *mine* and *thine* . . . our tables are supplied by our common industry, our wives have entered completely into these views' (ii, pp. 292–3). *Edmund Oliver* is a novel of its period, and on the whole a good one. Its quest for the just society and the good life may weigh a little heavily at times; but at his best, Lloyd handles plot, characterisation, dialogue, the epistolary form, with ease and elegance:

D'OYLEY TO CLAREMONT: His mind is certainly not a common one, but its growth is choked by prejudice – he was absurd enough to confess himself a Christian – would you believe it? a Christian . . . (i, p. 79)

OLIVER TO MAURICE: I could perceive in him the sneer of self-congratulating superiority, when he discovered that I was a Christian. 'You deem, then, Sir, that religion is convenient as a political restraint on the minds of the vulgar – ' 'No', I answered, 'I rather consider the possession of it as the sublimest prerogative of the human mind.' 'You are an enthusiast, Sir, I fancy'; and he changed the conversation, hastily turning his head to conceal a sarcastic smile. (i, p. 85)

# 24

## JAMES PLUMPTRE

---

# The lakers

*a comic opera*
1798

' "My dear, dear aunt", she rapturously cried' (Elizabeth Bennet in *Pride and prejudice* has just been asked to come on a tour of the Lakes),

what delight! what felicity! You give me fresh life and vigour . . . What are men to rocks and mountains? Oh, what hours of transport shall we spend! (Chapman, p. 154)

Though not published till 1813, *Pride and prejudice* was composed in 1796–7, the years in which the Reverend James Plumptre (pronounced *plum-tree*) of St Clare's College, Cambridge, made his first two northern tours, and wrote *The lakers*.

Elizabeth's tour was called off. The Gardiners took her to Derbyshire instead; where, for all her 'fresh life and vigour', she finally settled for a man in place of the promised rocks and mountains. Jane Austen, however, allows herself more prolonged satire of the picturesque in *Sense and sensibility*, drafted at the same period. It seems that she has read Gilpin's work, and is not wholly unsympathetic. 'Admiration of landscape scenery', Marianne Dashwood comments defensively to Edward Ferrars,

is become a mere jargon. Every body pretends to feel, and tries to describe with the taste and elegance of him who first defined what picturesque beauty was. I detest jargon of every kind, and sometimes I have kept my feelings to myself, because I could find no language to describe them in but what was worn and hackneyed out of all sense and meaning.

Edward replies as the plain man, who is not to be drawn into this contemporary fad:

I like a fine prospect, but not on picturesque principles. I do not like crooked, twisted, blasted trees. I admire them much more if they are tall, straight and flourishing. I do not like ruined, tattered cottages. I am not fond of nettles, thistles, or heath blossoms [heather]. I have more pleasure in a snug farm-house than a watch-tower – and a troop of tidy happy villagers please me better than the finest banditti in the world. (Chapman, pp. 97–8)

Gilpin's major *Tours* had appeared in succession in the Eighties: *The Wye*, 1782, *The lakes*, 1786, *The highlands*, 1789. *Three essays on picturesque beauty* followed in 1792. Austen and Plumptre were writing when the cult was at its height. On his first visit to the Lakes, Plumptre took with him Uvedale Price's more rarified *Essays on the picturesque* (1794), but Gilpin's would have been the name on everybody's lips. West, in his *Guide to the lakes*, had told the tourists what to visit; Gilpin, making constantly the analogy of painting, told them how to see:

Perhaps a sun-beam, half-suffused in vapour, darting between two mountains, may stretch along the water in a lengthened gleam, just as the skiff passes to receive the light upon its swelling sail; while the sea-gull, wheeling along the storm, turns its silvery side, strongly illumined, against the bosom of some lurid cloud; and by that single touch of opposition, gives double darkness to the rising tempest. (*Lakes tour*, i, p. 127)

Plumptre wrote to Gilpin in 1803 to apologise for *The lakers*, but he had taken no offence. The satire is good-natured, and not directed at Gilpin himself. Beccabunga Veronica, Plumptre's flamboyant comic heroine, is one of those who trade in the jargon that Marianne Dashwood so scrupulously avoids. 'Where's my Claude-Lorrain?' she cries (reaching for her Claude-glass):

I must throw a Gilpin tint over these magic scenes of beauty. (*Looks through the glass.*) How gorgeously glowing! . . . The effect is inexpressibly interesting. The amphitheatrical perspective of the long landscape; the peeping points of the many-coloured crags of the headlong mountains, looking out most interestingly from the picturesque luxuriance of the bowery foliage, margining their ruggedness, and feathering the fells . . . (p. 19)

Though guiltless of impropriety, Beccabunga knows a good deal about 'bowery foliage'. She is not merely a picturesque traveller, but a picturesque travelling botanist in search of a titled husband. With Erasmus Darwin as her guide, 'she has been studying the system of plants, till she now wishes to know the system of man'.

# James Plumptre

Botany, we are reminded in the Preface, is by no means 'a proper amusement for the more polished sex':

the false taste of a licentious age, which is gaining ground, and corrupting the soft and elegant manners of the otherwise loveliest part of the creation, requires every discouragement which can be given. (p. xii)

It is no joking matter that Darwin's *Loves of the plants*, 1789 (though designed merely to propagate the Linnaean system of classification), has introduced the loveliest part of Creation to the world of floral sexuality:

> With honey'd lips enamour'd Woodbines meet,
> Clasp with fond arms, and mix their kisses sweet.
> (Canto i, ll. 19–20)

Plumptre is serious in his disapproval, but humorous in his discouragement. Beccabunga's maid, Anna, proudly regards her mistress as 'a great schollard'. To the unsophisticated Billy Sample she confides, 'all ladies that know any thing study botamy now'. Nor is this all:

*Anna.* Such curious truths too contained in it – why, plants are all men and women.
*Sample.* Aye, there are sweet-williams; I'm a sweet-william . . .
*Anna.* No, no, I mean that they drink and sleep, and are like man and wife.
*Sample.* What, sleep in the same bed?
*Anna.* Yes, and in different beds . . . (p. 43)

'Deeply versed in the loves of the plants', Beccabunga is determined upon marriage to Sir Charles Portinscale, whose title and botany are impeccable – only to be preempted by her niece. Fobbed off with Speedwell, the gentleman's gentleman, she resorts again to her glass:

I fear I shall never get another offer half so good . . . He's a vastly clever man, he's a botanist, he's picturesque – I'll throw a Gilpin tint over him. (*Looks through her glass.*) Yes, he's gorgeously glowing . . . We will be *connate* like the twin flowers on the same *peduncle* . . . (pp. 58–9)

It may be that 'botamy' and the picturesque will never again be topical, but *The lakers* is a very funny play. Plumptre was unable to get it staged. With a good comic actress, and some good voices (it is full of catchy songs in the manner of *The beggar's opera*), perhaps it could yet have its première.

# 25

# SAMUEL TAYLOR COLERIDGE

## Fears in solitude

*written in 1798 during the alarm of an invasion; to which
are added France: an ode, and Frost at midnight*
1798

Coleridge's slim quarto, containing *Fears in solitude*, *Frost at midnight* and *France: an ode*, is a statement of personal faith emerging from a context of political despair. It was issued in the same month as *Lyrical ballads*, Coleridge's famous collaboration with Wordsworth, but printed over his own name, where *Lyrical ballads* was anonymous. The ballads were intended to reach a wide audience. If their revolutionary poetic method was to be accepted with sympathy, it was prudent not to associate them with Coleridge's Jacobin reputation. By contrast, the quarto (whose publisher, Joseph Johnson, was imprisoned during the summer) was intended for those who shared the poet's views.

*France: an ode*, written to protest against the invasion of republican Switzerland in March 1798, was first published in the *Morning post* of 16 April. Both the political context and Coleridge's own standing are made clear in the editorial note:

The following excellent Ode will be in unison with the feelings of every friend of Liberty and foe to Oppression; of all who, admiring the French Revolution, detest and deplore the conduct of France towards Switzerland.

'It is very satisfactory', the editor continues,

to find so steady and zealous an advocate for Freedom as Mr. Coleridge concur with us . . . What we most admire is the *avowal* of his sentiments, and public censure of the unprincipled and atrocious conduct of France.

There had been many trials for British sympathizers in the Revolution – the execution of Louis XVI and declaration of war on England

# Samuel Taylor Coleridge

(January–February 1793), the Reign of Terror, the policy of foreign conquest that followed Robespierre's death in July 1794, the refusal of British offers of peace in 1796 – but this time the French had gone too far. Switzerland was Europe's oldest republic, symbolic of the virtues of liberty and independence for which the Revolution had stood. The horror that Coleridge felt, and chose also to 'avow', had been felt by readers of the *Morning post* and others, up and down the country:

> When France in wrath her giant limbs uprear'd,
> And with that oath which smote earth, air, and sea,
> Stamp'd her strong foot and said, she would be free,
> Bear witness for me, how I hop'd and fear'd!
> With what a joy my lofty gratulation
> Unaw'd I sung amid a slavish band . . .
> For ne'er, O Liberty! with partial aim
> I dimm'd thy light, or damp'd thy holy flame;
> But blest the paeans of deliver'd France,
> And hung my head, and wept at Britain's name!
>
> (*France: an ode*, ll. 22–7, 39–42)

In April 1798 horror gave way to fear. England herself, it seemed, was about to be invaded. Coleridge responded with *Fears in solitude*, a complex and under-rated work that ranges from personal to public, from prayer and self-reproof to fluent satire against newspaper reporting of the war, and 'dainty terms for fratricide':

> Terms which we trundle smoothly o'er our tongues
> Like mere abstractions, empty sounds to which
> We join no feeling and attach no form,
> As if the soldier died without a wound;
> As if the fibres of this godlike frame
> Were gor'd without a pang; as if the wretch,
> Who fell in battle doing bloody deeds,
> Pass'd off to heaven, *translated* and not killed . . .
>
> (ll. 111–18)

Coleridge's vehemence is impressive. From east to west 'a groan of accusation' rises against imperialist Britain; whose ships have carried slavery, war, syphilis across the world:

> like a cloud that travels on,
> Steam'd up from Cairo's swamps of pestilence,
> Ev'n so, my countrymen! have we gone forth
> And borne to distant tribes slavery and pangs,

And, deadlier far, our vices, whose deep taint
With slow perdition murders the whole man,
His body and his soul! Meanwhile, at home,
We have been drinking with a riotous thirst
Pollutions from the brimming cup of wealth . . .

       (ll. 48–56)

Behind the vehemence is a patriotism based on personal faith in 'the
God in nature' – 'There lives nor form nor feeling in my soul /
Unborrow'd from my country' (ll. 189–90) – a faith that had found its
perfect expression two months earlier in *Frost at midnight*. In its original
form, this greatest of Coleridge's conversation poems is longer than the
1834 text that is normally read, and different in important ways. Unlike
Wordsworth, Coleridge was often a good reviser, but in this case he
sharpened, and moralized, his lines at the expense of a more generous
earlier vision. As the poet sits before his dying fire there is, in the later
text of *Frost at midnight*, a moment of incongruous self-blame. 'Me-
thinks its motion in this hush of nature', Coleridge writes, alluding to
the film of soot (or 'stranger') on the grate:

> Gives it dim sympathies with me who live,
> Making it a companionable form,
> Whose puny flaps and freaks the idling Spirit
> By its own moods interprets, every where,
> Echo or mirror seeking of itself,
> And makes a toy of Thought.
>    (1834 *Frost at midnight*, ll. 18–23)

The poet foists himself on his surroundings, and is reproved for selfish
lack of vision. In the terms of *Biographia literaria*, his behaviour is
presumably fanciful rather than imaginative.

  To read in the 1798 version (the poem that inspired the Wordsworth
of *Tintern abbey* and the *Prelude* 'spots of time') of 'the living spirit in
our frame / That loves not to behold a lifeless thing' is to be in a
different, more innocent, world:

> Methinks, it's motion in this hush of nature
> Gives it dim sympathies with me, who live,
> Making it a companionable form,
> With which I can hold commune. Idle thought!
> But still the living spirit in our frame,
> That loves not to behold a lifeless thing,
> Transfuses into all it's own delights

It's own volition, sometimes with deep faith,
And sometimes with fantastic playfulness.

(ll. 17–25)

The 'stranger' in this earlier, stronger, text is not merely 'a companion-
able form', but one with which the poet can – and rightly does – 'hold
commune'. The original version of *Frost at midnight*, like the original
version of *Dejection, an ode*, is more personal, more interesting, more
significant for its period, less formally satisfying. That Coleridge should
have cut the final lines of 1798, where the child Hartley comes to life,
will seem to many an improvement. There could be no more beautiful
ending than the 'silent icicles / Quietly shining to the quiet moon'. Its
effect is to round the poem off in utter peacefulness, where before it had
ended in joyful eagerness. The idealized child, who in his father's wish-
fulfilment will (in either text) 'wander like a breeze / By lakes and sandy
shores', is permitted in the original ending to shout, stretch and flutter,
in his mother's arms. In doing so, he claims the poem as his own,
demonstrating in his response to the world of frost the outgoing
imaginative sympathy that is his father's theme.

Truly understood, sympathy is the 'see[ing] into the life of things'
which, at this moment, Coleridge shared with Wordsworth. As portrayed in *Frost at midnight*, and implied in the other poems of this
volume, it is the principle of selfless love, founded on Coleridge's belief
in an immanent Unitarian God, 'who from eternity doth teach /
Himself in all, and all things in himself' (ll. 66–7). It is allied to the
original ideals of the Revolution, but opposed by now to political
solutions of any kind.

# Lyrical ballads
*with a few other poems*
1798

*Lyrical ballads* made no great impression on its first appearance, in September 1798. Its authors, Wordsworth and Coleridge, preferred to be anonymous, and were in fact on their way to Germany; its Bristol publisher, Joseph Cottle, felt so little confidence in their work that he transferred the copyright to the London firm of A. and J. Arch when less than two dozen copies had been sold. Sales, however, proved to be steady. In 1800 Cottle bought back the copyright and issued the two-volume second edition, with its famous Preface. Further editions appeared in 1802 and 1805. Among the early reviewers most were encouraging, though none understood the greatness of the poetry or the revolutionary nature of the volume. Only Southey (Coleridge's brother-in-law and erstwhile collaborator) was hostile, taking the opportunity of attacking in the *Critical* both his former friend, and his former friend's new partner. *The ancient mariner* is 'a Dutch attempt at German sublimity', *The idiot boy* 'resembles a Flemish picture in the worthlessness of its design and the excellence of its execution' (October 1798).

The authors of *Lyrical ballads* had been almost daily in each other's company since July 1797, when Coleridge arranged for Wordsworth and his sister Dorothy to rent Alfoxden House, four miles away from his cottage at Nether Stowey in Somerset. On Christmas Day 1797 (Dorothy's birthday) Wordsworth was twenty-seven, Dorothy, twenty-six, and Coleridge, twenty-five. Already their companionship had inspired *Kubla Khan* and a half-length version of *The ancient mariner*, written by Coleridge in November. The next six months would be a period of astonishing creativity for both poets, as well as producing the first of Dorothy's *Journals*, that tell of the day-to-day lives from which the poetry emerged, and establish her own powers as a writer. An impressive, and largely credible, account of the origins of *Lyrical ballads* is given by Coleridge in *Biographia literaria* (1817):

> During the first year that Mr. Wordsworth and I were neighbours, our conversations turned frequently on the two cardinal points of poetry, the power of exciting the sympathy of the reader by a faithful adherence to the truth of nature, and the power of giving the interest of novelty by the modifying colours of imagination. The sudden charm, which accidents of light and shade, which moon-light or sun-set diffused over a known and familiar landscape, appeared to represent the practicability of combining both. (ii. p. 1)

'In this idea', Coleridge continues, 'originated the plan of the *Lyrical ballads*' (ii, p. 2).

As early as 20 November 1797, Dorothy records that *The ancient mariner* (begun as a collaboration, but soon handed over to Coleridge) is to be published 'with some pieces of William's'. But the plan for *Lyrical ballads* – insofar as the volume ever was planned – must belong to spring 1798. Coleridge's account in *Biographia* is persuasive:

> it was agreed, that my endeavours should be directed to persons and characters supernatural, or at least romantic . . . Mr. Wordsworth, on the other hand, was to propose to himself as his object, to give the charm of novelty to things of every day, and to excite a feeling analogous to the supernatural, by awakening the mind's attention from the lethargy of custom, and directing it to the loveliness and the wonders of the world before us . . . (ii, p. 2)

Thoughts of a division of labour had probably arisen during the revisions to *The ancient mariner*, completed 23 March. In April, Coleridge started work on the supernatural *Christabel*, and Wordsworth began *Peter Bell*, designed as the *Mariner*'s non-supernatural twin. *Peter Bell*, however, grew too long for *Lyrical ballads*, and was left in manuscript till 1819; *Christabel* didn't at this stage get beyond Part One. Despite the impression of premeditation given in *Biographia*, it is unlikely that any of the four poems that Coleridge finally published in *Lyrical ballads* – the *Mariner*, the *Dungeon* and *Foster Mother's Tale* (both old work, excerpted from the play, *Osorio*), and the blank-verse *Nightingale* – was in fact conceived with the scheme in mind. By contrast, Wordsworth's building up of his stock of poems looks very purposeful. Terms for publication were agreed with Cottle at the end of May. In the preceding three months he had composed thirteen of the nineteen poems that make up his share of the volume; there was *Tintern abbey* still to come.

Coleridge's importance to *Lyrical ballads* should not be judged by the number of his poems. The *Mariner* makes an extraordinary impact at the beginning of the collection, and throughout there is the pervasive influence of Coleridge's thinking. As far back as October 1796 he had printed *Reflections on having left a place of retirement* in the *Monthly* as 'A Poem that affects not to be Poetry'. Unlike Wordsworth, who was later to comment, 'I never cared a straw for the theory' (and claimed to have written the 1800 Preface 'solely to please Mr. Coleridge, out of sheer good nature'), Coleridge was fascinated by theoretical concerns. It is surely his voice that we hear in the Advertisement to *Lyrical ballads* 1798, forerunner to the Preface. In terms that quietly plagiarize Joanna Baillie's *Series of plays* (*c.* March 1798), the 'majority' of the poems are defined as experimental,

written chiefly with a view to ascertain how far the language of conversation in the middle and lower classes of society is adapted to the purposes of poetic pleasure. (p. i)

It is likely that Coleridge's definitions came after the poetry and are to some extent a rationalization; his Unitarian pantheism had been there from the first. Conforming itself to the joyous moods of the Alfoxden spring, it underlies and underpins the poetry. Coleridge's belief in 'the vast family of love' (*Religious musings*, 1796) is to be seen equally in the Mariner's blessing of the water-snakes –

> O happy living things! no tongue
> Their beauty might declare:
> A spring of love gusht from my heart,
> And I bless'd them unaware!
> (ll. 273–6)

– and in the beautiful lines of Wordsworth's 'It is the first mild day of March':

> Love, now an universal birth,
> From heart to heart is stealing,
> From earth to man, from man to earth,
> – It is the hour of feeling.
> (ll. 21–4)

In *Tintern abbey* we learn of a 'something far more deeply interfused',

# Wordsworth and Coleridge

> Whose dwelling is the light of setting suns,
> And the round ocean, and the living air,
> And the blue sky, and in the mind of man . . .
>> (ll. 97–100)

*Tintern abbey* is in many ways a sequel to Coleridge's Unitarian *Frost at midnight*, yet Wordsworth nowhere names the in-dwelling 'something' as God. His concern is with intuition, religious instinct, not established belief. Through an act of imagination man is enabled to 'see into the life of things', of which he is a part. Such consciousness, however, is given to few. Others share unknowingly in 'the hour of feeling', finding the true self in the selflessness of love. Betty Foy of *The idiot boy*, whose name means 'faith' (compare Sans Foy in *The faerie queen*), is in a state of grace, as

> She gently pats the pony's side,
> On which her idiot boy must ride,
> And seems no longer in a hurry.
>> (ll. 79–81)

The gesture is worthy of Sterne, from whom Wordsworth learned both of a silent language of emotion, and of the potential of comic incongruity to embody love:

> She looks again – her arms are up –
> She screams – she cannot move for joy;
> She darts as with a torrent's force,
> She almost has o'erturned the horse,
> And fast she holds her idiot boy.
>> (ll. 382–6)

Johnny's idiocy (insisted on again and again in the poetry) makes him for Wordsworth a numinous figure, calling to his mind in 1802, 'the sublime expression of scripture . . . *Their life is hidden with God*'. At the same time, it makes Betty's love 'one of the great triumphs of the human heart' (to John Wilson, 7 June).

'We think the "experiment" has failed', Southey had the gall to write in the *Critical*, 'not because the language of conversation is little adapted to "the purposes of poetic pleasure", but because it has been tried upon uninteresting subjects.' The statement comes ill from one who had seen the manuscripts of *Lyrical ballads* while they were at the press, and actually borrowed from the poems he condemned. His *Idiot*, for instance, is a macabre combination of Wordsworth's *Idiot boy* and *We are seven*. Unable to comprehend the fact of death, a mongol digs up the corpse of his mother, brings it home, and attempts to warm it into life in front of the fire. As might be expected, Southey's jibes at the *Lyrical ballads* draw attention chiefly to the lack of drama. Poems designed 'to give the charm of novelty to things of every day' are seen as failed attempts at 'German sublimity'. Tacitly they are compared to Bürger, whose horror-ballads (translated by Taylor, Scott and others) they were designed to transcend.

The 'lyrical ballad', as defined by Wordsworth and Coleridge in opposition to Bürger, subordinates narrative to personal emotion. When in *The thorn* Wordsworth takes Bürger as his source, he turns the gothic improbabilities (a ghost, blue fire, ponds of toads) into a study of the superstitious mind. Goody Blake's curse has its effect not because she is a witch (as some of the reviewers assumed), but through the power of Harry Gill's imagination. In the words of the 1800 Preface, the feeling 'developed' in these poems, 'gives importance to the action and situation, and not the action and situation to the feeling' (p. xvii). Southey, whose *Inscriptions* and *Botany Bay eclogues* (1797) had been among the first experiments in the plain style, was not ready to accept the far more radical step taken in this new valuing of emotion and the workings of the mind.

To rate so highly the feelings of 'the middle and lower classes of society' had, of course, a political aspect. Chaucer, Spenser, Shakespeare, Milton, Pope, had known better than to take the lower orders seriously. To do so in the years following the Revolution was a threat to political stability. Fears over the effect of Coleridge's jacobin reputation lay behind the anonymous publication of *Lyrical ballads* (and led to his issuing the political work of 1798 separately in the *Fears in solitude* quarto). Wordsworth's reputation was no threat, but *The last of the flock* demonstrates as clearly as *Michael* his subversive wish 'to shew that people who do not wear fine cloaths can feel deeply' (letter to Fox, 14 January 1801). It is significant, however, that the shepherd's predicament could have no political solution: as Wrangham notes in the *British critic*, there are in *Lyrical ballads* few signs of 'enmity to present institutions' (October 1799).

Wordsworth turns to the lower classes not because of jacobin sympathies (though he still has them), but because he hopes to find purity of emotion, as well as purity of language, among the unsophisticated. For the same primitivist reason he turns to a Hudson Bay Indian, sick, and left behind in the snow by her companions, as a means of portraying the conflicting moods – resignation, resentment, persisting love – of a dying woman:

> Alas! you might have dragged me on
> Another day, a single one!
> Too soon despair o'er me prevailed;
> Too soon my heartless spirit failed;
> When you were gone my limbs were stronger . . .
> (*Forsaken Indian woman*, ll. 21–5)

# 27

# AUGUST VON KOTZEBUE

## Lover's vows
*adapted from the German by Elizabeth Inchbald*
1798 (1790)

*Lovers' vows* has a strange half-life in English literature, known to readers of Jane Austen as the play that all the fuss was about in *Mansfield Park*, but seldom read or placed in its original context. As Mrs Inchbald points out in 1798, despite the great number of German plays being translated, 'no person of talents or literary knowledge' had undertaken Kotzebue's *Das Kind der Liebe* (*Child of love*) since its publication in 1790. Her explanation – interesting in the light of *Mansfield Park* – is that the play is, in the original, discordant with an English stage. In particular, 'Amelia's love [as portrayed] by Kotzebue is indelicately blunt' (p. iii). Southey's view, expressed the following year, is that, 'though German plays have always something of the ridiculous', Kotzebue is possessed of 'unsurpassed and unsurpassable genius'. His work, however, has invariably a political message:

I wonder his plays are acted here; they are so Jacobinical in tendency. They create Jacobinical feelings, almost irresistibly. In every one that I have yet seen . . . some old prejudice or old principle is attacked. (to Wynn, 5 April 1799)

Though described on the title-page as 'From the German', *Lovers' vows* is a free adaptation, designed to please an English audience, and brought into line with English modesty. But even when adapted, the play remains an attack on old prejudice and principle. Amelia's directness is the central fact. It can be rendered less 'blunt', but nothing can make it by Austen's standards 'delicate':

*Amelia* [to her less-than-aristocratic tutor]: It is my father's will that I should marry – It is my father's wish to see me happy – If then you love me as you say,

# August von Kotzebue

I will marry; and will be happy – but only with you. – I will tell him this. – At first he will start; then grow angry; then be in a passion – In his passion he will call me 'undutiful'; but he will soon recollect himself, and resume his usual smiles, saying, 'Well, well, if he love you, and you love him, in the name of heaven, let it be'. – Then I shall hug him round the neck, kiss his hands, run away from him, and fly to you; it will soon be known that I am your bride, the whole village will come to wish me joy, and heaven's blessing will follow. (pp. 42–3)

Amelia has been taught by the young clergyman, Anhalt (descendant of Abelard and Rousseau's St Preux), that 'birth and fortune [are] old-fashioned things'. Love and integrity are what matter. Her 'indelicacy' is innocent, but there can be no doubt that she is defying class, defying parental authority, defying the taboo which says that a woman shall not make the running in matters of love. To judge from Inchbald's excessive rectitude at the time of Godwin's marriage to Mary Wollstonecraft in 1797, she was not one to write these matters off as 'old prejudice'. Nor would she be unaware of making a political statement. She must have been able to accept Kotzebue's jacobinical tendency, as (to Southey's surprise) British audiences accepted it. This despite the threat of French invasion in 1798, and a backlash against radical thinking. 'Kotzebue's *Child of Love*, in Germany', Inchbald boasts in her Preface, 'was never more attractive than *Lovers' Vows* has been in England' (p. i). After its run at Covent Garden, the play was staged frequently in London and elsewhere: during Austen's time in Bath, 1801–5, there were six productions at the Theatre Royal.

Austen knows *Lovers' vows* extremely well, and assumes that her audience does so too (among her characters, Fanny stands out as not having read or seen it). It is important that Edmund and Fanny, as representatives of the author, are against any theatrical presentation whatever. *Lovers' vows* is decided upon at a late stage: Austen's major objections would have been the same if the choice had been *King Lear*. It is wrong to do anything so radical as put on a play in the absence of the head of the family. It is wrong to bring guests from outside the family into the intimacy that drama implies. It is wrong for those of marriageable – that is to say (though Austen would never say it), sexually arousable – age to adopt roles that leave them unprotected. Acting overrides the safeguards devised by society to keep the sexes at a distance. 'Pray let me know my fate', says Mary Crawford, breaking every possible taboo. 'Who is to be Anhalt? What gentleman among

116

you am I to have the pleasure of making love to?' (*Mansfield Park*, ed. Chapman, p. 143).

*Lovers' vows* is chosen by Austen's characters as an acceptable compromise; by Austen herself, it is chosen for its impropriety, and for the sinuous way in which it can be interwoven with her own plot. Certain correspondences are neat but of little interest: Mr Yates, who plays Baron Wildenhaim, will seduce, and finally marry, Julie Bertram, as Wildenhaim seduces and finally marries Agatha. Agatha is played by Maria, who will be betrayed by Henry Crawford as Agatha is (initially) betrayed by the Baron. Count Cassel and Mr Rushworth are a perfect match in their silliness. The pairing of Amelia and Mary, Anhalt and Edmund, is of quite a different kind. Here there is scope for development, and interaction, and the subtle examination of values. The scene of Amelia's proposal to Anhalt is central both to *Lovers' vows* and to Austen's novel. In its portrayal of the different values of Fanny and Mary, and their fight for the soul of Edmund, *Mansfield Park* narrows down to the episode of the play. And the episode of the play narrows down to the scene in the chilly East Room, as Mary and Edmund come in turn to make use of Fanny as prompter.

'Have you ever happened to look at the part I mean?' Mary asks, oblivious of Fanny's love for Edmund, and of her painful brooding over the scene in question:

Here it is. I did not think much of it at first – but, upon my word – . There, look at *that* speech, and *that*, and *that*. How am I ever to look him in the face and say such things? Could you do it? But then he is your cousin, which makes all the difference . . . (Chapman, p. 168)

Edmund arrives, also unbidden. Together he and Mary play out before Fanny the declaration of love that she can never make. The Mansfield theatricals tend to be regarded as a quaint and slightly inexplicable episode: why the fuss, when the Austen children themselves had enjoyed acting? The more one looks at the coincidence of play and novel, however, the more likely it seems that *Lovers' vows* was Austen's starting-point. Edmund (as clergyman, in effect tutor) forms the character and values of Fanny, as Anhalt had formed Amelia; Fanny repays him with all Amelia's staunchness and love. But social positions have been reversed. Fanny, as poor relation, is required to depend wholly upon her own worth; Edmund, meanwhile, is given enough standing to make him an attractive match. Austen is thus enabled to complicate her plot by introducing in Mary the sort of woman who, within the contemporary English scene, might indeed have the forwardness that Amelia is permitted to show. Kotzebue has been neatly turned to the *defence* of an 'old principle'.

# 28

## MARY ROBINSON

═══════════════════════

# Lyrical tales
1800

'Perdita' Robinson's *Lyrical tales* almost had the distinction of changing literary history. 'My Brother William', wrote Dorothy Wordsworth on 10 September 1800,

is going to publish a second Edition of the *Lyrical ballads*, with a second volume. He intends to give them the title of 'Poems by W. Wordsworth', as Mrs Robinson has claimed the title and is about publishing a volume of *Lyrical tales*. This is a great objection to the former title, particularly as they are both printed at the same press, and Longman is the publisher of both the works.

The Preface to *Lyrical ballads* (inserted in the second edition of 1800) might never have been the Preface to *Lyrical ballads*! The Wordsworths didn't know Robinson personally, but Coleridge did, and must have been aware that her 'claiming' of the title had a certain appropriateness. With the *Lyrical ballads* in mind, she was attempting a similar fusion of narrative and lyricism.

In the event, Wordsworth changed his mind. *Lyrical tales* appeared just before Christmas, *Lyrical ballads* five weeks later (though with 1800 on the title page). Some confusion there must surely have been. Robinson, however, did not live to see it. 'Poor dear Mrs Robinson', Coleridge wrote to Thomas Poole on 1 February 1801, 'you have heard of her Death. She wrote me a most affecting, heart-rending Letter a few weeks before she died, to express what she called her death bed affection and esteem for me'. 'Perdita' had died on Boxing Day 1800, aged 43. She is remembered now as the actress who in 1779 caught the eye of the Prince of Wales (later to be Prince Regent) as he watched *A winter's tale*. But she was also a successful and singularly brave writer. Married to a trickster at the age of fifteen, she turned herself three years later into the star of Drury Lane, then lost the use of her legs after an illness in her early twenties. For the rest of her life she suffered from rheumatic fever. Despite this she established a second career, making a reputation as both poet and novelist, and becoming in 1797 Coleridge's fellow contributor to *The morning post*. In her last months, though she knew she was dying, she enjoyed a mild flirtation with him, carried out in the pages of the Poetry Section.

Coleridge, whose contributions to the *Post* were frequently by Wordsworth, set things in motion on 14 October with *The solitude of Binnorie* and a fulsome introduction. Given that the poem was not his own, his opening words may seem misleading:

Sir, it would be unpardonable in the author of the following lines if he omitted to acknowledge that the metre . . . is borrowed from *The Haunted Beach* of Mrs Robinson, a most exquisite poem . . . This acknowledgement will not appear superfluous to those who have felt the bewitching effect of that absolutely original stanza . . . and who call to mind that the invention of a metre has so widely diffused the name of Sappho, and almost constitutes the present celebrity of Alcaeus.

The names of the two Greek metre-makers would return with added significance. On 24 November Coleridge published Wordsworth's love-poem, 'How sweet when crimson colours dart / Across a breast of snow' (not his greatest or most characteristic work), under the heading of *Alcaeus to Sappho*. Meanwhile on 17 October Robinson had contributed an ode that was rather more explicit in its title, and showed her to be closely in touch with domestic events in the north: *Ode, inscribed to the infant son of S. T. Coleridge, esq. born Sept. 14, at Keswick*:

> Sweet Baby Boy! accept a Stranger's song;
> An untaught Minstrel joys to sing of thee . . .

Nor was this all. Coleridge sent to the *Post* stanzas that were never printed, written 'immediately on the perusal of Mrs Robinson's beautiful poem, *The Snow Drop*', and she in turn contributed what is surely the first example of 'the bewitching effect' of *Kubla Khan* (in manuscript till 1816), signing her poem 'Sappho', but addressing it to Coleridge by name:

> Spirit Divine! with Thee I'll trace
> Imagination's boundless space!
> With thee, beneath thy *sunny dome*
>     I'll listen to the minstrel's lay
>     Hymning the gradual close of day,
> In *Caves of Ice* enchanted roam . . .

On 18 December *Lyrical Tales* was published; next day, Daniel Stuart, editor of the *Post*, included the wistful opening poem, *All alone*. Eight days later the author was dead:

> My Father never will return,
>   He rests beneath the sea-green wave;
> I have no kindred left, to mourn
>   When I am in yonder grave!
> *Not one!* to dress with flow'rs the stone –
> *Then – surely,* I AM LEFT ALONE!
>
> (st. xxv)

Stuart's view that *All alone* was 'one of the most affecting productions that [had] lately issued from the English press' was probably justified. In the late 1780s Robinson had come to know Robert Merry and been through a phase of Della Cruscan artifice that obscured her naturalness, yet showed at the same time an extraordinary skill and versatility. Her later work owes most to Southey, whose humanitarian concern was close to her own, and whose *Poems* 1797 include such 'lyrical tales' as *Mary*, *Donica* and *Rudiger*. Coleridge was right to point to the metre of *The haunted beach* (and right too that the tale itself ends feebly). Robinson had an exceptional ear and her poetry was improving all the time. Like almost all minor poets she was imitative, and not till the very end of her life were there models available to whom she could deeply respond. The tones we hear in *All alone* are those of Wordsworth's *Forsaken Indian woman* from *Lyrical ballads* 1798. Another month, and there would have been the edition of 1800 (advertised in the back of her own volume) with the new inspiration of *Michael* and the Lucy poems. Another year or two, and – with Coleridge there to help – 'Imagination's boundless space' might not have seemed so out of reach.

———————

Poems chiefly written
in retirement
1801

'John Thelwall had something very good about him', Coleridge remarked in *Table talk* (1832), and added a reminiscence that goes back to
July 1797, and his first meeting with a man whose career had been
closely parallel to his own:

> We were once sitting in a beautiful recess in the Quantocks, when I said to him,
> 'Citizen John, this is a fine place to talk treason in!' 'Nay, Citizen Samuel', replied
> he, 'it is rather a place to make a man forget that there is any necessity for treason!'
> (27 July 1830)

The conversation – between two of the most outspoken radicals of the
mid-1790s – took place at Alfoxden House, Somerset, where Coleridge
had just installed Wordsworth and his sister Dorothy. Though they
would hardly have put it to themselves in such terms, the three men
were in the processes of switching their energies from politics to poetry.
During the following year Coleridge and Thelwall would both write
most of their finest work; Wordsworth too would come into his own,
with *Lyrical ballads* and *Tintern abbey*.

To the authorities, whose legislation had effectively brought an end
to the reform movement, it would have seemed that the three poets
held similar treasonable views. Thelwall and Coleridge, however, were
long-standing opponents. And though Wordsworth would have been
closer to Thelwall – both had been at one stage disciples of Godwin,
whom Coleridge denounced – he differed from the others because he
had learned his politics in France. The two 'Citizens' had been in correspondence for over a year. Citizen Samuel drew his radicalism from

the New Testament and Priestleyan Unitarianism. He looked forward to a Christian Second Coming, and could advise the poor: 'Rest awhile, Children of Wretchedness' (*Religious musings*). Citizen John, by contrast, was an atheist, prompted by a deep sense of social injustice, and by the need to get things done. Coleridge had lectured vehemently in Bristol until gagged by the Two Bills of December 1795; Thelwall had found a means to continue his denunciation of Government policy in London until April 1796, and then in the provinces for almost another year. According to his own account, meetings at Yarmouth, Lynn, Wisbech, Derby, Stockport and Norwich, had been broken up by organized violence, and at four of these places he 'narrowly escaped assassination' (p. xxx).

Thelwall was a man of exceptional abilities. Before being drawn into politics in 1792 he had trained briefly as both painter (cf. his 1801 frontispiece) and lawyer, and established his literary career with *Poems on various subjects* (1787); *The peripatetic* followed in 1793. While on a charge of high treason in 1794 (along with Hardy, Horne Tooke and other leading dissidents) he had compiled a quarto volume, *Poems written in close confinement in the Tower and Newgate*. In 1795–6 he had written and published a journal, *The tribune*, as well as composing the *Address to the king* for the Copenhagen Fields meeting of the London Corresponding Society (12 November 1795). After the banning of political assemblies, he had lectured to packed audiences on Classical History, at once escaping prosecution and giving his hearers the pleasure of construing the reference to contemporary events.

As he journeyed away from Alfoxden in July 1797, Thelwall composed a conversation poem showing the influence both of Wordsworth's *Yew-tree lines* and of Coleridge's *Lime-tree bower*, and significantly entitled *Lines, written at Bridgewater . . . during a long excursion in quest of a peaceful retreat*. Meanwhile the 'peaceful retreat' he had just left was under surveillance. Early in August reports were received by the Home Office that 'French people' had 'contrived to get possession of a Mansion House at Alfoxden' and were mapping the local river as the possible site for an invasion. French troops had landed at Fishguard the previous February, and news of suspicious activity close to the Bristol Channel could not be ignored. On 15 August, James Walsh – by chance, the agent who had arrested Thelwall in 1794 – arrived to investigate. Walsh knew his job, reporting to his superiors that this was

# John Thelwall

'no French Affair but a mischiefuous [*sic*] gang of disaffected English-
men'. The 'Spy Nozy' episode of *Biographia literaria* (1817) makes light
of the incident, but being spied on would hardly have seemed so
amusing at the time.

Though he found a retreat at Llys-Wen in Wales, turning farmer,
and composing there the bulk of his *Poems, chiefly written in retirement*,
Thelwall was consistently harrassed. *Written at Bridgewater* shows a
certain wistfulness, as he permits himself to dream of taking his family
to live near Coleridge in a latter-day version of Pantisocracy:

> And 'twould be sweet, my Samuel . . .
> To share our frugal viands, and the bowl
> Sparkling with home-brew'd beverage: – by our sides
> Thy Sara, and my Susan, and, perchance,
> Alfoxden's musing tenant, and the maid
> Of ardent eye, who, with fraternal love,
> Sweetens his solitude.
>
> (p. 130)

There was, as Coleridge said, 'something very good' about Thelwall.
His Prefatory Memoir – an important document for those who wish
to gain an understanding of the period – is entirely without rancour.
His political career was truly disinterested. His poems embody values
that would make the world a better place.

Thelwall had never ceased to be a writer, but the visit to Alfoxden
seems to have reconfirmed him in his role as poet. As might be expected from one who became a specialist on elocution, and who in
1814 marked in the cadence of every line of *The Excursion*, his poetry is
especially sensitive in its musical effects. If one leaves aside the strange
Arthurian *Fairy of the lake* and the attempts at an epic voice in *The hope
of Albion*, Thelwall often seems a lesser Coleridge – Coleridge without
the high moments of inspiration, but also without the fustian, the
posturing. It is clear that he knows *Religious musings*, but his poetry
bangs no drums. The new voice he has heard is that of the conversation
poem, yet for him there can be no 'infinite and intellectual breeze, /
At once the soul of each and God of all' (*Eolian harp*), no 'Great Universal Teacher' (*Frost at midnight*) who will presently make all things
well. It is characteristic of Thelwall, both as poet and as man, that the
most moving sequence in *Poems, chiefly written in retirement* is *Paternal
tears*, an expression of heart-felt personal emotion.

## 30

## THOMAS MOORE

## The poetical works of the late
## Thomas Little esq

1801

'I have just been turning over *Little*', Byron wrote to Moore on 9 June 1820, 'which I knew by heart in 1803, being then in my fifteenth summer.' It had been the summer of his first, entirely hopeless, love, for his eighteen-year-old cousin, Mary Chaworth. 'I cannot get him to return to school', his mother had written, 'though I have done all in my power for six weeks past. He has no indisposition that I know of, but love, desperate love' (Prothero, i, p. 16). 'Heigho', Byron's letter continues, 'I believe all the mischief I have ever done, or sung, has been owing to that confounded book of yours.' Moore's 'confounded book' had appeared in 1801, pompously entitled *The poetical works of the late Thomas Little, Esq*, and with a Preface blandly telling of the death of the writer 'in his one-and-twentieth year'. Moore, who was the son of a Dublin grocer, had less claim than many to the title of 'Esquire'; he was also perfectly alive.

The *Poetical works* was an immediate success, going through fifteen London editions by 1822, as well as being published in Ireland and America. Whatever mischief Moore's songs may have done to the adolescent Byron, there was no doubting their seductive charm. 'Without any of the grossness of Lord Rochester', the *Literary journal* warned its readers in June 1806 when a new volume (*Epistles, odes, and other poems*) came out,

he touches the same strings with no less energy and success. In short, if we were desirous to render a wife unfaithful to her marriage-bed, or to habituate a virgin to listen to the language of seduction: if we were desirous to convey to her the loosest wishes without startling her by corresponding language; and to afford an excuse to herself for indulging in these emotions, in the apparent purity of what she read, we should certainly put Mr. Moore's amatory poems into her hands.

So strong was the pressure to disapprove, that Byron himself adopted the highest moral tones in *English bards and Scotch reviewers*:

> Who in soft guise, surrounded by a choir
> Of virgins melting, not to Vesta's fire,
> With sparkling eyes, and cheek by passion flush'd,
> Strikes his wild Lyre, whilst listening dames are hush'd?
> 'Tis LITTLE! young Catullus of his day,
> As sweet, but as immoral in his lay!
>
> (ll. 283–8)

Byron was just twenty-one, and given to striking attitudes in the manner of Pope. 'Grieved to condemn', he continues, 'the Muse must still be just, / Nor spare melodious advocates of lust.' (ll. 289–90)

Hunt, in *The feast of the poets*, though noting (like everyone else) the 'pernicious tendency' of Moore, saw also a 'redeeming something – a leaning after the better affections' (p. 73). 'You feel at once', he wrote, 'that his songs are indeed to be sung, – a happy propriety, which he seems to share exclusively with Dryden' (p. 75). Not since Dryden, and his younger contemporary, Prior, had there been such lightness of touch:

> Oh! why should Platonic control, love,
>   Enchain an emotion so free?
> Your soul, though a very sweet soul, love,
>   Will ne'er be sufficient for me.
> If you think, by this coldness and scorning,
>   To seem more angelic and bright,
> Be an angel, my love, in the morning,
>   But, oh! *be a woman tonight!*
>
> (p. 40)

Though it seems harsh to describe him as an 'advocate of lust', Moore was unashamedly erotic. What was the virgin, yet unhabituated to the language of seduction, to make of *An ode upon morning*:

> Turn to me, love! the morning rays
>   Are glowing o'er thy languid charms;
> Take one luxurious, parting gaze,
>   While yet I linger in thine arms.
>
> (p. 106)

What was the wife, yet faithful to her marriage-bed, to make of 'Remember him thou leav'st behind':

> And though ungenial ties have bound
>   Thy fate unto another's care;
> That arm, which clasps thy bosom round,
>   Cannot confine the heart that's there.
>
> No, no! that heart is only mine
>   By ties all other ties above,
> For I have wed it at a shrine
>   Where we have had no priest but love!
>
> (p. 121)

Playing down the eroticism, and emphasizing instead the musical and national qualities of his song, Moore produced in the years 1808–34 ten collections of *Irish melodies* (the first seven with tunes by Sir John Stevenson). To Hazlitt, it seemed that he was 'heedless, gay, and prodigal of his poetic wealth . . . another Ariel, as light, as tricksy, as indefatiguable, and as humane a spirit'. He had harsher things to say as well: 'The infinite delight he takes in such an infinite number of things, creates indifference in minds less susceptible of pleasure than his own.' And more damning: 'His mind does not brood over the great and permanent; it glances over the surfaces' (Howe, v, p. 151). But this was to judge Moore on Wordsworth's ground. He was not a Romantic, but an elegant poet, and elegant social climber, of the Regency. Though not commanding Byron's loyalty – 'Do but give Tom a good dinner, and a lord . . . TOMMY loves a Lord' (*Tatler*, 15 January 1831) – he came to be one of his closest friends. 'An Epitome of all that's delightful', was Byron's comment on 15 November 1811, after their first meeting. It was to Moore that he entrusted his *Memoirs*, and it was Moore who reluctantly consented that they must be burned.

Despite the popularity of his oriental romance, *Lalla Rookh* (six editions in 1817, and many later), the songs are Moore's claim to immortality. Predicting this in June 1821, Baldwin's *London magazine* added charmingly, 'immortal he must be, as long as English ladies can *love*, or Irish gentlemen can *drink*, which, we take it, is as much immortality as any modern bard can consider himself equitably entitled to.'

# 31

## JEAN-JACQUES ROUSSEAU

———

# Eloisa

*or a series of original letters.*
*Translated by William Kenrick*
1803 (1761)

To Byron, the Rousseau of *La nouvelle Héloïse* (*Eloisa*, in Kenrick's excellent translation) is the 'apostle of affliction'. With more than a hint of self-identification, he sees the love of St Preux for Julie (Eloisa) as 'passion's essence'. 'As a tree / On fire by lightning', he writes in *Childe Harold* Canto III,

> with ethereal flame
> Kindled he was, and blasted; for to be
> Thus, and enamoured, were in him the same.

Strictly speaking, Byron suggests, the love that Rousseau evoked was not for woman at all, but for an 'ideal beauty'

> which became
> In him existence, and o'erflowing teems
> Along his burning page, distempered though it seems.
>
> *This* breathed itself to life in Julie, *this*
> Invested her with all that's wild and sweet . . .
> (ll. 734–7, 740–4)

Shelley was actually reading *La nouvelle Héloïse* as Byron composed these lines in their boat on Lake Geneva. He too uses the word 'overflowing' in his account of Rousseau's abundant creativity. 'I read *Julie* all day', he writes to Peacock in his journal-letter of 16 July 1816, 'an overflowing, as it now seems, surrounded by the scenes which it has so wonderfully peopled, of sublimest genius, and more than human sensibility' (*Six weeks' tour*, pp. 127–8). Looking across the water at the landscapes in which Rousseau had sited his story, he muses on imagination and the achievement of 'a mind so powerfully bright as to cast a shade of falsehood on the records that are called reality.'

There can be no doubt that the two poets see Rousseau in their own terms. Byron is the tree 'blasted' by passion; Shelley, meanwhile, is at work in July 1816 on a *Hymn to intellectual beauty*, inspired by Wordsworth's *Intimations* and addressed to an 'unseen power' that is in the highest, Platonic sense, 'ideal'. Yet there is an appropriateness in this Romantic reading of the greatest of all forerunners of Romanticism. *Eloisa* is indeed a work of 'sublimest genius ... more than human sensibility'. To the modern reader the 'more than human' smacks of exaggeration – and exaggeration, because it is larger than life, is regarded as telling less than the truth. Writing his novel in 1762, Rousseau was bound by no such tradition of realism. As a thinker he valued precision, but as a creative writer he refused to be constricted. Byron and Shelley recognized in him a fellow poet, for whom passion was a lifeforce, an absolute not to be qualified by experience or lessened by time.

Eloisa sets out to discipline her passion, giving herself ungrudgingly to the service of others; yet she dies acknowledging that her love for St Preux has never been subdued:

Long have I indulged myself in the salutary delusion, that my passion was extinguished; the delusion is now vanished, when it can be no longer useful. You imagined me cured of my love; I thought so too. Let us thank Heaven that the deception hath lasted as long as it could be of service to us. In vain, alas! I endeavoured to stifle that passion which inspired me with life; it was impossible: it was interwoven with my heart strings. It now expands itself, when it is no longer to be dreaded; it supports me now my strength fails me; it cheers my soul even in death. (iv, p. 277)

Passion, however, is allowed this supremacy only because it has been tested by the most exacting standards. The 'new' Eloisa is not, like the old, forced to take the veil, but she lives a life consecrated to duty – duty to her father who has thwarted her love, duty to the husband whom he has imposed upon her, duty to friends and children and servants and beggars at the door. St Preux, the new Abelard, is not, like the old, physically gelded, but is forced to endure first exile, then the castrating friendship and proximity of the lover whom he can never again possess:

When I bewailed her at a distance, the hope of seeing her again was comfort to my soul; I flattered myself that the sight of her would banish all my sorrows in an instant, at least, I could conceive it possible to be in a more cruel situation than my own. – But to be by her side, to see her, to touch her, to talk to her, to love her, to adore her, and, whilst I almost enjoyed her again, to find her lost to me for ever . . . (iii. pp. 220–1)

To a scarcely lesser degree the integrity that validates passion in the lovers is seen also in the minor characters who surround them. Eloisa's husband, Wolmar, has extraordinary wisdom and compassion; Clara, her cousin and confidante, is exalted finally almost to the tragic level of passion; though his portrait is less convincing, St Preux's English bene-factor, Lord B., is generous from first to last. Inevitably there are times when Rousseau the philosopher, observer, advocate of natural wildness and benevolent paternalism, is too obviously present. Certain parts of the book – St Preux's satirical reflections on Paris in volume two, the accounts of rural economy in three – can be read very fast. Yet to skip them altogether is to risk losing the thread of a narrative that is artfully controlled and always capable of the unexpected.

Like Wordsworth in *Michael*, Rousseau is concerned to define the simple way of life, yet fascinated by motivation and emotional com-plexity. With the exception of Lord B., his characters have the capacity to change and develop, or at least are presented to us in changing lights that retain our interest. His use of the epistolary form, while never achieving the delicate characterization through style of Richardson's *Clarissa*, enables him to reveal the letter-writers' inmost thoughts and to tell his story from different points of view. The novel was immensely popular in its own time – far more so that any of Rousseau's other works – and occupies a unique position in the history of Romanticism. As a translator, Kenrick has lived up to the standards of his Preface. In place of the normal 'thin gauze spread over the original, the French language appear[ing] through every paragraph' (p. viii), he has pro-vided a strong, clear, thoroughly English version, that is true to the spirit of Rousseau and remains extremely readable.

# 32

# WILLIAM BLAKE

---

# A descriptive catalogue

*of pictures, poetical and historical inventions,*
*painted by William Blake in water colours*
1809

'I was amusing myself', Crabb Robinson notes (looking back to the spring of 1810), 'by writing an account of the insane poet, painter, and engraver, Blake':

Before I drew up this paper I went to see a gallery of Blake's paintings which were exhibited by his brother, a hosier, in Carnaby Market. These paintings filled several rooms of an ordinary dwelling-house. The entrance was two shillings and sixpence, catalogue included. I was deeply interested by the catalogue as well as the pictures. I took four, telling the brother, I hoped he would let me come in again. He said, 'Oh, as often as you please.' I dare say such a thing had never happened before, or did afterwards. (Morley, i, p. 15)

By a happy chance Robinson gave a copy of the *Descriptive catalogue* to Lamb, who knew at least two of the *Songs of experience*, and was encouraged to pay a visit to Carnaby Market. 'He paints in water colours', Lamb recalls in a letter of 16 May 1824,

marvellous strange pictures, visions of his brain, which he asserts that he has seen . . . His Pictures – one in particular [of] the Canterbury Pilgrims (far above Stothard's) – have great merit, but, hard, dry, yet with grace. He has written a Catalogue of them, with a most spirited criticism on Chaucer, but mystical and full of Vision. His poems have been sold hitherto only in Manuscript. I never read them, but a friend at my desire procured the *Sweep Song*. There is one to a tiger, which I have heard recited, beginning

Tiger, Tiger, burning bright,
Thro' the desarts of the night,

which is glorious.

Printed in May 1809, the *Descriptive catalogue* is unusual among

Blake's writings both in being a commercial publication, and because it is so clearly an attempt to reach an audience. Almost all his poetry had by now been written. The illuminated books, if not precisely 'manuscript' as Lamb imagined, were hand-made and sold in tiny numbers. Though they aspire to prophecy, their mythic complexities are private and unexplained. Now suddenly Blake comes into the open, revealing his techniques and intentions, challenging the public to see whether he is not indeed superior to the fashionable Thomas Stothard. It is not a case merely of rivalry between artists. Behind Stothard is the publisher, Cromek, who in 1805 had paid Blake twenty guineas for the designs to Blair's *Grave*, then abruptly transferred the contract for engraving (worth sixty guineas a plate) to Schiavonetti. If we are to believe the story as told by Alexander Gilchrist, 'shifty Cromek' went on to steal Blake's idea for a picture of the Canterbury Pilgrims, commissioning from Stothard the oil that was shown up and down the country in 1807. In fact it seems quite as likely that Blake copied Stothard, then convinced himself and his friends that the idea had been his. Either way Chaucer became the centrepiece of an exhibition which Blake saw in the grandest terms:

If Italy is enriched and made great by RAPHAEL, if MICHAEL ANGELO is its supreme glory, if Art is the glory of a Nation, if Genius and Inspiration are the great Origin and Bond of Society, the distinction my Works have obtained from those who best understand such things, calls for my Exhibition as the greatest of Duties to my Country. (Advertisement to Exhibition, p. 2)

Blake's belief in his country and his art could lead to some fairly extreme statements – 'England expects that every man should do his duty, in Arts, as well as in Arms, or in the Senate' (p. 61) – but the *Descriptive catalogue* shows a remarkable consistency in his thinking. The allusion to Nelson at Trafalgar ('England expects . . .') has special appropriateness. Pride of place in the Exhibition is given to the 'spiritual forms' of Nelson and Pitt, the one 'guiding Leviathan, in whose wreathings are enfolded the Nations of the Earth' (p. 1), the other 'guiding Behemoth . . . who rides on the whirlwind, directing the storms of war' (p. 2). The two pictures, Blake tells us,

are compositions of a mythological cast, similar to those Apotheoses of Persian, Hindoo, and Egyptian Antiquity, which are still preserved on rude monuments, being copies from some stupendous originals now lost or perhaps buried till some happier age. (p. 3)

'The Artist', Blake adds, 'having been taken in vision into the ancient republics, monarchies, and patriarchates . . . has seen those wonderful originals', which are 'terrific and grand in the highest degree' (p. 4). In his own words he 'has endeavoured to emulate the grandeur of those seen in his vision, and to apply it to modern Heroes, on a smaller scale' (p. 4). Nelson and Pitt are represented not as the recently dead Lord Admiral and Prime Minister, but as manifestations of the spirit ('A Spirit and a Vision are not, as the modern philosophy supposes, a cloudy vapour or a nothing: they are organized and minutely articulated beyond all that the mortal and perishing nature can produce', (p. 37). Blake's audience is asked to see these eccentric but magnificent pictures with the eye of vision. 'If the doors of perception were cleansed', he had written in plate 14 of *The marriage of heaven and hell* (1790), 'everything would appear to man as it is, infinite.'

Like the Wordsworth of the Preface to *Lyrical ballads*, Blake is concerned with permanence. But where Wordsworth's archetypes are of the natural world ('To his mind / The mountain's outline and its steady form / Gave simple grandeur', *In storm and tempest*, ll. 23–5), Blake's are of an unperceived spiritual existence, that is reality. Both poets shocked the susceptible Robinson with their comments about Christ: Wordsworth with the statement 'I have no need of a Redeemer' ('in the mountains did he FEEL his faith', *Pedlar*, 122), Blake with the words, '[Jesus] is the only God – and so am I, and so are you' (Morley, i, 158 and 326). For Wordsworth, man is godlike in his imaginative power; for Blake, he is God – 'a portion of Eternity' – did he but know it. The *Descriptive catalogue* makes clear that in this fallen, or vegetative, world, the artist's role is prophetic: 'Painting, as well as poetry and music, exists and exults in immortal thoughts' (p. 36). As visionary, the artist is an inhabitant of the 'happy country' of Eden. His task is to aid the process by which 'the world of vegetation and generation may expect to be opened again to Heaven, through Eden, as it was in the beginning' (p. 41).

Chaucer's importance lies in his observation, not of transient human nature, but of

the physiognomies or lineaments of universal human life, beyond which Nature never steps. Names alter, things never alter . . . As Newton numbered the stars, and as Linneus numbered the plants, so Chaucer numbered the classes of men. (p. 10)

'Every age' Blake announces memorably, 'is a Canterbury Pilgrimage; we all pass on, each sustaining one or other of these characters; nor can a child be born, who is not one of these characters of Chaucer' (pp. 19–20). Stothard's version of the Pilgrims is an affront. He cannot perceive the universal, and the 'mis-execution' of his picture 'is equal to its misconception'. Blake's feelings are summed up in a phrase of magnificent derision: 'he has jumbled his dumb dollies together' (p. 30). 'Jumbling' is no random term of abuse; it allies Stothard to the 'blotting and blurring demons', Titian and Correggio, Rubens and Rembrandt, whose influence in Blake's view is destroying the art of painting. We are taken back to the remarkable opening words of his Preface:

THE eye that can prefer the Colouring of Titian and Rubens to that of Michael Angelo and Rafael, ought to be modest and to doubt its own powers ... Colouring does not depend on where the Colours are put, but on where the lights and darks are put, and all depends on Form or Outline. (pp. iii–iv)

Wordsworth had sought a language whose permanence could match, and convey, the abiding qualities of human emotion; for Blake the interaction of form and content is predictably more complex:

The great and golden rule of art, as well as of life, is this: That the more distinct, sharp, and wirey the bounding line, the more perfect the work of art; and the less keen and sharp, the greater is the evidence of weak imitation, plagiarism, and bungling. (pp. 63–4)

The wirey, bounding ('containing') line characteristic of Blake's work as engraver and watercolourist, becomes his criterion of excellence in painting. That sharpness of outline should also be the 'golden rule' of life has to be explained in different terms. 'Energy is the only life', Blake had written in plate 4 of *The marriage of heaven and hell*, 'and Reason is the bound or outward circumference of Energy. Energy is Eternal Delight.' The 'wirey' line of reason bounds the eternal delight of energy (often in Blake to be equated with imagination), giving it form, and enabling it to be energetic by providing it with something to push against:

Without Contraries is no progression. Attraction and Repulsion, Reason and Energy, Love and Hate, are necessary to Human existence. (plate 3)

No wonder Robinson was 'deeply interested' by the *Descriptive catalogue*. Though limited in his understanding of 'the insane poet, painter and engraver', he was impressed by his powers. The *Catalogue*, while relating to a specific group of pictures, is the nearest that Blake came to providing a key to his thought. Alongside the 'spirited criticism of Chaucer', the vehement discussion of painting and painters, and of the nature of history ('Mr. B. has ... given the historical fact in its poetical vigour; so as it always happens, and not in that dull way that some Historians pretend', p. 43), Blake takes us into the world of his Prophetic Books. Commentary on *The ancient Britons* includes a version of the central myth of Albion, the Great Humanity Divine, and the fall into division that leaves him powerless to resist his four component Zoas. To Robinson it must have seemed wholly incomprehensible, but in terms of *Vala* it makes excellent sense. 'How he became divided', Blake concludes, 'is a subject of great sublimity and pathos. The Artist has written it under inspiration, and will, if God please, publish it ... In the mean time he has painted this Picture' (p. 42).

Painting and poetry are identical in their function, both existing to convey prophetic truth. To one with Blake's passionate conviction, art would indeed be 'the Glory of a Nation', 'Genius and Inspiration' could be nothing less than 'the great Bond and Origin of Society'. For the rest of us, it may be that reading the *Descriptive catalogue* – getting to know its author in this forthcoming mood – finally leaves more questions than it answers. How do we cope with what Robinson baldly refers to as Blake's insanity? We value him not only for his beauty and power (in *The tyger*, for instance, so elegantly misquoted by Lamb), but for his rightness (in *London* and *The garden of love* and elsewhere); how are we to react to paintings of spirits, and judgments that are plainly crazy? Pity, we know, 'divides the soul', but how is indulgence (at the least) to be avoided when we hear that Titian and Rembrandt must be got rid of (p. iv), on the grounds that their colours merge? And what of poor Stothard, whose 'dumb dollies', if the truth be told, are grouped with skill, and painted with a sense of life and drama and variety that Blake has forsworn? There can be few more brilliantly uncomfortable expressions of praise than Lamb's description of Blake's own *Canterbury pilgrims* as 'hard, dry, yet with grace'.

# 33

## SAMUEL TAYLOR COLERIDGE

---

# Remorse
### 1813 (1797)

*Remorse* was a success. Turned down by Sheridan in 1797, it was put on at Drury Lane in January 1813, and ran for twenty nights. Coleridge had worked hard during the rehearsals, writing in passages, and also cutting, to make the play more actable. On 25 January he claimed to have been 'pleading strenuously for more and more excisions' while the actors, and even the manager, argued that his lines were too good to go. It was all very gratifying. 'You will have heard', he wrote to his (estranged) wife two days later,

that on my entering the Box on Saturday Night I was discovered by the Pit [stalls] – and that they all turned their faces towards our Box, and gave a treble chear of Claps.

There were dark suggestions that he had packed the audience, but on 13 February, Coleridge was able to report:

It has been a good thing for the Theatre. They will get 8 or 10,000£ – and I shall get more than all my literary Labors put together, nay, thrice as much . . . 400£: including the Copy-right.

With the money assured, he was prepared to be surprisingly frank: '*Remorse* has succeeded in spite of bad Scenes, execrable Acting, and Newspaper Calumny'.

Immediate calumnies varied from '*infernal* Lies' in *The Times*, and 'dirty malice' in the *Morning herald*, to open prejudice in the *Satirist* against the Lake Poets:

The author belongs to a school of sentimental whiners, or affectors of babyish simplicity – of amateurs of pretty touches of Nature – of descriptive bardlings –

the whole scope and tendency of whose writings are as dissimilar as can be conceived to whatever has been or can be effective upon the stage. (23 February 1813)

In addition to its successful run, however, the play went through three editions within the year. Reviews were mixed, but by no means as hostile and uncomprehending as those that were to greet *Kubla Khan* and *Christabel* in 1816. 'Of Shakespeare we are frequently reminded', writes the *Monthly*, 'not by any paltry plagiarism, but by bold and *original imitation*' (May 1813). To the *Christian observer*, *Remorse* appears a rival to the Germans in its 'philosophical spirit and passionate energy', yet 'has no resemblance to them in their affectation of strained and extravagant sentiment' (April). 'To the merits of incident and character', the *Quarterly* notes, 'we have to add the charm of a rich and glowing poetry' (April). It has to be said that the reviewer was probably Coleridge's nephew.

It is 'the nakedness of the plot' that comes in for most criticism, together with the improbability of the remorseful villain-hero. 'Ordonio', the *Pamphleteer* comments in May 1815,

thinks like one of Shakespeare's loftiest characters; but then he must go and tell all he thinks in the set speeches of Racine. He is a metaphysical villain, who justifies to himself the vileness of his actions by the subtleties of his perverted reason.

The reviewer's comments are fair enough. It is Ordonio who chiefly reminds us that *Remorse* is an old play, written in the Nineties and revamped sixteen years later. Like Rivers in Wordsworth's *Borderers* – whose 'perverted reason' he at times dangerously adopts ('What? if one reptile sting another reptile? / Where is the crime?' p. 42) – he belongs, not to the Regency, but to the years of earnest moral questioning that followed the Revolution.

Sheridan in January 1797 had passed a message to Coleridge, through Bowles, asking him 'to write a tragedy on some popular subject'. Why he thought the author of *Religious musings* could learn to be 'popular' we cannot know. Coleridge, however, was flattered. He wrote on 6 February to lecture Sheridan on 'the four most popular Tragedies of Shakespeare', and on the success of Schiller's *Robbers*, and ended with a flourish of happy pomposity:

# Samuel Taylor Coleridge

I shall not cease to remember this your kind attention to me; and am pleased,
that I have to add the feeling of individual obligation to the deeper and more
lofty gratitude, which I owe you in common with all Europe. –

S. T. Coleridge.

By June, when Coleridge paid his visit to the Wordsworths at Racedown, he had written two-and-a-half acts of his play, then entitled
*Osorio*. By 16 October, he was through: 'It is done; and I would rather
mend hedges and follow the plough, than write another.'

A month later *Kubla Khan* had been composed, and by 20 November
there was a first version of *The ancient mariner*. At the same time,
*Osorio* was turned down. Coleridge's sense of injury was aggravated
when Sheridan failed to return the manuscript, and in 1806 was said to
be misquoting it to entertain his friends: 'Drip! drip! drip! there's nothing here but dripping' (accurately, 'Drip! drip! a ceaseless sound of
water-drops'). Hurt feelings were paraded at length in the Preface to
the 'infamously incorrect' first edition of *Remorse*; by the time of the
second – 'corrected and augmented' – they had subsided into a strangely
garbled opening paragraph. Success had been a vindication.

For modern readers, it must be the 'rich and glowing poetry' of
*Remorse* that is chiefly of interest. As the *British review* commented in
May 1813,

Mr Coleridge, though entitled undoubtedly to the praise of genius for many
truly poetical and brilliant passages in this piece, sinks very much in a comparison
with Mrs Joanna Baillie, as a delineator of the passions.

Critics were not wrong to see confusion in plot and motive; the 'weak
Scenes' that Coleridge himself referred to in *Remorse* are evident
enough. Added to which, there are too frequent moments when the
language strains for dramatic effect: Ordonio: 'Forgive me, Alvar! –
*Curse* me with forgiveness!' (p. 70). Yet a play completed between
*This lime-tree bower my prison* and *Kubla Khan* could hardly be without
redeeming features. The beautiful but undramatic excerpt from *Osorio*
printed in *Lyrical ballads* as *The foster-mother's tale* appears as an appendix
in *Remorse*, but Alvar's speech – *The dungeon* in 1798 – keeps its position
in the revised play (pp. 62–3). Among many other fine passages are the
speeches of Alhadra in Acts I and IV, Teresa's

There are woes
Ill bartered for the garishness of joy . . .
(p. 6)

and Alvar's

> On a rude rock,
> A rock, methought, fast by a grove of firs,
> Whose threaddy leaves to the low-breathing gale
> Made a soft sound most like the distant ocean . . .
>
> (p. 16)

# 34

## PERCY BYSSHE SHELLEY

# Queen Mab
### 1813

On 30 June 1822, a week before they were drowned together in the Gulf of Spezia, Edward Williams sat aboard the *Don Juan* reading a pirated copy of Shelley's *Queen Mab*. 'An astonishing work', he noted in his *Journal*: 'The enthusiasm of his spirit breaks out in some admirable passages in the poetry, and the notes are subtle and elegant as he could now write'. The poem had been composed ten years earlier when Shelley was nineteen, and is extraordinarily ambitious. Written chiefly in blank verse, but also anticipating *Prometheus* in its use of lyric-metres, it offers a vision of the past, present and future of mankind, reinforcing its polemic with 120 pages of scientific and philosophical notes. According to the poet, who, it should be remembered, was the elder son of a Whig baronet (and who on his Irish expedition of 1812 had found the lower orders lacking in Godwinian reason), *Mab* was intended to reach the sons and daughters of the aristocracy. Two hundred and fifty copies were printed in 1813 for private circulation, and seventy distributed. In 1816 a cut-down version was published as *The daemon of the world*, but made little impression. The piracy that brought *Mab* to a working-class audience, making it far and away Shelley's best-known poem, came in 1821, after stocks of the first edition had been disposed of (without the author's knowledge) to the radical bookseller, William Clark, who sold them off, pasting his own name over Shelley's imprint.

Out in Italy, Shelley knew little of this – and of course nothing of the long series of editions by Richard Carlile (including useful translations of French, Greek and Latin in the notes) that were to make his poems a 'bible' for the Chartists twenty years after his death. Indignation at the news of Clark's piracy was soon followed by amusement. '*Queen Mab*', Shelley wrote to Gisborne on 16 June 1821, a poem written by me when very young, in the most furious style, with long notes against Jesus Christ, & God the Father and the King & the Bishops & marriage & the Devil knows what, is just published by one of the low book-sellers in the Strand, against my wish & consent . . .

Unlike Southey, however, whose republican *Wat Tyler*, written in 1794, had emerged to embarrass him as Poet Laureate in 1817, Shelley had not gone back on his political views. He was worried that the un-revised *Mab*, with its violent attack on Christianity, might be 'better fitted to injure than to serve the cause which it advocates' (11 June 1822).

For advocating equality, and portraying the treachery of a king, *Wat Tyler* had been denounced in the House of Commons as 'the most seditious book ever written'. *Mab* was no less seditious, and by the standards of the day it was blasphemous as well. Subsumed in the notes was *The necessity of atheism*, the pamphlet for which Shelley had been sent down from Oxford in 1811: 'God is an hypothesis, and, as such, stands in need of proof' (p. 172). In the event, Clark was prosecuted by the Society for the Prevention of Vice (and dropped out, to be replaced as pirate by the hardier Carlile). Further publicity was provided by the scandalized reviewers. In affronting the traditional readership of poetry Shelley had gained one that was far more important to his cause than the scions of the aristocracy. Unintentionally he had reached the new working-class audience, politicised by Paine, from which even the 'leveller' Wordsworth was debarred.

Like Erasmus Darwin's *Botanic garden* (1789-91), on which it some-times draws, *Queen Mab* is a compendium in which the notes are fre-quently as important as the poetry. Darwin knew personally most of the scientists and thinkers on whom he depends; Shelley's learning is bookish. His major sources are Godwin (later to be his father-in-law, but at this stage known chiefly through his writing), Holbach and Newton (not the physicist, but a passionate vegetarian). Among the many others on whom he draws are: Homer, Plato, Lucretius, Pliny, Bacon, Milton, Spinoza, Locke, Hume, Rousseau, Volney, Gibbon, Condorcet, Drummond and Monboddo. It is impossible not to be impressed by the breadth and seriousness of his concerns. The fairy Mab, who bears no obvious relation to Mercutio's mischief-maker in *Romeo and Juliet*, conducts the soul of the sleeping Ianthe (female, but in some ways representative of Shelley himself) on a tour of the heavens.

As her chariot proceeds, earth and its goings-on dwindle into proportion:

> The magic car moved on.
> Earth's distant orb appeared
> The smallest light that twinkles in the heaven;
> Whilst round the chariot's way
> Innumerable systems rolled . . .
>
> (pp. 13–14)

'The indefinite immensity of the universe', Shelley comments in his note,

is a most awful subject of contemplation. He who rightly feels its mystery and grandeur, is in no danger of seduction from the falsehoods of religious systems, or of deifying the principle of the universe. It is impossible to believe that the Spirit that pervades this infinite machine, begat a son upon the body of a Jewish woman . . . (p. 126)

Like Blake (whose work he did not know), Shelley was angered by organized religion and its turning of the 'pervading spirit' of the universe into a Nobodaddy. Even his tones are sometimes remarkably Blakean. When in Canto VII of *Queen Mab* Jehovah speaks, it is the voice of Urizen, Blake's truculent Eternal Priest, that we are hearing:

> 'From an eternity of idleness
> I, God, awoke; in seven days' toil made earth
> From nothing; rested, and created man:
> I placed him in a paradise, and there
> Planted the tree of evil, so that he
> Might eat and perish, and my soul procure
> Wherewith to sate its malice . . .'
>
> (p. 90)

More obviously than Blake, Shelley writes as a Platonist. As such, he has affinities with the Unitarian early Coleridge, whose denunciation of 'priests idolatrous' is as vehement as his own, and who similarly rejects the divinity of Jesus, while admiring him as a man. Coleridge, though, is prepared to equate the Platonic world soul (or its scientific equivalent, 'Nature's vast ever-acting energy') with a personal, 'deified', God the Father. In this respect at least, Shelley may be closer to the Wordsworth of *Tintern abbey*, who feels an immanent 'presence', a 'something far more deeply interfused', a 'motion and a spirit', but nowhere mentions God.

Several of the major influences on *Queen Mab* – Hume, Drummond, Paine – are deists, and it is significant that Shelley's pervading spirit is one who requires no prayer or praises, and takes no account of human action. Governing the universe of the poem, and complicating Shelley's view of human potential, is the force of impersonal necessity, Platonic in origin, but deriving immediately from Holbach, who is quoted at length in the notes. Evil and good are both predetermined by an end-less chain of cause and effect: as things are as they are, they couldn't have been otherwise. Godwin's social determinism ('the assassin cannot help the murder he commits any more than the dagger', 1793 *Political justice* ii, p. 690) reinforces, and to some extent qualifies, the influence of Holbach, permitting a confidence in human perfectibility that his bleaker system denies. At times Shelley can write with a full Godwinian optimism –

> when reason's voice,
> Loud as the voice of nature, shall have waked
> The nations . . .
>
> ( p. 37)

– but he does not feel able to conclude his poem in the rationalist millenium that *Political justice* would imply. The emptiness of Holbach's definition of necessity imposes a limit on his portrayal of human achievement and aspiration. Of all things, the climax of *Mab* turns out to depend on vegetarianism. Anatomy shows man to be naturally a fructivor. When he ceases to eat his fellow animals his blood will cool, his aggression will disappear, conflict will cease:

> no longer now
> He slays the lamb that looks him in the face,
> And horribly devours his mangled flesh . . .
>
> (p. 109)

Though not in this form, suffering and injustice have been central to Shelley's poem, explaining not only his hatred of monarchy and tyranny, but also his horror of organized religion. 'It is a history of wickedness', Paine commented of Christianity in *The age of reason*, Part I (1794), 'that has served to corrupt and brutalize mankind; and, for my part, I sincerely detest it as I detest everything that is cruel'. The words might be Shelley's own. In his denunciation of tyranny, slavery, the 'legal butchery' of war, he is more extravagant than Paine, but the

detestation of cruelty is the same. Ahasuerus, the Wandering Jew cursed
by Christ with immortality, becomes his type of the suffering individual, struggling Prometheus-like

> with whirlwinds of mad agony,
> Yet peaceful, and serene, and self-enshrined,
> Mocking [his] powerless tyrant's horrible curse
> With stubborn and unalterable will . . .
>
> (p. 98)

Despite the flamboyancy of the twenty-year-old (and the improbability of his vegetarian solution to human troubles), the Shelley of *Queen
Mab* is impressively clear-thinking: 'Time is our consciousness of the
succession of ideas in our mind' (p. 208). Fossil evidence leads Shelley
to deduce that the poles have changed their position. The claims of the
French Revolution and its period are beautifully put into context by his
comment:

I will not insult common sense by insisting on the doctrine of the natural equality
of man. The question is not concerning its desirableness, but its practicability: so
far as it is practicable, it is desirable. (p. 140)

And no wonder the Chartists valued a poet who could write succinctly,
'There is no real wealth but the labour of man' (p. 138). It is perhaps
difficult to claim that *Queen Mab* is a great work, but in Williams's
phrase it is certainly an 'astonishing' one. The notes may or may not be
as 'subtle and elegant' as Shelley could have written at the end of his
life, but they form the basis of any examination of his later views. The
poetry, meanwhile, is high-flown, but rarely falters, capable of many
different moods from indignation to beauty and peace:

> Look on yonder earth:
> The golden harvests spring; the unfailing sun
> Sheds light and life; the fruits, the flowers, the trees,
> Arise in due succession; all things speak
> Peace, harmony, and love. The universe
> In nature's silent eloquence, declares
> That all fulfil the works of love and joy –
> All but the outcast man.
>
> (p. 41)

# 35

## LEIGH HUNT

═══════════════

# The feast of the poets
### 1814 (1811)

Like Byron's *English bards and Scotch reviewers* (1809), Leigh Hunt's *Feast of the poets* (first published in *The reflector*, 1811) is a clever, funny, biased, enjoyable view of the literary scene, written by a cocksure young man with no respect for his elders. Both writers damned the vast majority of their contemporaries, and both later regretted some of the judgments they had made. 'With this effusion', Hunt commented in his *Autobiography* (1850), 'while thinking of nothing but showing my wit . . . I made almost every living poet and poetaster my enemy' (i, p. 239):

> I offended all the critics of the old or French school by objecting to the monotony of Pope's versification, and all the critics of the new or German school, by laughing at Wordsworth, with whose writings I was then unacquainted, except through the medium of his deriders. (p. 248)

Hunt did not of course go on, as Byron did (with the publication of *Childe Harold* in 1810) to become the great literary success of his day. In radical circles, however, he became something of a hero, by spending two years in prison for libelling the Prince Regent. The first few nights were disturbing, as the jailer had put him in a room where he could hear the working-class prisoners clanking their chains. He was then considerably moved to rooms out of earshot on the ground floor, which he had decorated with floral wallpaper, and which opened onto a garden all his own. There he was joined by his wife and increasing family, visited by Byron, Hazlitt and others, and had leisure to revise his poem for the first edition of 1814.

Though more than a hundred lines of verse were added to *The feast*, they altered the tone very little. It is the hundred pages of additional notes that transform the work. The poem depends no more than *The dunciad* on being just or charitable, yet the notes admit to an anxiety to get things right which the verse conceals. It was a period in which attitudes were changing. Jeffrey's attacks on the Lake School in the *Edinburgh* had carried all before them in the reviews of Southey's *Thalaba* (1802) and Wordsworth's *Poems* (1807); by the time of the *Excursion* review of 1814, Jeffrey himself was beginning to look isolated. The value of Hunt's work is partly as a barometer. His notes form a separate and highly important piece of literary criticism, which shows him to be anxious chiefly about his assessment of Scott, the Lakers and Byron.

To Scott, it seems, he has been too kind. In *The feast* itself he is awarded a place at Apollo's table – alongside Moore, Campbell and Southey. In the notes he is crushed. The novels have yet to appear, and despite the sales of Scott's poetry (which apparently weighed with the god), Hunt as critic refuses to be convinced by the sequence of long romantic historical poems which followed *The lay of the last minstrel* (1805):

Of Mr Walter Scott's poetry the estimate is sufficiently easy, and will now perhaps, after the surfeit he has given us of it, be pretty generally acknowledged. It is little more than a leap back into the dress and the diction of rude but gorgeous times, when show concealed a great want of substance, and a little thinking was conveyed in a great many words.

'Thus it is not invidious', Hunt continues, 'to call the late demand for it a fashion' (p. 65). Scott, it seems, is doubly a thing of the past!

Southey (who since *The feast* was first written has accepted the Laureateship when Scott turned it down) also retains his seat at the table. In the notes he is treated with relative indulgence – 'let his praises remain; – it is not worth while to alter them' (p. 81) – but Hunt cannot forgive the Lakers for degenerating 'like the others, into servile place-hunters':

Mr Southey, and even Mr Wordsworth have both accepted offices under government, of such a nature, as absolutely ties up their independence; Mr Coleridge, in pamphlets and newspapers, has done his best to deserve likewise . . . (p. 78)

As place-men, Southey and Wordsworth are on an equal footing; as poets, they are not. Hunt is uneasy – willing to make amends in the notes, but not to rewrite his poem. 'Though Mr Southey . . . is admitted', we are told, 'where Mr Wordsworth is not, it is not meant to insinuate that he is a better poet, but merely that he has not so abused the comparative little that was expected of him' (p. 81). Hunt's prose becomes convoluted as he strives at once to do Wordsworth justice and to maintain his convenient earlier position:

> [Southey] is no more to be compared with Mr Wordsworth in real genius than the man who thinks once out of a hundred times is with him who thinks the whole hundred; but that he is at the same time a poet, will be no more denied, than that the hundredth part of Mr Wordsworth's genius would make a poet. His fancy perhaps has gone little beyond books, but still it is of a truly poetical character; he touches the affections pleasingly though not powerfully . . . (p. 81)

If Hunt in 1811 was as ignorant of Wordsworth as he later claimed, it is surprising that he should have been such an elegant parodist. *The feast* is for the most part hurried along by its anapaest rhythms, but pauses at one point for a version of Wordsworthian simplicity that shows its author to have been no common 'derider':

> And t'other some lines he had made on a straw,
> Shewing how he had found it, and what it was for,
> And how, when 'twas balanc'd, it stood like a spell! –
> And how, when 'twas balanc'd no longer, it fell!
> A wild thing of scorn he describ'd it to be,
> But said it was patient to heaven's decree: –
> Then he gaz'd upon nothing, and looking forlorn,
> Dropt a *natural* tear for that *wild thing of scorn*!
>
> (p. 12)

'I am told, on very good authority', Hunt added in a note, 'that this parody upon Mr Wordsworth's worst style of writing has been taken for a serious extract from him, and panegyrized accordingly, with much grave wonderment how I could find it ridiculous' (p. 87).

The notes are not commonly so mischievious. Hunt is at a loss. Wordsworth, with no place at Apollo's table, is awarded a critical note of twenty-two pages. At one moment he is praised as the greatest poet of the age, at the next he is blamed (with Coleridge) for misuse of his talents:

> Mr Wordsworth is capable of being at the head of a new and great age of poetry; and in point of fact, I do not deny that he is so already, as the greatest poet of the present; – but in point of effect, in point of delight and utility, he appears to me to have made a mistake unworthy of him, and to have sought by eccentricity and

by a turning away from society, what he might have obtained by keeping to his proper and more neighbourly sphere. (p. 90)

Placing Byron is the other major problem. Wordsworth's great work – though Hunt perhaps could not have known it – had all been written by 1814; Byron's was still to come. While rightly looking to the future, Hunt beautifully categorizes the romances, refusing to rate them at their current disproportionate value:

The characteristics of Lord Byron's poetry are a general vein of melancholy, – a fondness for pithy, suggesting, and passionate modes of speech, – and an intensity of feeling, which appears to seek relief in it's own violence. (pp. 130–1)

Writing in the *Examiner* in October 1819, Hunt was to be among the first to recognize, and to accept, the mode of *Don Juan*. Meanwhile it is to *Childe Harold* that he turns for Byron at his truest to himself:

Of all his lordship's productions, I confess I am still most taken with the little effusions at the end of the *Childe Harold* [canto II]. It is here, I think, that the soul of him is to be found, and that he has most given himself up to those natural words and native impressions, which are the truest test of poetry. (p. 133)

WILLIAM WORDSWORTH

Poems

*(Poems by William Wordsworth: including Lyrical ballads, and the miscellaneous pieces of the author, with additional poems, a new preface and a supplementary essay)*
1815

*Poems* 1815 is not the Wordsworth publication that comes to everybody's mind. *An evening walk* stands out in 1793 as his first major published work. *Lyrical ballads* 1798 has a special place in literary history; the 1800 'second edition' (with its newly inserted Preface, and twice the original number of poems) is scarcely less famous; *Poems in two volumes*, 1807, is known for its Wordsworthian blend of power and idiosyncrasy, and for the first publication of both *Resolution and independence* and the *Ode*. As merely the 'first collected edition', embodying little that is new, *Poems* 1815 would seem to have less claim to our attention.

Yet it was these two handsome octavo volumes, comprising 775 pages of verse and prose, that established Wordsworth's position as the great poet of his day. Here was something evidently substantial. Faced by the 1815 collection, it was no longer sufficient to jeer at Wordsworth's puerility, hold him up to ridicule for his affectation of simplicity, and degrading tendency to choose his heroes and heroines among the lower classes. *1815* was the edition that Shelley took with him, first to Switzerland, and then to Italy. It was in this form that Wordsworth inspired in Byron the unusual responsiveness of *Childe Harold* Canto Three: 'to me / High mountains are a feeling'. This was the text that prompted Keats to regard Wordsworth as 'deeper than Milton', and that brought forth Blake's passionate marginalia – half admiring ('This is all in the highest degree Imaginative and equal to any Poet'), half indignant:

# William Wordsworth

Natural Objects always did & now do weaken deaden and Obliterate Imagination in Me Wordsworth must know that what he Writes Valuable is Not to be found in Nature.

Wordsworth in 1815 was taking stock. It was thirty years since his fluent couplets on the bicentenary of Hawkshead Grammar School, and fifteen since his return to Cumbria in December 1799, intent upon putting together his great composite philosophical work, *The recluse*. A full-length version of *The prelude* had been completed in 1804–6, and in 1814 Wordsworth had gone on to publish *The excursion* (with 'A Portion of *The recluse*' on the titlepage). As autobiography ('a thing unprecedented in Literary history that a man should talk so much about himself'; 1 May 1805), *The prelude* would have to stay in manuscript till *The recluse* could be printed as a whole. Nonetheless, it was a contribution. How could the shorter poems too be included? Wordsworth's image of his poetry as a cathedral is remarkably imaginative. Cathedrals are sacred and organic. If any buildings can be said to grow, they do. The product of different plans, periods and styles, they are nevertheless felt to be harmonious. Major sections of *The recluse*, Wordsworth told readers of *The excursion*, would form the body of his gothic church. *The prelude* would be an ante-chapel. Minor poems, when 'properly arranged', would be seen to resemble 'cells, oratories and sepulchral recesses'.

No doubt there had to be a more practical arrangement for *Poems* 1815. Building on the section of *Poems in two volumes* (1807) entitled 'Moods of My Own Mind', Wordsworth introduced four major categories: 'Poems Founded on the Affections', 'Poems of the Fancy', 'Poems of the Imagination' and 'Poems Proceeding from Sentiment and Reflection'. Not surprisingly Wordsworth's categories tend to overlap. Fancy, which he sees as lively and frequently tender, is more important to him than to Coleridge, and (because it has its own vitality) cannot be distinguished from imagination when it comes to a borderline. *Tintern abbey*, which 'Proceeds from Sentiment and Reflection' if ever anything did, is placed (according to an alternative logic) at the end of 'Poems of the Imagination'. The *Ode* could have fitted happily into either of these categories. Instead it is held back – rather as the Climbing of Snowdon is held back in *The Prelude* – to form a climax. Or does it perhaps form a 'sepulchral recess'? The poet has distinctions in his mind that are less clear to his readers. How, one wonders, could a Wordsworthian poem of the affections ever not be a work of sentiment and reflection? Most would surely be imaginative as well?

Though less obviously so, the poet's thinking is again metaphorical. *Poems* 1815 is not a building, or a part of a building, but a journey through life. 'As far as it was possible', the Preface tells us, poems have been arranged 'according to an order of time, commencing with Child-hood, and terminating with Old Age, Death, and Immortality' (p. xiv). Poems are grouped because they evoke a particular phase of existence, not because their composition belongs to a given period. The first poem of volume one is *The rainbow* ('The Child is Father of the Man'), the last of volume two is the *Ode*, with its message of 'faith that looks through death', and 'years that bring the philosophic mind'. Interven-ing sections form a proof – at least for the poet himself – of days 'Bound each to each by natural piety'. The collection has, we are told, 'a beginning, a middle, and an end'. We mount from Childhood, through the Affections, to Fancy, and the high-point of Imagination; we decline (though that is perhaps too strong a word) through Sentiment and Reflection (effectively, 'the philosophic mind') to Old Age, Epitaphs and Elegiac Poetry. Loss and death are confronted in tributes to John Wordsworth, the brother who died at sea in 1805. First the beautiful *Elegiac stanzas* ('A deep distress hath humaniz'd my Soul'), then *To the daisy*, with its anticipation of the death of the poet himself, and its strained yet meaningful syntax:

> SWEET Flower! belike one day to have
> A place upon thy Poet's grave,
> I welcome thee once more:
> But He, who was on land, at sea,
> My Brother, too, in loving thee,
> Although he loved more silently,
> Sleeps by his native shore.
>
> (ii, 341, ll. 1–7)

It is left to the *Ode* to offer – as *The daisy* does not – Intimations of Immortality. Through his 'Recollections of Early Childhood', Words-worth, like Donne in another valediction forbidding mourning, 'draws [his] circle just', and ends where he begun.

In practice the arrangement of *Poems* 1815 enables Wordsworth to replace a chronological sequence with a logic depending on affinities of

mood, emotion, personal association. *The brothers*, incorporating tender
memories of John's visit to Grasmere in 1800, stands in 'Poems of the
Affections' next to *The sparrow's nest*, with its moving tribute to
Dorothy:

> The Blessing of my later years
> Was with me when a Boy;
> She gave me eyes, she gave me ears;
> And humble cares, and delicate fears;
> A heart, the fountain of sweet tears;
>  And love, and thought, and joy.
>
>  (i, 115, ll. 15–20)

At the end of the same group, a great Alfoxden comic ballad in the
manner of Sterne (*The idiot boy*, 1798) is followed by a tragic Grasmere
narrative in low-style blank verse (*Michael*, 1800) and a sombre
Virgilian tale expanding an episode of the Trojan War (*Laodamia*,
1814). For Wordsworth, it is love that forms the link: a mother's, a
father's, and a wife's. With impeccable logic that few would recognize,
the heightened drama of *Goody Blake and Harry Gill* (1788) is followed
in 'Poems of the Imagination' by *I wandered lonely as a cloud* (1804). The
first reveals the power of a curse on an ignorant, superstitious mind:

> The cold, cold moon above her head
> Thus on her knees did Goody pray,
> Young Harry heard what she had said:
> And icy cold he turned away.
>
>  (i, 326, ll. 101–4)

The second shows memory, joy, imagination in the poet himself:

> They flash upon that inward eye
> Which is the bliss of solitude,
> And then my heart with pleasure fills,
> And dances with the Daffodils.
>
>  (i, 329, ll. 21–4)

Both equally show the mind as 'lord and master'.

It was Coleridge with whom Wordsworth, at Alfoxden in 1798, had
first discussed the analogy of superstition and the imagination. The
Preface to *Lyrical ballads*, though published over Wordsworth's name,
had been written from Coleridge's notes in 1800, and claimed by him
two years later as 'half the child of [his] own brain'. *The prelude* had
depended in its most exalted moods on Coleridge's thinking. By 1815

such interdependence is long past. There has been a patching-up of the quarrel of 1810, but no return to collaboration. In the new Preface Wordsworth is on his own. He may engage with the fancy-imagination distinction proposed by Coleridge in *Omniana* (1812), but he is writing to please himself. The result is an important critical work, enlightening for a sequence of major Romantic definitions, and not least for its bearing on Wordsworth's own poetry. Piqued by the reviewers and the slow reception of his work, Wordsworth comes out into the open, tells us, rightly and forthrightly, that his imaginative writing has 'the same ennobling tendency' as the Bible, Milton and Spenser. In support he offers an account of *There was a boy* that shows just how odd, and how powerfully new, was his genius. His is not a sprightly prose, but few poets have written so thoughtfully either about the nature of their own writing, or about the workings of the mind:

Guided by one of my own primary consciousnesses, I have represented a commutation and transfer of internal feelings, co-operating with external accidents to plant, for immortality, images of sound and sight in the celestial soil of the Imagination. The Boy, there introduced, is listening, with something of a feverish and restless anxiety, for a recurrence of the riotous sounds which he had previously excited; and, at the moment when the intenseness of his mind is beginning to remit, he is surprised into a perception of the solemn and tranquillizing images which the Poem describes. (i, pp. xxxi–ii)

'I do not know who wrote these Prefaces', Blake commented in the margin of the 'Essay Supplementary to the Preface', 'they are very mischievous & direct contrary to Wordsworths own Practise'. Though intuitively he agreed with Blake, Wordsworth the critic was putting too little stress on imagination as 'The Divine Vision': 'the Natural Man' was 'rising up against the Spiritual Man'. For all this, the 'Essay' contains some of his most perceptive criticism, taking his discussion of imagination and the workings of poetry into a study of language itself. The boy who has blown 'mimic hootings' to the owls of Windermere will forever associate their calls with 'the visible scene' that has 'enter[ed] unawares into his mind' (i, 298, ll. 21–2). He has received a precious gift, but the imaginative power he demonstrates is taken no further. The poet, in offering a parallel experience to his readers, has to cope with the fact that language is personal, and therefore anarchic, 'subject to endless fluctuations and arbitrary associations'. 'The genius of the Poet', we are told, 'melts these down for his purpose; but they retain their shape and quality to him who is not capable of exerting, within his own mind, a corresponding energy' (i, p. 372). Readers too must be imaginative. It is for this reason that,

in every thing which is to send the soul into herself, to be admonished of her weakness, or to be made conscious of her power . . . *there*, the Poet must reconcile himself for a season to few and scattered hearers'. (ii, p. 373)

Not that Wordsworth does reconcile himself to such an audience. The idiosyncratic groupings of *Poems* 1815 enable him to lay before potential readers an extraordinary range of poetry that 'send[s] the soul into herself': narrative poetry, meditative poetry, political poetry, lyrics of astonishing power, and hybrids so much his own that they defy categorization (*Resolution and independence*, for one). In poem after poem he emerges as the great poet of the sublime, Milton's natural successor, save that Milton (as Keats pointed out on 3 May 1818) 'did not think into the human heart as Wordsworth has done.' It is a poetry grounded in actuality,

> in the very world, which is the world
> Of all of us, – the place where in the end
> We find our happiness, or not all!
> (ii, p. 71; *French Revolution*, ll. 38–40)

yet for this reason the more convincing in its strangeness:

> And hers shall be the breathing balm,
> And hers the silence and the calm
> Of mute insensate things.
> (i, p. 313; *Three years she grew*, ll. 16–18)

There are poems of monosyllabic tenderness:

> There is a blessing in the air,
> Which seems a sense of joy to yield
> To the bare trees, and mountains bare,
> And grass in the green field.
> (ii, p. 113; *Lines*, ll. 5–8)

And there are poems of memorable grandeur:

> O THOU! whose fancies from afar are brought;
> Who of thy words dost make a mock apparel,
> And fittest to unutterable thought
> The breeze-like motion and the self-born carol . . .
> (i, p. 42; *To H.C.*, ll. 1–4)

But in all there is a vision – and with it, a voice – that is utterly individual. Wordsworth was not wrong when, in the 'Essay Supplementary', he defined genius as 'the introduction of a new element into the intellectual universe.'

---

# Poems
## 1816

Byron's 1816 *Poems* came out in early June, six weeks after he left England for what proved to be the last time. It is quite unlike his other publications, and has sometimes been dismissed as opportunism – Murray cashing in on the scandal surrounding the poet's departure, building a slim volume round verse that was already the subject of gossip and rumour. Yet Byron provided the material, and Byron corrected the proofs. In truth it is a defiant volume, a quiet putting of the record straight. Byron had been hounded out of the country, turned on by the press, cut by the Regency society whose hero he had been since 1810 and the appearance of *Childe Harold*. His close friends had stood by him, however, and truest of all had been his half-sister, Augusta, on whom the gossip centred.

It is Augusta's poem, written two days before they parted on Easter Sunday 1816, that is given pride of place in the volume:

> When fortune changed – and love fled far,
>    And hatred's shafts flew thick and fast,
> Thou wert the solitary star
>    Which rose and set not to the last . . .
>
> And when the cloud upon us came,
>    Which strove to blacken o'er thy ray –
> Then purer spread its gentle flame;
>    And dashed the darkness all away.
>
> (p. 10)

To mention the 'cloud' (accusations of incest) in a poem written for publication was extraordinary. Yet Byron passed the *Stanzas to Augusta* over to Murray almost at once. To his annoyance one immediate result was a letter from Lady Caroline Lamb, to whom Murray had unwisely shown them. 'I do implore you', she wrote, 'for God's sake not to publish . . . you will draw ruin on your own head and hers'. (Prothero, ii, p. 450)

Sent the stanzas by Hobhouse after Byron's departure, Augusta herself said merely, 'I think them most beautiful . . . I need not add they are most gratifying to me, who doat upon dear B' (6 May 1816). Byron had said what he wanted to say, and she had accepted it. There is a curious sense in which they look like innocents. 'To me she was, in the hour of need', Byron told Lady Blessington, 'a tower of strength . . . Augusta knew all my weaknesses, but she had love enough to bear with them.' (Blessington, p. 198) For him there had presumably been a *frisson* attached to their love-making, but it was experienced within a relationship of unusual purity. Neither felt any remorse, till Annabella took upon herself the duty of imposing it on Augusta.

Not surprisingly, Annabella's poem is more complex. Byron was slow to understand his wife's implacable nature. On 26 February, when she was far advanced in her plans for a separation, he wrote pathetically,

Dearest Pip – I wish you would make it up – for I am dreadfully sick of all this – and cannot foresee any good that can come of it. If you will, I am ready to make any penitential speech or speeches you please – and will be very good and tractable for the rest of my days – and very sorry for all that have gone before . . .

*Fare thee well*, which forms the centrepiece of *Poems* 1816, was sent to Annabella, 20–25 March (or perhaps 8–9 April), still with the hope of bringing about a reconciliation: 'I send you the first verses that I ever attempted to write upon you, and perhaps the last that I may ever write at all.' The poem, like the note, is emotional and extreme, but there is no reason to think it ungenuine:

> All my faults – perchance thou knowest –
>  All my madness – none can know . . .
> Fare thee well! – thus disunited –
>  Torn from every nearer tie –
> Seared in heart – and lone – and blighted –
>  More than this, I scarce can die.
>
> (pp. 23–4)

Tom Moore's is the best commentary. Suspicious at first, he came after reading Byron's *Memoranda* to accept that the poem was written amid 'the swell of tender recollections'. Byron in truth was hurt and confused. Rejection was something new, and he had not expected it to happen.

Annabella returned the verses without a comment; Byron showed them to his friends, and sent them to Murray. It was Brougham who supplied them to the *Champion*, where they were printed a week before Byron left, alongside a lampoon on Annabella's confidante, Mrs Clermont, which showed him in a peculiarly revengeful and unpleasant mood. The effect – certainly intended by the editors – was to degrade the love poem, imply that it was a sham. In Cruikshank's cartoon, entitled *Fare thee well* and published two weeks later, the lines quoted above appear in a bubble as Byron gestures towards Annabella, child in arms on the cliffs at Dover. The word 'lone' is double-underlined; three women are solacing the poet in his dinghy; leaning over the rail of Byron's ship, a sailor comments, 'I say Jack, I hope he's got enough on 'em aboard!'

In *Poems* 1816, *Fare thee well* has more decorous company, preceded by exquisite lyrics, followed by political poems designed to make clear Byron's allegiances as he goes into exile. Especially moving among the first, are the two sets of *Stanzas for music*: the lament for his schoolfellow, Dorset, 'There's not a joy the world can give', with its poignant echo of Wordsworth's *Elegiac stanzas* (also for a young life pointlessly ended) –

> Oh could I feel as I have felt, – *or be what I have been,*
> Or weep as I could once have wept, o'er many a vanished scene . . .
> (p. 18)

– and the song that may be a tribute to the voice of Claire Clairmont, Mary Godwin's step-sister, who at this time claimed enough of Byron's attention to conceive his child, Allegra:

> There be none of Beauty's daughters
>   With a magic like thee;
> And like music on the waters
>   Is thy sweet voice to me:
> When, as if its sound were causing
> The charmed ocean's pausing,
> The waves lie still and gleaming,
> And the lulled winds seem dreaming.
> (p. 19)

The *Champion*'s attack on Byron in April was partly as author of the ode, 'We do not curse thee, Waterloo', first of the group of alleged translations ('From the French') that form the second half of *Poems* 1816. The *Ode* too had appeared in the press, but rather than being leaked by friends, it had been planted by Byron himself – with a whimsical attribution to Chateaubriand. True to his republican youth, Wordsworth had greeted the coronation of Napoleon in 1804 as 'the dog / Returning to his vomit' (1805 *Prelude* x, ll. 934–5). For all his admiration of Napoleon, Byron in the *Ode* takes a similar view. Under 'the soldier citizen' France had been invincible. Defeat came when 'The Hero sunk into the King':

> Her Safety sits not on a throne,
> With CAPET or NAPOLEON!
> But in equal rights and laws,
> Hearts and hands in one great cause . . .
> (p. 29)

Republican or not, Byron – as events turned out – had no alternative to ending the 1816 volume in the grand swelling rhythms of *Napoleon's farewell*:

> Farewell to the Land, where the gloom of my Glory
> Arose and o'ershadowed the earth with her name –
> She abandons me now, – but the page of her story
> The brightest or blackest, is filled with my fame.
> (p. 37)

The lines had been defiant at the time of writing, four weeks after Waterloo; now they seemed prophetic as well.

# 38

ROBERT SOUTHEY

---

## Wat Tyler
### *a dramatic poem*
### 1817 (1794)

The first that Southey heard of the publication of *Wat Tyler* in February 1817 was when he received in Keswick an advertisement published in the *Morning chronicle*. His response on Valentine's Day has a certain dignity:

God be thanked that the worst which malice can say of me is no more than what I was once proud to say of myself, and never shall be ashamed of saying – that I was a Republican in my youth.

The confidence, however, proved to be misplaced. Not only was he vulnerable as Poet Laureate, and a servant of the Crown, he was known to be the author of an unsigned article in the *Quarterly* for October 1816, denouncing 'incendiaries' who stirred the lower orders to rebel. When 'the man of free opinions' turns author, Southey had permitted himself to say, 'his very breath becomes venomous, and every page which he sends forth carries with it a poison to the unsuspicious reader.'

On 14 March the words of the *Quarterly* were quoted in the Commons, with due gravity, by William Smith, a member of the whig Opposition. Appropriately the House was debating the Seditious Meetings Bill. The scene is reported in *Hansard*. Sustaining the pretence of Southey's anonymity, Smith asked permission to read an extract from a poem recently published, to which he supposed the writer of his quotation must have been alluding, as 'a part of the virus with which the public mind had been infected':

> My brethren, these are truths, and weighty ones:
> Ye are all equal; nature made ye so.
> Equality is your birthright; – when I gaze

# Wat Tyler

On the proud palace, and behold one man,
In the blood-purpled robes of royalty,
Feasting at ease, and lording over millions;
Then turn me to the hut of poverty,
And see the wretched labourer, worn with toil,
Divide his scanty morsel with his infants,
I sicken, and, indignant at the sight,
'Blush for the patience of humanity.'

(p. 31)

*Wat Tyler* had come into the hands of the booksellers, Sherwood, Neely and Jones, and been pirated by them on 13 February. Other radical publishers had joined in, and a great many copies had been sold. Southey's tory friends, as well as the whigs, would have known that he was the author. Why, Smith asked guilelessly, 'had not those who thought it necessary to suspend the Habeas corpus act taken notice of this poem?'

*Wat Tyler* appeared to him to be the most seditious book that was ever written; its author did not stop short of exhorting to general anarchy; he vilified kings, priests, and nobles, and was for universal suffrage and perfect equality.

Southey's seditious poem suggesting the horrors of equality (but not in fact of universal suffrage) had been written in November 1794, when he was twenty. He and Coleridge were still hoping to establish a commune, or 'pantisocracy', on the banks of the Susquehanna. Priestley and many other British radicals had already emigrated. The letter in which Southey announces the composition of his play opens, 'Would we were in America!' It was the time of the Treason Trials. Hardy, first of the accused, and Secretary of the London Corresponding Society, had just been acquitted. Southey was in high spirits. 'I am writing a tragedy', he told his brother,

on my Uncle Wat Tyler, who knocked out a tax-gatherer's brains, then rose in rebellion. Our toast today was: May there never be wanting a Wat Tyler whilst there is a Tax-gatherer. (6 November 1794)

Later he was to claim that the play had been written in three mornings; yet the poetry is heartfelt and shows little sign of haste. In taking the Peasants' Revolt for his subject, Southey had hit on an historical period that closely paralleled his own. The difference was that in 1381 the revolution that never quite happened in the 1790s, had indeed taken place. Protesting against a poll-tax levied to fight a needless war with France, the peasants had asserted their rights, and even, through weight of numbers, briefly gained control of London.

Four hundred years later there was still the unjust taxation that fell most heavily on the lower orders, still the war in which they were killed or maimed with no benefit to their class; but repression was more efficient. 'When', Paine commented in Part Two of *The rights of man* (his great blueprint for the welfare state), 'we see age going to the work-house and youth to the gallows, something must be wrong in the system of government.' Through industrialization, and the Corresponding Societies' mass distribution of Paine, the working-class had become politicized. Pitt and his ministers, however, were not to be taken by surprise as the counsellors of Richard II had been. The Treason Trials of 1794 were a warning. Twelve of England's leading radicals stood to be hanged, drawn and quartered (the fate reserved for John Ball in Southey's play) on an absurd charge of conspiring against the life of George III.

As it happened there was a similar political situation when Southey's play reappeared in 1817. Twenty years of war had given an extra poignancy to Tyler's final speech:

> King of England
> Why are we sold like cattle in your markets? . . .
> The Parliament for ever asks more money:
> We toil and sweat for money for your taxes:
> Where is the benefit, what food reap we
> From all the councils of your government?
> Think you that we should quarrel with the French?
> What boots to us your victories, your glory?
>
> (pp. 43–4)

As in 1794, Habeas corpus had been suspended (this time in response to Luddite machine-breaking). *Wat Tyler* could not have been published at a more appropriate moment. To the delight of the radicals, Southey's injunction to stop the piracy was refused, Lord Chancellor Eldon deciding that damages could not be recovered for a work that was 'in its nature calculated to do an injury to the public'. Southey in *A letter to William Smith* retained his dignity, and did in fact care about the condition of the poor. Hone came out with his New Edition and remarkable 'Preface Suitable to Recent Circumstances'. Hunt, Coleridge, Hazlitt, Byron, all had their say. Amid the fuss, what nobody seems to have noticed is that political indignation had inspired the Poet Laureate in his youth to write a very passable play.

# 39
## JOHN KEATS

━━━━━━━━━━

# Poems
## 1817

Keats was twenty-one when his first collection of poems was published on 3 March 1817. Four years, and two books, later he was dead. None of the three books sold, but the fate of *Poems* 1817 was especially ignominious: W. C. Hazlitt records that unbound copies were remaindered at a penny-halfpenny each to a bookseller, who 'paid tuppence-halfpenny for boarding and sold the lot very slowly at eighteen-pence' (quarter of the original price). Shelley had advised against hurrying into print, but, as Cowden Clarke recalled, the volume was 'launched amid the cheers and fond anticipations' of the inner circle of Keats's friends:

Every one of us expected (and not unreasonably) that it would create a sensation in the literary world; for such a first production (and a considerable portion of it from a minor) has rarely occurred . . . Alas! the book might have emerged in Timbuctoo with a far stronger chance of fame and approbation . . . The whole community, as if by compact, seemed determined to know nothing about it. (*Recollections*, p. 140)

Keats's own rueful comment was that the book 'was read by some dozen of [his] friends, who liked it, and some dozen whom [he] was unacquainted with, who did not'. *Poems* 1817 was ignored by the *Edinburgh* and *Quarterly*, but reviews elsewhere were in fact largely favourable. No one found fault gratuitously as Croker would do the following year with *Endymion*, and even the 'unacquainted' found much to praise. Friends were a greater problem – not because they were wrong, but because they were tactless. The assumptions they shared with the writer were in many cases not yet acceptable to the public. Reynolds on 17 March listed Byron, Moore, Rogers and Campbell, in the *Champion*, and prophesied (rightly in three cases out of four) that Keats would 'eclipse them all'. Bailey went further. Writing to the *Oxford herald* from his rooms in Magdalen Hall (where parts of *Endymion* were drafted), he claimed on 30 May 1818 that Keats's first volume contained 'the richest promise' he had ever seen 'of an etherial imagination maintained by vast intellectual power'. Perhaps the dons saw intellectual power as their own prerogative; at any rate, the University that had sent Shelley down seven years before did not make amends by flocking to the bookshops.

More important for its long-term implications was Hunt's proprietary review in the *Examiner* for 1 June 1817. Keats's volume, he tells his readers, 'is the production of the young writer whom we had the pleasure of announcing to the public a short time since'. The essay contains much that is shrewd and perceptive, as Hunt develops the position that he had taken up in *The feast of the poets* (1814). Keats is placed for the *Examiner*'s readers in terms both of contemporary poetry, and of the still dominant Augustan decorum:

The school which existed till lately since the Restoration of Charles the 2d, was rather a school of wit and ethics in verse than any thing else . . . Pope distilled as much real poetry as could be got from the drawing-room world in which the art then lived . . .

'It was the Lake Poets', Hunt continues (showing how far his own views, though ahead of the times, were also changing with them), 'that were the first to revive a true taste for nature'. Keats, as 'a young poet giving himself up to his own impressions, and revelling in real poetry for its own sake', is, like Wordsworth, a 'successor of the true and abundant poets of the older time. Poetry, like Plenty, should be represented with a cornucopia'.

To be type-cast as a follower of Hunt (which he partly was) did Keats no good. For the next thirty years he would be treated as a disciple, a member of the Cockney School, and therefore excessive in both principles and poetic technique. Yet Hunt understood the imaginative power and abundance of Keats's writing as no one else did. The characteristics he noted especially were 'a fine ear, a fancy and imagination at will, and an intense feeling of external beauty in its most natural and least expressible simplicity.' *I stood tiptoe* and *Sleep and poetry* (first and last poems of the 1817 volume) are singled out, as showing Keats

# John Keats

'at his best advantage'. They display 'that fertile power of association and imagery which constitutes the abstract poetical faculty as distinguished from every other.'

'I find I cannot exist without poetry – without eternal poetry', Keats tells Reynolds on 18 April 1817. He is 'all in a Tremble from not having written anything of late'. Hunt's influence by now was on the wane (criticisms begin to creep into the letters in May), but there is no doubt that his encouragement had been very important. Keats had been writing for only two years when *Poems* 1817 was published, and had still to withdraw from his surgical courses at Guy's Hospital. The ill effects of Hunt's poetic style have been too much stressed. Keats under his influence was quietly developing his own strengths – breaking through to become the writer who in *Sleep and poetry* maps out his future with such prescience, and who in the one truly great poem of this first collection offers us an imaginative vision that is entirely new:

> Then felt I like some watcher of the skies
>  When a new planet swims into his ken;
> Or like stout Cortez when with eagle eyes
>  He star'd at the Pacific – and all his men
> Look'd at each other with a wild surmise –
>  Silent, upon a peak in Darien.

# 40

MARY SHELLEY AND P. B. SHELLEY

———————

History of a six weeks' tour
*through a part of France, Switzerland, Germany and Holland:
with letters descriptive of a sail round the lake of
Geneva, and of the glaciers of Chamouni*
1817

Appearing in 1817, the year before *Frankenstein*, *History of a six weeks' tour* is Mary Shelley's first venture into print. The *Tour* takes its name from the trip to Geneva which she had made with Shelley and her step-sister, Claire Clairmont, in July–August 1814. On its own Mary's journal of this 'elopement-journey' would have been too short, so she fills out the volume with material from their travels two years later in the summer of 1816. First she writes two 'letters' herself, purporting to have been sent from Geneva in May and June 1816; then she adds Shelley's two magnificent (and genuine) letters to Peacock of July. Finally, in smaller print, and with no mention on the title-page, there comes the first publication of *Mont Blanc*.

The result is a composite volume, opening with the reflections of the sixteen-year-old Mary, showing her development into the author of *Frankenstein*, recording Shelley's companionship with Byron on Lake Geneva and first impressions of the Alps, and concluding in one of the greatest of all Romantic poems. Though the *Tour* is published anonymously, initials printed at the end of each section reveal the joint authorship. Mary writes well from the first. Personal details appear entirely natural: 'I was dreadfully sea-sick' (p. 3); 'Our beds were too uncomfortable to allow a thought of sleeping in them' (p. 33). There is little straining for effect, but at times she will permit herself a small literary flourish: 'we were still far distant [from Calais], when the moon sunk in the red and stormy horizon, and the fast-flashing lightning became pale in the breaking day' (p. 3). The small adventures of the journey are told with engaging matter-of-factness, and we gain a vivid sense of what it was all like. At Charenton they sell their donkey and buy a mule for ten Napoleons:

About nine o'clock we departed. We were clad in black silk. I rode on the mule, which carried also our portmanteau; S[helley] and C[laire] followed, bringing a small basket of provisions. At about one we arrived in Gros Bois, where, under the shade of the trees, we ate our bread and fruit, and drank our wine, thinking of Don Quixote and Sancho. (p. 16)

In point of time the two journeys recorded in the *Tour* are divided by the Hundred Days and Waterloo. Amid much shrewd and delightful observation, it is the revenge of the Cossacks that most impresses Mary as she travels through France in 1814:

Nothing could be more entire than the ruin which these barbarians had spread as they advanced . . . the distress of the inhabitants, whose houses had been burned, their cattle killed, and all their wealth destroyed, has given a sting to my detestation of war . . . (p. 19)

Two years later her political comments are sharper. Since 'the last invasion of the Allies' there is a different attitude among the French:

the discontent and sullenness of their minds perpetually betrays itself. Nor is it wonderful that they should regard the subjects of a government which fills their country with hostile garrisons, and sustains a detested dynasty on the throne, with . . . acrimony and indignation . . . (pp. 86–7)

Shelley is no doubt present in all this. His own letters have similar observations (a blackened beam from which prisoners of Chillon were hanged suggests 'that cold and inhuman tyranny, which it has been the delight of man to exercise over man', p. 130), but the new friendship with Byron gives to the writing of this summer a special quality. Sailing together on Lake Geneva, the two poets distance themselves from past and present relationships – from Claire, for instance, who had imposed herself on Byron in London, and is now pregnant and demanding. Near Mellorie they are almost drowned in a sudden squall that 'produced waves of a frightful height, and covered the whole surface [of the lake] with a chaos of foam' (p. 120). Shelley cannot swim, Byron has swum the Hellespont; together they sit with arms crossed 'every instant expecting to be swamped' (p. 121). 'He don't lack courage', was Byron's approving comment.

Chillon, with dungeons under the lake, produces its horrors, Clarens its delights. While Byron composes *Childe Harold* Canto Three, Shelley has been reading Rousseau's *La nouvelle Héloïse* (*Eloisa*) in the boat. Entirely captivated, Shelley enters into the fantasy of the people of Clarens 'that the persons of [the] romance had actual existence':

A thousand times, thought I, have Julia and St. Preux walked on this terrassed road, looking towards these mountains which I now behold; nay, treading on the ground where I now tread. From the window of our lodging our landlady pointed out 'le bosquet de Julie' . . . In the evening we walked thither. It is indeed Julia's wood. The hay was making under the trees: the trees themselves were aged, but vigorous, and interspersed with younger ones, which are destined to be their successors, and in future years, when we are dead, to afford a shade to future worshippers of nature, who love the memory of that tenderness and peace of which this was the imaginary abode. (pp. 131–2)

At the Castle of Clarens the two poets gather roses on the terrace 'in the feeling that they might be the posterity of some planted by Julia's hand' (p. 133). In the 'decayed summerhouse' at Lausanne, however, where Gibbon had completed *Decline and fall*, there is a parting of the ways. Byron gathers acacia leaves 'to preserve in remembrance' of Gibbon, Shelley refrains from doing so, 'fearing to outrage the greater and more sacred name of Rousseau'. Gibbon for him has a 'cold and unimpassioned spirit' (pp. 137–8).

Commenting on the *Six weeks' tour* in a letter to Moore of 16 December 1817, Shelley sees Byron's company as throwing 'the light of an enchantment which can never be dissolved'. The climax of the summer (and of the book), however, is the trip to Chamouni, made only with Mary and Claire. In prose and in verse, the Alps bring from Shelley his deepest imaginative response. As they enter the Vale of Chamouni Shelley becomes aware of Mont Blanc and what is to be the landscape of his poem:

I never knew – I never imagined what mountains were before. The immensity of these aerial summits excited, when they suddenly burst upon the sight, a sentiment of extatic wonder, not unallied to madness. And remember this was all one scene, it all pressed home to our regard and our imagination. Though it embraced a vast extent of space, the snowy pyramids which shot into the bright blue sky seemed to overhang our path; the ravine, clothed with gigantic pines, and black with its depth below, so deep that the very roaring of the untameable Arve, which rolled through it, could not be heard above – all was as much our own, as if we had been the creators of such impressions in the minds of others as now occupied our own. (pp. 151–2)

# Mary Shelley and P. B. Shelley

'Nature', he adds, 'was the poet, whose harmony held our spirits more breathless than that of the divinest' (p. 152).

'The Poem, entitled *Mont Blanc*', we are told in the Preface to the *Six weeks' tour*, 'was composed under the immediate impression of the deep and powerful feelings excited by the objects which it attempts to describe'. It is 'an undisciplined overflowing of the soul', and rests its claims 'on an attempt to imitate the untameable wildness and inaccessible solemnity from which those feelings sprang' (p. vi). Shelley is not given to self-deprecation, but has chosen to present one of his most profound, complex and beautifully crafted poems as a mere effusion. Rivalling the poet, Nature, the Shelley of *Mont Blanc* takes as his subject not merely the ravine and 'untameable Arve', but the mind for which, and of which, these physical actualities become symbolic:

> Thou art the path of that unresting sound –
> Dizzy Ravine! and when I gaze on thee
> I seem as in a trance sublime and strange
> To muse on my own separate phantasy,
> My own, my human mind, which passively
> Now renders and receives fast influencings,
> Holding an unremitting interchange
> With the clear universe of things around.
>
> (p. 177)

The poetry creates an impression at once of the Alpine scene itself, and of the human mind that (in the act of perception) creates the scene. More distantly it evokes the possibility of a Universal Mind – the 'secret strength of things' that 'governs thought' and inhabits the snows of Mont Blanc – creative both of the landscape and of the poet's imagination. Shelley, however, never loses sight of mountain scenery that drew from him the great prose of his letter. The glaciers especially haunt him with their 'work of desolation'. 'One would think', he had written in one inspired image, 'that Mont Blanc, like the god of the Stoics, was a vast animal, and that the frozen blood for ever circulated through his stony veins' (p. 167). The poetry is less whimsical, but no less powerful and strange:

> the glaciers creep
> Like snakes that watch their prey, from their far fountains,
> Slow rolling on; there, many a precipice,
> Frost and the Sun in scorn of mortal power
> Have piled: dome, pyramid, and pinnacle,
> A city of death ...
>
> (p. 180)

# 41

# SAMUEL TAYLOR COLERIDGE

## Sibylline leaves
*a collection of poems*
1817

' "Sibylline", says our Dictionary, [means] "of or belonging to a Sibyl or *Prophetess*": the word cannot therefore, we hope, be appropriated by Mr Coleridge, who is not so humble a poet as to assume, voluntarily, the character of an old woman' (*Literary gazette*, 26 July 1817). The *Gazette* was among the first with its review of *Sibylline leaves*, and found the title more pleasurable than the contents:

But on refreshing our classic memory we grasp the very essence and soul of this mysterious title. The Sibyl wrote her prophecies on leaves; so does Mr Coleridge his verses – the prophecies of the Sibyl became incomprehensible, if not instantly gathered; so does the sense of Mr Coleridge's poetry . . .

*Sibylline leaves* appeared in the same week of July 1817 as *Biographia literaria*, but had been in print for two years. Had it come out at once the volume might have been more favourably received. Reviewers brought to it the incomprehension they had felt over *Christabel* and *Kubla Khan*, published with Byron's help in 1816.

As the *Monthly review* pointed out in January 1819, Coleridge's lack of recognition had much to do with bad marketing. For a start, the writer suggests, he should have spun his narratives out into quartos, like Southey and Scott. The case of *The ancient mariner* was particularly unfortunate:

he compresses matter enough for *a handsome volume* into a two-penny pamphlet; then he lets his friend bury his jewels in a heap of sand of his own; then he scatters his 'Sibylline Leaves' over half a hundred perishable news-papers and magazines . . .

The point was a serious one. Before 1816–17 hardly any of Coleridge's major poems had been available to the public. *Kubla Khan* and *Christabel* had circulated in manuscript. *The ancient mariner* had been published anonymously in *Lyrical ballads* 1798, then 'buried' (with insulting obsequies: 'The Poem of my Friend has indeed great defects') under Wordsworth's name in subsequent editions. *Frost at midnight* was almost as deeply interred in the rare *Fears in solitude* volume of 1798. *Dejection: an ode* was among many poems printed only in newspapers; *This lime-tree bower* was tucked away in Southey's *Annual anthology* (1800), and *The nightingale* (like *The ancient mariner*) in *Lyrical ballads*. Even the miscellaneous early poems had not been reprinted since 1803.

*Sibylline leaves*, however, was more than a mere gathering together of scattered poetry. Wordsworth's two-volume *Poems* 1815 had consolidated his reputation; Coleridge was at last taking thought for his own. In the new collection *The ancient mariner* is given pride of place, and thoroughly revised. Famous lines make their first appearance:

> The Night-Mair LIFE-IN-DEATH was she
> Who thicks man's blood with cold.
>
> (p. 14)

Marginal glosses are introduced that prompt an interpretation – sometimes rather flatly, sometimes with enhancing beauty:

In his loneliness and fixedness, he yearneth towards the journeying Moon, and the stars that still sojourn, yet still move onward; and every where the blue sky belongs to them, and is their appointed rest, and their native country, and their own natural homes, which they enter unannounced, as lords that are certainly expected, and yet there is a silent joy at their arrival. (p. 19)

*Frost at midnight* achieves its perfect form. The luxuriance of 1798 is pruned away, but the strength retained, and there is no hint yet of the 'puny flaps and freaks' of the moralized final text (1834). Though little changed from the *Morning post* version of October 1802, *Dejection: an ode* is addressed now to a 'Lady' in place of the Wordsworth pseudonym, 'Edmund' (a step back towards the love-poem it originally was), and includes the magnificent new transition:

> Hence, viper thoughts, that coil around my mind,
> Reality's dark dream!
>
> (p. 242)

No ambitious distinctions – such as Wordsworth's 'Poems of the Imagination', 'Poems of the Fancy' – are attempted in *Sibylline leaves*.

The term 'Conversation Poem', however, is used for the first time (replacing 'A Conversational Poem' as subtitle to *The nightingale*), and Coleridge's heading, 'Meditative Poems in Blank Verse', points the way to the now traditional grouping. Ignoring chronology, the sequence in *Sibylline leaves* opens with *Hymn before sunrise* and includes (among other poems), *Lines written at Elbingerode, The Eolian harp, Reflections on having left a place of retirement, This lime-tree bower, To William Wordsworth* (here called *To a gentleman*), *The nightingale* and *Frost at midnight*.

Hazlitt remarked of Coleridge in *The spirit of the age*: 'All that he has done of moment, he had done twenty years ago' – adding, a little unkindly, 'since then, he may be said to have lived on the sound of his own voice' (p. 64). Like *Biographia, Sibylline leaves* was an apologia for the writer's literary life. Leaves from the past had to be collected and arranged to establish a pattern, find out what was the message of his undoubtedly prophetic voice. Almost all the poetry that Coleridge was working with in 1815 belonged to the years 1793–1803. Much of it proclaimed the Unitarian pantheism to which he still felt drawn, but which he had long been trying to talk himself out of. As in the definitions of *Biographia*, the result was a compromise, but one that leaned heavily in the direction of his early views.

*Religious musings* – climax of *Poems on various subjects* (1796), and great Unitarian statement of belief – is left out of *Sibylline leaves*. Yet in its place Coleridge inserts *The destiny of nations*, written in 1795 as part of Southey's *Joan of Arc*, and no less assertive in its Priestleyan view of a world charged (as by electricity) with the presence of God:

> Glory to Thee, Father of Earth and Heaven!
> All conscious PRESENCE of the Universe!
> Nature's vast Ever-acting ENERGY!
> In Will, in Deed, IMPULSE of All to All!
> (p. 302)

That Coleridge should choose in 1815 to print material of this kind might be explained as his being true to a former self. That the greatest of all his pantheist statements should actually have been written at this late period is inexplicable except in terms of his being still emotionally committed to the Unitarianism he believed himself to have renounced.

It is in the *Errata* of *Sibylline leaves* (added in 1817) that *The Eolian*

*Harp* acquires the great central lines, so often read as typifying the work of Coleridge's pantheist youth:

> O! the one Life, within us and abroad,
> Which meets all Motion, and becomes its soul,
> A Light in Sound, a sound-like power in Light,
> Rhythm in all Thought, and Joyance every where –
> Methinks, it should have been impossible
> Not to love all things in a world so fill'd . . .
>
> (p. xi)

# 42

## WILLIAM HAZLITT

---

# Political essays

*with sketches of public characters*
1819

Hazlitt, whose flair for opening sentences makes him a Donne among prose-writers, begins *Political Essays* with the words, 'I am no politician'. It is not a case of modesty:

Still less can I be said to be a party-man . . . I have a hatred of tyranny, and a contempt for its tools; and this feeling I have expressed as often and as strongly as I could. I cannot sit down quietly under the claims of barefaced power, and I have tried to expose the little arts of sophistry by which they are defended. (p. vii)

The essays that follow this plain-speaking Preface show Hazlitt to be very much his own man. He is an acute and disdainful observer of different tools of 'barefaced power', and different political sophistries:

A Tory is one who is governed by sense and habit alone. He considers not what is possible, but what is real; he gives might the preference over right . . . He says what others say; he does as he is prompted by his own advantage. He knows on which side his bread is buttered . . . (p. xxvi)

What then of the Opposition? 'A modern Whig', we are told, with no less sharpness and no more charity, 'is but the fag-end of a Tory',

a coward on both sides of a question, who dare not be a knave nor an honest man, but is a sort of whiffling, shuffling, cunning, silly, contemptible, unmeaning negation of the two . . . He is on bad terms with the Government, and not on good ones with the people. (p. xxxiii)

Perhaps the reformers – non-party men, like Hazlitt himself – will be treated with more sympathy? They, at least, should be on good terms with the people. But no:

# William Hazlitt

> Tory sticks to Tory: Whig sticks to Whig: the Reformer sticks neither to him-
> self nor to any body else . . . He would rather have slavery than liberty, unless it
> is a liberty precisely after his own fashion: he would rather have the Bourbons
> than Buonaparte; for he is truly for a Republic, and if he cannot have that, is
> indifferent about the rest. (pp. xxi–iii)

The last comment is a reminder of Hazlitt's passionate Bonapartism.
As a republican, Wordsworth had denounced Napoleon's coronation
in 1804 as restoration of the hated French monarchy. For Hazlitt,
monarchy or no monarchy, Napoleon rises from the Revolution and
remains an embodiment of its principles. To some extent he has Byron
on his side. But neither Byron's identification in *Poems* 1816 with the
Satanic fallen Bonaparte, nor his contempt in *Childe Harold* for the
Allies' replacement of one great tyrant by numerous petty ones, is to
be compared with Hazlitt's principled stand. There can be no doubt
that allegiance to Napoleon led to some of his less balanced judgments,
but Hazlitt is to be seen (with Shelley) as the Romantic who stuck to
his beliefs. Southey, author of the republican *Wat Tyler* in 1794, had
twenty years later become Poet Laureate and a notable turncoat.
Coleridge, his brother-in-law, had taken in middle age to lying to himself and others about never having been a jacobin. Wordsworth, though
he never renounced his faith in the French Revolution, was not above a
little toadying to the British aristocracy, and by the time of the 1818
election was campaigning for his tory patron. Like Shelley (for whom
Wordsworth was the 'lone star' of liberty who deserted his post)
Hazlitt remains a political thinker from first to last. He appears in many
roles – philosopher of the mind, literary theorist, essayist and critic,
inspired commentator on his age – but never retreats from the fight
against tyranny and social injustice.

The articles gathered together in *Political essays* derive from many
sources, notably the *Morning chronicle* and *Examiner*, but also the
*Champion, Morning post, Yellow dwarf* and even the *Edinburgh*. Most
belong to the years 1813–18, that straddle the battle of Waterloo and
highlight the social problems caused by war. Towards the end of the
volume, however, is a group of 'Sketches from Public Characters'
(Chatham, Burke, Fox and Pitt) written in 1807, and a series of essays
from the same year on Malthus and population. A footnote to the
sketch of Burke suggests that Hazlitt has not come unscathed through
the twelve intervening years: 'This character was written in a fit of

extravagant candour, at a time when I thought I could do justice, or more than justice, to an enemy, without betraying a cause' (p. 361). The sketch is astonishingly generous. One might say of the young Hazlitt who wrote it, as he himself said of Fox, 'He judged of every thing in the downright sincerity of his nature' (p. 387).

Pitt and Malthus have placed themselves beyond such generosity. If Fox is Hazlitt's Antony, Pitt is the cold and scheming Octavius Caesar. Making the most of his 'few talents and fewer virtues', he has lived a life that was successful, manipulative, null:

He has not left behind him a single memorable saying – not one profound maxim – one solid observation – one forcible description – one beautiful thought – one humorous picture – one affecting sentiment. (p. 391)

Pitt's influence died with him; Malthus lives on, his Pharisaic message welcome for all time to those best placed to help their fellow human-beings: the poor man and his family have been doomed to starve by 'the laws of nature, which are the laws of God' (p. 425). It is Malthus's concern for the rising cost of poor-relief that brings forth Hazlitt's most passionate indignation:

Do [the poor] work less hard? Are they better fed? . . . Have they got so much as a quarter of an hour's leisure, a farthing candle, or a cheese-paring more than they had? Has not the price of provisions risen enormously? Has not the price of labour almost stood still? Have not the government and the rich had their way in every thing? Have they not gratified their ambition, their pride, their obstinacy, their ruinous extravagance? Have they not squandered the resources of the country as they pleased? (p. 427–8)

Hazlitt raises journalism to an art form, the brilliance of his prose being matched by a fierce personal integrity that refuses to kowtow. Though not republished until 1990 as a separate volume, *Political essays* gives us the best of all opportunities to see him at work: 'A Poet-laureate is an excrescence even in a Court' (*On court influence*, p. 283); Coleridge is governed by 'fantastic impulse' and 'his own specific levity' (*On Mr Coleridge's lay sermon*, p. 123); the 'dog-kennels [of the wealthy] are glutted with food which would maintain the children of the poor' (*What is the people?*, p. 312); 'the liberty and independence of nations [in Castlereagh's view] are best supported abroad by the point of the bayonet; and morality, religion, and social order, are best defended at home by spies and informers' (*On the spy-system*, p. 242);

certainly the Bourbons form a contrast to Bonaparte, 'a tortoise placed upon the throne of France would do the same thing' (*Dottrell-catching*, p. 7); 'instead of applying for an injunction against *Wat Tyler*',

Mr Southey would do well to apply for an injunction against Mr Coleridge, who has undertaken his defence in *The Courier*. If he can escape from the ominous patronage of that gentleman's pen, he has nothing to fear from his own. (*The Courier and Wat Tyler*, p. 200)

# 43

## JOHN WILLIAM POLIDORI

───────────

# The vampyre
*a tale*
1819


John Polidori, whose father was an Italian emigré, was twenty-one
when in April 1816 Byron hired him in London as his travelling
physician. He seems to have been talented, but vain, and not as aware
as he might have been of the distinguished company he was keeping.
In June he was present with Byron, Shelley and Mary Godwin on the
rainy evening at the Villa Diodati near Geneva, described by Mary in
her 1831 introduction to *Frankenstein*. It was Byron who suggested
that each of the party should write a ghost story to while away the
time. According to her own account, several days passed before Mary
experienced the waking-dream (so close in effect to Coleridge's dream
of *Kubla Khan*) in which the early scenes of *Frankenstein* materialized in
her mind 'with a vividness far beyond the usual bounds of reverie': 'I
saw – with shut eyes but acute mental vision – I saw the student of un-
hallowed arts kneeling beside the thing he had put together' (p. x).
Shelley had meanwhile begun a story 'founded on the experiences of
his early life'. As the author of *Zastrozzi* (written at the age of seventeen), he was the only member of the group with experience as a gothic
writer. On this occasion, however, he seems not to have got very far.
Polidori and Byron both made significant progress.

'Poor Polidori', Mary recalls,

had some terrible idea about a skull-headed lady who was . . . punished for peeping through a key-hole – what to see, I forget – something very shocking and
wrong of course . . . (p. viii)

Byron's idea was more sophisticated: nothing less, it appears, than

# John William Polidori

the first-ever literary tale of a vampire. It is Moore who gives the fullest account of his progress:

During a week of rain at this time, having amused themselves with reading German ghost-stories, they agreed, at last, to write something in imitation of them. 'You and I', said Lord Byron to Mrs Shelley, 'will publish ours together.' He then began his tale of the Vampire; and having arranged the whole in his head, repeated to them a sketch of the story one evening . . . From his remembrance of this sketch, Polidori afterwards vamped up his strange novel of the Vampire.

Polidori's 'vamping up' of Byron's sketch may well have been suggested by the publication of *Frankenstein* early in 1818. *The vampyre* appeared anonymously a year afterwards, prefaced by an account of Byron's life in Geneva, and followed by an entirely fanciful account of his 'residence' at Mitylene. As a silent comment on the situation Murray three months later printed with *Mazeppa* the 'Fragment' of Byron's story that had been written down on 17 June 1816.

There is no reason to think that Polidori in 1816 would have been shown what Byron was writing. It is easy to see, however, why the 'sketch' should have stayed in his mind. The eleven printed pages of the *Fragment* tell a compelling story, building up a portrait of Augustus Darvell that is never openly sinister. Byron's prose is complex and sensitive, capable of hints, qualifications, second thoughts and dissimulations, that suggest an almost Jamesian depth of character.

It was evident that he was prey to some cureless disquiet; but whether it arose from ambition, love, remorse, grief, from one or all of these, or merely from a morbid temperament akin to disease, I could not discover: there were circumstances alleged, which might have justified the application to each of these causes; but, as I have said before, these were so contradictory and contradicted, that none could be fixed upon with accuracy. (1819 *Mazeppa*, p. 61)

Subject to a wasting away that has no obvious physical cause, Darvell agrees to accompany the unnamed young narrator on a Mediterranean tour, leading him (as it turns out) to a Moorish cemetery between Smyrna and Ephesus, that is his chosen place of death. There he binds the narrator by an oath, first to throw his ring on the ninth day of the month (at noon) 'into the salt springs that run into the Bay of Eleusis', then to wait an hour the following day at the ruins of the temple of Ceres. In the final pages of the *Fragment* Darvell dies, amid further suggestions of magical power. The exact place of his grave is ordained by a stork with a snake writhing in its beak, come (it would seem) to summon him to Hades. Nothing is ever explained.

Though his condition is such that he might well be resuscitated by vampirism, Darvell is nowhere described as a vampire. Polidori's Lord Ruthven, by contrast, feeds in the course of the story upon three different girls – the daughter of his hostess in Rome, the beautiful Greek, Ianthe, and finally Aubrey's sister. Between the second episode and the third, he dies, binding Aubrey, not to Darvell's magic behests, but simply by an oath not to reveal his death for a year. Much else is different in the two accounts, but it may of course be that Byron's sketch differed from the *Fragment*. Interestingly, Byron spoke of Polidori in 1819 not as stealing his idea, but as 'appropriating' his 'story'. Certain details seem too clumsy to come from Byron: Ruthven's charity, for instance, to the undeserving, and his ruining of innocent families by gambling. On the whole, however, Ruthven, if not very complex, is convincingly portrayed. That his name should be drawn from Caroline Lamb's *Glenarvon* (1816) would have brought Byron to the minds of Polidori's readers, even if they were not already making the identification.

Polidori writes a strong, simple prose, sufficient for a story that moves fast, and shocks by virtue of the novelty and horror of its ideas rather than a pleasure in hints and hesitation:

all who were anxious to bask in the smile of royalty, hastened thither. Aubrey was there with his sister. While he was standing in a corner by himself, heedless of all around him, engaged in the remembrance that the first time he had seen Lord Ruthven was in that very place – he felt himself suddenly seized by the arm, and a voice he recognised too well, sounded in his ear – 'Remember your oath'. (p. 60)

*The vampyre* appeared first in the *New monthly magazine* (May 1819), then in book form, and had the distinction of being produced (over Byron's name) as a *melo-drame* in Paris. A sequel, *The modern Oedipus*, appeared within the year. Polidori, however, failed to establish himself as a writer. Disappointed and in debt, he took prussic acid in December 1821. To literary history he is known as the uncle of Christina and Dante Gabriel Rossetti, and originator of the more famous vampire-stories of Le Fanu (1872) and Bram Stoker (1897). It is a strange thought that *Dracula* as well as *Frankenstein* should come from the single evening at Villa Diodati.

# John William Polidori

How much of *The vampyre* is owed to Byron we shall never know, but he certainly had no part in the sections of the book that purport to be biography. However indulgent he might feel about the appropriation of his story, he was forced to a public denial of authorship by the naivety of Polidori's praise. The account of Geneva 1816 had at least some basis in fact (including as it does the first account of the ghost-story competition); not so Polidori's picture of the eccentric English 'milord' living and doing good in secret in a Greek island-paradise:

we were told, the lord passed many of his evenings and nights till twelve o'clock, reading, writing, and talking to himself. 'I suppose', said the old man, '*praying*, for he was very devout, and always attended our church twice a week, besides Sundays.' (p. 80)

Though he may have been content that *The vampyre* should be bought in error, Polidori can hardly have intended to pass off such propaganda as Byron's own. The skull-headed lady would have seen nothing more improbable through her key-hole.

# 44

# JOHN KEATS

━━━━━━━━━━━

## Lamia

*Isabella, The Eve of St Agnes,*
*and other poems*
1820

Keats's 1820 volume has come to epitomise the second wave of English Romanticism, as the 1798 *Lyrical ballads* of Wordsworth and Coleridge epitomised the first. In the Odes and *Eve of St Agnes* – as in *Tintern abbey* and *The ancient mariner* – we hear a voice that is individual, yet profoundly characteristic of the age:

> Darkling I listen; and, for many a time
>   I have been half in love with easeful Death,
> Call'd him soft names in many a mused rhyme,
>   To take into the air my quiet breath;
> Now more than ever seems it rich to die,
>   To cease upon the midnight with no pain,
>     While thou art pouring forth thy soul abroad
>       In such an ecstasy!
>   Still wouldst thou sing, and I have ears in vain –
>     To thy high requiem become a sod.
>
>                                        (pp. 110–11)

Keats's poignant lines from *Ode to a nightingale* were written in May 1819, at the mid-point of his great creative year (after *The eve of St Agnes, La belle dame sans merci* and *Ode to Psyche*; before the *Grecian urn, Melancholy, Lamia* and *Autumn*). He did not know himself to be ill, but almost certainly had contracted tuberculosis as he nursed his dying brother, Tom, at the end of the previous year. In February 1820 would come the appalling moment when Keats (a medical student till 1817) recognized that the blood he had coughed onto his pillow showed his lungs to be infected: 'I cannot be deceived in that colour; that drop of

# John Keats

blood is my death-warrant; I must die' (Brown, p. 65). Keats's fully-trained doctors were less perceptive. Thinking his illness merely nervous, they told him to rest. And they bled him – as Byron's physician would bleed him at Missolonghi, fatally weakening his resistance.

Anxious about money, and never truly reassured about his health, Keats decided to put together his next collection at once. Since his illness, he tells Fanny Brawne in an undated note of February 1820, she has had to share his thoughts with 'That last infirmity of noble mind', the wish for fame:

'If I should die', said I to myself, 'I have left no immortal work behind me – nothing to make my friends proud of my memory – but I have lov'd the principle of beauty in all things, and if I had had time I would have made myself remember'd.'

'Perhaps on your account', he writes, more hopefully, a month or so later,

I have imagined my illness more serious than it is: how horrid was the chance of slipping into the ground instead of into your arms . . . Take care of yourself dear that we may both be well in the Summer.

'I do not at all fatigue myself with writing', he adds, 'having merely to put a line or two here and there . . .' He had been forbidden to write new poetry, just as he had been forbidden to spend any length of time with Fanny (so close at Hampstead that her movements could be watched through the window), in case excitement should bring on an attack.

Revision was completed by April, and copy sent off to Taylor and Hessey, publishers of *Endymion. Isabella; or the pot of basil* went back two years to spring 1818. The original *Hyperion* was included, though it had been written chiefly in the days of Tom's illness, and Keats had tried hard to rewrite it. The bulk of the volume, however, belonged to 1819, the period between the poet's contracting of tuberculosis and his becoming too ill to write. In June 1820 he had another severe hemorrhage, and for the first time there was talk of his going to Italy. The poems came out at the beginning of July. Lamb's review in the *New Times* appeared on the 19th, setting a favourable trend, though unusual in singling out *Isabella* as 'the finest thing in the volume'. The *Monthly* followed at once, proclaiming *Hyperion* 'decidedly the best of Mr Keats's productions'. His writing, we are told, is 'obscure', shocking to 'our ideas of poetic decorum', yet 'displays the ore of true poetic genius'. The *Guardian*, on 6 August, was almost slavish: 'We open this volume with an indescribable feeling of reverence and curiosity.' Keats's lack of decorum seldom went unnoticed, jibes at the Cockney School continued, but there could be no doubt that he had won acceptance.

His fellow cockney, Hunt, knew him best, and offered the most thoughtful assessment. *'Endymion'*, he wrote on 2 August,

with all its extraordinary powers, partook of the faults of youth, though the best ones; but the reader of *Hyperion* and these other stories would never guess that they were written at twenty. The author's versification is now perfected, the exuberances of his imagination restrained, and a calm power, the surest and loftiest of all power, takes place of the impatient workings of the younger god within him. The character of his genius is that of energy and voluptuousness, each able at will to take leave of the other, and possessing, in their union, a high feeling of humanity . . . Mr Keats undoubtedly takes his seat with the oldest and best of our living poets.

The praise was just, but came too late. Keats's thoughts on the five-week voyage to Italy, and during the sad heroic months in Rome, were wholly with Fanny. 'I can bear to die – I cannot bear to leave her', he wrote to Brown on 1 November: 'I am afraid to write to her – to receive a letter from her – to see her handwriting would break my heart'. Two weeks before he died at the age of twenty-five on 23 February 1821, Keats suggested to Severn his bleak epitaph: 'Here lies one whose name was writ in water.'

Shelley had written while Keats was still in England to suggest he come to Livorno; learning now of his death, he composed for him the great funeral-elegy, *Adonais*. 'My spirit's bark', the poem ends,

> is driven,
> Far from the shore, far from the trembling throng
> Whose sails were never to the tempest given . . .
> I am borne darkly, fearfully, afar;
> Whilst, burning through the inmost veil of Heaven,
> The soul of Adonais, like a star,
> Beacons from the abode where the Eternal are.

That a copy of Keats's poems should have been in Shelley's pocket in August 1822 when his body was washed ashore on the Italian coast must be among the most touching details of literary history. Metaphor

had become fact. Half in love with death, Shelley had 'given' the un-
furled sails of the *Don Juan* to a Mediterranean tempest – driven the
boat under in the eye of the storm.

It is Arthur Hallam who defines both Shelley and Keats for the next
generation, shows how they will come to be valued. Unlike Hunt,
'who did little more than point the way', they 'were born poets, lived
poets, and went poets to their untimely graves'. Reviewing Tennyson's
*Poems chiefly lyrical* in *The Englishman's magazine* of August 1831 (two
years before his own untimely death), Hallam draws attention first to
the poets' 'opposite genius', then to their special kinship. Shelley, as we
might expect, is 'vast, impetuous, and sublime'; by contrast, 'the tenderness of Keats cannot sustain a lofty flight'. There is, however, 'a
ground-work of similarity'. For all their difference, the two men have
attained 'a remarkable point in the progress of literature', a mode of
feeling that leads into Tennyson, and on:

Susceptible of the slightest impulse from external nature, their fine organs
trembled into emotion at colours, and sounds, and movements, unperceived or
unregarded by duller temperaments. Rich and clear were their perceptions of
visible forms; full and deep their feelings of music. So vivid was the delight
attending the simple exertions of eye and ear, that it became mingled more and
more with their trains of active thought, and tended to absorb their whole being
into the energy of sense. Other poets *seek* for images to illustrate their conceptions;
these men had no need to seek: they lived in a world of images . . .

# 45

## LORD BYRON

---

# Three plays
### (*Sardanapalus, a tragedy. The two Foscari,
a tragedy. Cain, a mystery*)
### 1821

Byron was in Ravenna, waiting to take part in a revolution, when
*Sardanapalus* was started. It was January 1821, and he was almost thirty-
three. In December *Don Juan* Canto Five had gone off to Kinnaird in
London. The ménage with Teresa Guiccioli was looking remarkably
settled, not least because of Byron's liking for her father and brother,
aristocratic fellow-conspirators in the Carboneria. 'I must put more
love into *Sardanapalus* than I intended', he noted in his journal after
going over the preliminary sketch with Teresa on the evening of the
13th. Byron had portrayed romantic love many times since *The Giaour*
of 1813, but in Sardanapalus and the Ionian slave girl, Myrrha, he
offers both passion and sustained relationship. Myrrha brings out qualities in the King that would otherwise be unperceived, enabling Byron
to present an extraordinary array of his own thoughts, doubts, questions, weaknesses and strengths.

Salamenes' opening speech tells us at once not to expect the swash-
buckling earlier Byronic hero:

> He must not perish thus. I will not see
> The blood of Nimrod and Semiramis
> Sink in the earth, and thirteen hundred years
> Of empire ending like a shepherd's tale;
> He must be roused. In his effeminate heart
> There is a careless courage which corruption
> Has not all quench'd, and latent energies,
> Repress'd by circumstance, but not destroy'd –
> Steep'd, but not drown'd, in deep voluptuousness.
>
> (p. 5)

187

# Lord Byron

Sardanapalus is partly Byron, part Mark Antony. Like Richard II he dallies, yet dies 'As full of valour as of royal blood'. Other parallels suggest themselves: Arbaces is taunted into treachery by the Chaldean priest, Beleses, as Macbeth is taunted by his wife. Yet the presence of Shakespeare is less dominant than in much Romantic drama. Byron does not work by allusion, and is too experienced to fall into the pastiche to be seen at times in Wordsworth's *Borderers*. Like Shelley in *The Cenci*, he consciously avoids the richness of Shakespeare's style, developing a blank verse that is vivid but plain, without conceit or extended metaphor. It is the interplay of ideas that sustains our interest in *Sardanapalus*. Much of the dialogue is not inherently dramatic, but running through it is a discussion of values that thickens the texture of the play.

Myrrha represents not merely passion, but a Greek independence of mind:

> King, I am your subject!
> Master, I am your slave! Man, I have loved you! –
> Loved you, I know not by what fatal weakness,
> Although a Greek, and born a foe to monarchs –
> A slave, and hating fetters – an Ionian,
> And, therefore, when I love a stranger, more
> Degraded by that passion than by chains!
> Still I have loved you.
>
> (pp. 32–3)

Choosing to die with Sardanapalus, she offers for Ionia a final prayer:

> Then farewell, thou earth!
> And loveliest spot of earth! farewell Ionia!
> Be thou still free and beautiful . . .
>
> (p. 166)

Her last thoughts, however, will be for the 'barbarian' king by whom she has been enslaved, 'abased', yet whom she has freely loved. Like Richard II, Hamlet, Antony, Sardanapalus is unfit to rule. Yet no one denies that he has given peace to his vast empire. And despite the emphasis on 'voluptuousness' (scarcely borne out in monogamous love), his motives have been good: 'To me war is no glory – conquest no / Renown' (p. 132). What unfits him is apparently that the ruled see peace as weakness. Forced into action, he rouses the 'careless courage' noted by Salemenes, and dies with Marlovian grandeur.

Byron had provided arms for his 'fellow Carbonics', and in January 1821 was expecting to display his own 'latent energies' in fighting alongside them. Teresa had reason to think herself a model for the passionate Myrrha. At every level the ideas, emotions, drama, of *Sardanapalus* owe more to the Italian present of the writer than to the distant Assyrian past. *The two Foscari*, by contrast, is genuinely 'An Historical Tragedy'. Byron wrote it in less than a month (12 June–9 July), condensing French sources that are printed as an appendix to show how close he kept to the facts. It is a story of vindictive revenge, long drawn-out endurance and duty that suffers in silence. Among the characters, Marina comes to life in her indignation, but the play is starved of a Byronic presence. There was scope for identification neither in the three-times tortured Jacopo Foscari, nor in the Doge, his father, who so sternly presides over the sufferings of his son.

'What think you of Lord Byron's last Volume', Shelley wrote on 26 January 1822, 'In my opinion it contains finer poetry than has appeared in England since the publication of *Paradise Regained*'. '*Cain*', he adds, 'is apocalyptic – it is a revelation not before communicated to man.' The more usual response is expressed by Lockhart in the January issue of *Blackwood's*: 'taken altogether, it is a wicked and blasphemous performance, destitute of any merit sufficient to overshadow essential defects of the most abominable nature.' To the *Gentleman's magazine* for December 1821, the play is 'neither more nor less than a series of wanton libels on the Supreme Being'. In the circumstances it is interesting that Scott should have accepted Byron's dedication. Writing to Murray as he did so on 17 December 1821, he was flattered and untroubled:

I do not know that his Muse has ever taken so lofty a flight amid her former soarings. He has certainly matched Milton on his own ground. Some part of the language is bold, and may shock one class of readers ... But then they must condemn *Paradise Lost* if they have a mind to be consistent.

Byron himself was from the first pleased with his play. 'I have a good opinion of the piece as poetry', he told Murray on 12 September 1821, 'it is in my gay metaphysical style, and in the *Manfred* line'. To Moore, on the 19th, he gave an account of Cain's 'voyage among the stars, and afterwards to Hades'. 'You may suppose', he adds, 'the small talk which takes place between him and Lucifer upon these matters is not quite canonical':

# Lord Byron

The consequence is, that Cain comes back and kills Abel in a fit of dissatisfaction, partly with the politics of Paradise . . . partly because (as it is written in Genesis) Abel's sacrifice was the more acceptable to the Deity. I trust that the Rhapsody has arrived – it is in three acts, and entitled 'A Mystery', according to the former Christian custom, and in honour of what it probably will remain to the reader.

*Cain* is many things: a confronting of the text of *Genesis*, and of the concept of divine benevolence; a blending of *Paradise lost* with the legend of Faust; a vision of how Eve would have aged; a sci. fic. voyage into space and earlier worlds (presupposed by Cuvier on the basis of fossil remains); a reconstruction of events leading to the first murder; a portrayal of the perfect (and perfectly inevitable) incestuous relationship; a challenge to settled opinion; a vehicle for the questioning mind of the writer. No doubt Byron did intend to shock, but his play is brilliantly thoughtful:

> *Cain*              I lately saw
> A lamb stung by a reptile: the poor suckling
> Lay foaming on the earth, beneath the vain
> And piteous bleating of its restless dam;
> My father pluck'd some herbs, and laid them to
> The wound . . .
> Behold, my son! said Adam, how from evil
> Springs good!
> *Lucifer*              What didst thou answer?
> *Cain*                 Nothing; for
> He is my father: but I thought, that 'twere
> A better portion for the animal
> Never to have been *stung at all*, than to
> Purchase renewal of its little life
> With agonies unutterable . . .
>
> (p. 400)

# 46

## THOMAS DE QUINCEY

## Confessions of an English
## opium-eater
### 1822

*Confessions of an English opium-eater* must be the strangest of the great works of English literature. De Quincey writes from no settled position, and his confessions, though broadly autobiographical, fit into no established genre. Medical details, and warnings of the evils of drug addiction, may at any moment turn to boastfulness, or become a paean of praise for 'just, subtle, and mighty opium' (p. 114). Though on one level opium is 'the true hero of [the] tale' (pp. 180–1), on another it is almost an irrelevance. As a disciple of Wordsworth – and the only Romantic, other than Coleridge, to have read the unpublished *Prelude* – De Quincey is fascinated by the workings of memory and consciousness. The form that he adopts is an enactment of the moods, probings, compulsions, associations, of the mind that is its own true subject:

> Of this, at least, I feel assured, that there is no such thing as *forgetting* possible to the mind; a thousand accidents may, and will interpose a veil between our present consciousness and the secret inscriptions on the mind ... but alike, whether veiled or unveiled, the inscription remains for ever ... (p. 160)

The dreams that form the climax of *Confessions* seem in fact to have been its starting-point. It was through them that opium revealed to De Quincey, as the intensity of childhood memories revealed to Wordsworth, the powers and potential of his own imagination. Both writers find their inspiration in the past, but where Wordsworth is concerned chiefly with the interaction of mind and Nature, De Quincey sees past and present as bound together 'by subtle links of suffering' (p. 81). His father, a Manchester businessman, had died of tuberculosis when he was seven. Still earlier, and still more important, were the deaths of his sisters, Jane and Elizabeth, with whom he had briefly shared security and love. Adolescence only compounded the loneliness of childhood. Running away from Manchester Grammar School just before his seventeenth birthday, De Quincey was prepared to lead a penniless, half-starved existence in London rather than go back to his mother and guardians.

At first De Quincey had intended to head for Westmorland, but 'accident', as he put it, gave his steps 'a different direction'. In his pocket as he left the school were two books that tell us much about his temperament, forming in effect the poles between which his adult life would swing: *Lyrical ballads* and a copy of Euripides. A year later he would write to Wordsworth in terms of hero-worship, expressing his 'admiration', 'reverential love', and a willingness 'to sacrifice even his life' to promote the poet's interest and happiness (31 May 1803). As a runaway in London his consolation was 'to gaze from Oxford-street up every avenue in succession which pierces through the heart of Marylebone to the fields and woods', saying as he did so, '*that* is the road to the north, and therefore to [Grasmere], and if I had the wings of a dove, *that* way I would fly for comfort' (p. 82).

For De Quincey, writing *Confessions* in 1821 (and once again in London), Euripides embodies the tragic irony that it was in Grasmere that the Furies hunted him down:

Thus I said, and thus I wished, in my blindness; yet, even in that very northern region it was, even in that very valley, nay, in that very house to which my erroneous wishes pointed . . . that for years I was persecuted by visions as ugly, and as ghastly phantoms, as ever haunted the couch of an Orestes . . . (p. 82)

De Quincey had committed no crime, there was nothing on his conscience comparable to the blood-guilt of the House of Atreus. Yet the Eumenides had found him. In 1807 he had plucked up courage to arrive at Dove Cottage; two years later, when the Wordsworths moved out, he had taken the tenancy. In 1813 (according to his own account) he had become a confirmed opium addict. In 1817 he bid 'farewell – a long farewell to happiness'. Rooms associated with the poetry he had so much admired, and the peaceful life he so much envied, became the setting of dreams of 'unimaginable horror':

I was stared at, hooted at, grinned at, chattered at, by monkeys, by paroquets, by cockatoos. I ran into pagodas: and was fixed, for centuries, at the summit, or in secret rooms; I was the idol, I was the priest; I was worshipped; I was sacrificed. I fled from the wrath of Brama through all the forests of Asia: Vishnu hated me: Seeva laid wait for me. I came suddenly upon Isis and Osiris: I had done a deed, they said, which the ibis and the crocodile trembled at. I was buried for a thousand years, in stone coffins, with mummies and sphinxes, in narrow chambers at the heart of eternal pyramids. I was kissed, with cancerous kisses, by crocodiles; and laid, confounded with all unutterable slimy things, amongst reeds and Nilotic mud. (pp. 170–1)

The opium-dreams single De Quincey out, confirming that he, like the Wordsworth of the *The prelude*, is 'a chosen son'. His sense of self – strong from the first – is validated by the special nature of his suffering. Through the grander myth-making of *Suspiria de profundis* (written in the 1840s) he will seek to understand this, fitting experience into a Christian pattern of the God who cares, and seeing life in its entirety as an education through pain. *Confessions* is more immediate. De Quincey knows that the 'subtle links' of his suffering derive 'from a common root', but this he associates with adolescence and the loss of his 'youthful benefactress', Ann, not (as will be the case in *Suspiria*) with childhood and the death of his sister, Elizabeth. Ann, the fifteen-year-old prostitute who befriends him in Oxford Street, is central to *Confessions*. It is her book. We read of De Quincey's separation from her, and his desperate never-ending search, unaware that in the background lies the earlier deprivation:

to this hour, I have never heard a syllable about her. This, amongst such troubles as most men meet with in this life, has been my heaviest affliction. – If she lived, doubtless we must have been sometimes in search of each other, at the very same moment, through the mighty labyrinths of London; perhaps even within a few feet of each other – a barrier no wider than a London street, often amounting to a separation for eternity! (p. 78)

No logic underlies De Quincey's sense of being punished. It is as if hope itself has betrayed him into the power of the Furies – hope that Wordsworth's paradise of Grasmere could be paradise for him, hope that life could be lived on the level of his pleasure in *Lyrical ballads*. Many aspects of De Quincey's life at Dove Cottage were in fact positive and enhancing. Peggy Simpson from Nab Scar became not just his wife, but the Electra to his Orestes (Electra's role in the *Oresteia*, and Euripides' 'beautiful exhibition of the domestic affections', being spelt out in a footnote for the unlearned). The cottage itself is affectionately

# Thomas de Quincey

described: 'candles at four o'clock, warm hearth-rugs, tea, a fair tea-maker, shutters closed, curtains flowing . . .' (p. 137). On his unexpected arrival, the Malay (who runs so terribly 'a-muck', creating the Oriental dreams, and introducing 'the cursed crocodile') takes part in a scene of charming incongruity, 'his turban and loose trousers of dingy white relieved upon the dark panelling', and his face, 'enamelled or veneered with marine air', contrasting with the 'exquisite fairness' of the servant-girl, Barbara Lewthwaite. Still more striking is the juxtaposition of horror and domesticity as De Quincey wakes (like Lear with Cordelia) to find his children, 'come to show their coloured shoes':

All the feet of the tables, sofas, &c. soon became instinct with life: the abominable head of the crocodile, and his leering eyes, looked out at me, multiplied into a thousand repetitions: and I stood loathing and fascinated . . . many times the very same dream was broken up in the very same way: I heard gentle voices speaking to me (I hear every thing when I am sleeping); and instantly I awoke: it was broad noon; and my children were standing, hand in hand, at my bed-side; come to show me their coloured shoes, or new frocks, or to let me see them dressed for going out. (p. 172)

Like the opium with which it is so closely linked, Grasmere can bring 'an assuaging balm' to 'wounds that will never heal' (p. 114). There are moods in which the 'good and gracious nature' of Margaret (p. 86) can make it seem right to have been looking towards the North for comfort. But the wounds remain. (In fact – though we do not see it in these terms in *Confessions* – they are compounded, by the death in 1812 of yet another version of Elizabeth, the six-year-old Catharine Wordsworth.) In the double dream of Easter Sunday (pp. 174–7), De Quincey at last finds Ann. Seated 'upon a stone, and shaded by Judean palms', she is beautiful as ever, yet 'with unusual solemnity of expression'. She partakes, it seems, of 'the first fruits of resurrection'. The dream ends in touching wish-fulfilment:

I now gazed upon her with some awe, but suddenly her countenance grew dim, and, turning to the mountains, I perceived vapours rolling between us; in a moment, all had vanished; thick darkness came on; and, in the twinkling of an eye, I was far away from the mountains, and by lamp-light in Oxford-street, walking again with Ann – just as we walked seventeen years before, when we were both children. (p. 177)

Hints of Mary Magdalen at the tomb on Easter Morning, of the penitent Magdalen redeemed, of a heavenly future togetherness, are

194

suppressed as De Quincey's dreaming mind takes him back to Ann as she was. Only the actuality of the past can truly assuage. Thus it is that the final dream of *Confessions* ends in apocalyptic battle and 'everlasting farewells':

Some greater interest was at stake; some mightier cause than ever the sword had pleaded, or trumpet had proclaimed. Then came sudden alarms: hurryings to and fro: trepidations of innumerable fugitives. I knew not whether from the good cause or the bad: darkness and lights: tempest and human faces: and at last, with the sense that all was lost, female forms, and the features that were worth all the world to me, and but a moment allowed . . .

Ann appears, but only in the moment of 'eternal separation':

clasped hands, and heart-breaking partings, and then – everlasting farewells! and with a sigh, such as the caves of hell sighed when the incestuous mother uttered the abhorred name of death, the sound was reverberated – everlasting farewells! and again, and yet again reverberated – everlasting farewells! (pp. 178–9)

In the early text of *Confessions* (lengthened and weakened in 1856) De Quincey emerges unmistakably as one of the great Romantics. It was his fate to write prose in an age of poetry – but prose of astonishing intensity. To use his own more intelligent distinction, between the literature of knowledge and the literature of power, he stands among the most powerful writers of the day.

# 47

# WILLIAM HAZLITT

---

## The spirit of the age
### *or contemporary portraits*
### 1825

Nobody has written a more brilliant, more enviable, English prose than Hazlitt. No one has matched his ability to evoke, at the time and on the spot, the spirit of an age. Few can have lived in a period of greater literary and political interest. Hazlitt's masterpiece emerges from a series of individual portraits published in the *New monthly magazine* in 1824 as the (plural) 'Spirits of the Age'. Augmenting the series, and publishing it in book-form, he altered the title to suggest the presence of a *zeitgeist* – a single spirit, shared (in whatever degree) by contemporaries as disparate as Bentham and Coleridge, Godwin and Wordsworth, the Reverend Mr Irving and Sir Walter Scott.

Hazlitt allows his definitions to emerge, but the portraits of Bentham and Coleridge – first respectively of the 'reasoners' and the poets – set the tone for much that is to follow. Bentham 'meditates the coming age' and 'writes a language of his own that *darkens knowledge*':

He turns wooden utensils in a lathe for exercise and fancies he can turn men in the same manner. He has no great fondness for poetry, and can hardly extract a moral out of Shakespeare. His house is warmed and lighted by steam. He is one of those who prefer the artificial to the natural in most things, and think the mind of man omnipotent. He has a great contempt for out-of-door prospects, for green fields and trees, and is for referring every thing to Utility.

'There is', Hazlitt comments with delicious understatement, 'a little narrowness in this' (p. 28). Coleridge has been far from narrow. Possessing the genius that Bentham lacked, he has squandered it in a rake's progress through philosophy, theology, literature and intoxicating dreams:

Next, he was engaged with Hartley's tribes of mind, 'etherial braid, thought-woven,' – and he busied himself for a year or two with vibrations and vibratiuncles and the great law of association that binds all things in its mystic chain, and the doctrine of Necessity (the mild teacher of Charity) and the Millennium, anticipative of a life to come – and he plunged deep into the controversy on Matter and Spirit, and, as an escape from Dr. Priestley's Materialism, where he felt himself imprisoned by the logician's spell, like Ariel in the cloven pine-tree, he became suddenly enamoured of Bishop Berkeley's fairy-world, and used in all companies to build the universe, like a brave poetical fiction, of fine words – and he was deep-read in Malebranche, and in Cudworth's Intellectual System (a huge pile of learning, unwieldy, enormous) and in Lord Brook's hieroglyphic theories, and in Bishop Butler's Sermons, and in the Duchess of Newcastle's fantastic folios, and in Clarke and South and Tillotson . . . (pp. 68–9)

And so it goes on – and on – evoking in one breathless, beautiful sentence of more than four pages, such as no one else would have dared to write, the profusion, and the confusion, of Coleridge's intellectual life. Pleasure in his momentum carries Hazlitt along, at first with a semblance of chronology, then doubling back again and again (as Coleridge did himself) to take into account more and more disparate reading. The tone is affectionate, but knowing, and not uncritical. When Hazlitt comes to make judgments, some of them seem harsh: 'If our author's poetry is inferior to his conversation, his prose is utterly abortive' (p. 75). Yet they are seldom wholly unjust. For Hazlitt, Coleridge is the fallen idol, a disappointment in many different ways. Yet he is the author of *The ancient mariner*, 'unquestionably a work of genius – of wild, irregular, overwhelming imagination' (p. 74).

Oppositions come so naturally to Hazlitt that they almost seem to constitute his method. Gifford, who (as editor) is held responsible for the *Quarterly*'s damning review of *Endymion*, is doomed to have his own pedestrian verses quoted alongside *The Eve of Saint Agnes*. Scott and Byron are played off against each other: 'If the one defers too much to the spirit of antiquity, the others panders to the spirit of the age' (p. 176). Mackintosh and Coleridge, we are told, 'have a nearly equal range of reading and topics of conversation'. 'The first', Hazlitt adds, 'knows all that has been said upon a subject; the last has something to say that was never said before' (p. 225). It is a habit that could lead to black-and-white distinctions and judgments that are too snappy to be true. But even those whom Hazlitt most admires are touched by his shrewd deflating wit. And, though he is unconcernedly partisan, he can see qualities in surprising places. Gifford is unforgivable, but Jeffrey, for all the bigotry of his attacks on the Lakers, brings out the rueful comment, 'He ought to have belonged to us!' (p. 321).

'For my part', Hazlitt writes in *The feeling of immortality in youth* (1827),

I set out in life with the French Revolution . . . Youth was then doubly such. It was the dawn of a new era, a new impulse had been given to men's minds . . . the sun of Liberty rose with the sun of Life in the same day, and both were proud to run their race together. (Howe xvii, pp. 196–7)

To 'belong to us' is to be true to the Revolution – or true to the spirit of the Revolution. Like his fellow Lakers, Coleridge and Southey (now Poet Laureate), Wordsworth is a jacobin who has made compromises with the establishment. His genius nonetheless is 'a pure emanation of the Spirit of the Age' (p. 231). His poetry

is one of the innovations of the time. It partakes of, and is carried along with, the revolutionary movement of our age: the political changes of the day were the model on which he formed and conducted his poetical experiments. His Muse . . . is a levelling one. (p. 233)

Byron, by contrast, 'is that anomaly in letters and in society, a Noble Poet' (p. 177). He was born too late, of course, to be politically a follower of the Revolution, but Hazlitt requires that in his writing at least he shall put aside his rank. Failing to do so, Byron lays himself open to criticism that has an evident bias, and yet is so astute as hardly to seem unfair:

He raises his subject to himself, or tramples on it; he neither stoops to, nor loses himself in it. He exists not by sympathy, but by antipathy. He scorns all things, even himself. Nature must come to him to sit for her picture: he does not go to her. (p. 160)

It is not just lordliness that is a betrayal. The spirit of the age demands to be taken seriously – and demands that a writer shall take himself seriously. Hazlitt gives credit where it is due, but sees the 'drollery' as 'an utter discontinuity of ideas and feelings':

Don Juan indeed has great power; but its power is owing to the force of the serious writing, and to the oddity of the contrast between that and the flashy passages with which it is interlarded. (p. 173)

Death the leveller puts an end to the commentary on Byron. It is typical of Hazlitt that, hearing of Missolonghi as he writes, he should have retained the early vehement pages of his essay, and yet made noble amends:

Death cancels every thing but truth; and strips a man of every thing but genius and virtue. It is a sort of natural canonization. It make the meanest of us sacred – it installs the poet in his immortality, and lifts him to the skies. (pp. 179–80)

In his life Byron has trampled upon the spirit of the age, but his death has cancelled all. Whether or not his money and horses could have affected the nationalist war in Greece, he has 'died a martyr to his zeal in the cause of freedom, for the last, best hopes of man' (p. 181).

# 48

## JAMES HOGG

## Songs by the Ettrick shepherd
### 1831

James Hogg – famous as the Shepherd of the *Noctes ambrosianae* (*Black-wood's*, 1822–35), and truly a manual labourer for much of his life – was born in 1770, beside the Yarrow in the Forest of Ettrick. He died there in 1835. Though he claimed to have been at school for six months, he was almost entirely self-educated, working as a shepherd from the age of seven (half-yearly wages consisting of a ewe-lamb and a pair of shoes). During the 1790s he saved £200, but chances of bettering himself disappeared in 1804 when he lost everything in a scheme to buy a farm in the Hebrides. Two years later, Allan Cunningham, attracted by the reputation of his songs and tales, found him ragged and barefoot on a hillside amongst his master's ewes. Not until 1810, when he was thirty-nine, did Hogg go to Edinburgh in the hopes of making his living as a writer. Even then, there were many ups and downs – and many attempts (some unwise, some unlucky) to use his earnings to establish himself as a farmer.

Though Blackwood and Christopher North (John Wilson) were immensely important in Hogg's Edinburgh life, it was Scott whose friendship was the stable influence. The two poets seem to have met briefly in 1802. Hogg's first letter is an attempt to stay in touch: 'it would be presumption in me to expect that you will visit my cottage, but I will attend you in any part of the Forest if you will send me word.' Hogg is 'perusing' Scott's recent publication, *The minstrelsy of the Scottish border*. His letter is full of the awkward forthrightness that is so characteristic, reflecting at once his sense of self and awareness of class distinction:

I am far from supposing that a person of your discernment – damn it, I'll blot out that word, 'tis so like flattery – I say I don't think that you would despise a shepherd's 'humble cot and hamely fare', as Burns hath it; yet though I would be extremely proud of a visit, yet hang me if I know what I would do wi' ye. (30 June 1802)

In 1814 Hogg was introduced to Wordsworth at a dinner in Edinburgh. Not knowing the Lake Poet to be in Scotland, he had expected his fellow-guest to be a celebrated local horse-dealer who shared the surname. Wordsworth at the time had just published *The excursion*; Hogg (who, for all his confusion, knew Wordsworth's shorter poems well) had established his own reputation the previous year with *The queen's wake*. Wordsworth warmed to Hogg's genuineness, and Hogg noted Wordsworth's 'great good humour'. Together they paid a visit to Hogg's father in his Ettrick cottage, and 'traced the windings of the pastoral Yarrow', before heading separately for the Lakes. Unfortunately, when they met up again at Rydal Mount, Wordsworth injured Hogg's feelings (and, if the story is true, showed his own vanity) in a clumsy aside to De Quincey. Hogg was mortified, but there seems to be no ill-will in the brilliant parodies he published in *The poetic mirror* as 'portions' and 'extracts' of *The recluse* (the never-completed philosophical work of which *The excursion* was a part). No one has caught Wordsworth's tones so exactly, no one understood so perfectly *The excursion*'s uneasy blending of lofty and trivial:

> And lo! a vision bright and beautiful . . .
>                a beauteous ass.
> With panniers hanging silent at each side;
> Silent as cage of bird whose song is mute;
> Though silent yet not empty, filled with bread,
> The staff of life, the means by which the soul,
> By fate obedient to the powers of sense,
> Renews its faded vigour and keeps up
> A proud communion with the eternal heavens.
> (*James Rigg*, 16, ll. 27–34)

'Me an Wordsworth', the Shepherd comments at the beginning of the *Noctes ambrosianae*, 'are aboon the age we live in – it's no worthy of us' (*Blackwood's*, March 1825). Though writing a great deal himself, including what now seems his masterpiece, the *Confessions of a justified sinner* (1824), Hogg was for the last thirteen years of his life to be known chiefly through the pages of *Blackwood's* strange literary soap-opera.

## James Hogg

He was the star of the *Noctes*, a series of seventy-one imaginary conversations, to which he contributed as a writer (though forty-one were
by Wilson, and most of the others by Lockhart) and as talker, but
which expanded on his character in a way that amounted to fiction.
Letters suggest that there were difficulties, and show too the condescension of his witty, well-bred friends – Blackwood to Wilson,
1823: 'he will be a most unreasonable porker if he attempts to raise his
bristles' – but on the whole, Hogg was pleased. Wilson's half-serious
view was that the *Noctes* had spread the fame of his genius and virtues
'all over Europe, America, Asia and Africa'.

Hogg's thirty-five major publications cover many forms, but none
came to him so naturally as song. He taught himself to play the fiddle
among his sheep at the age of fifteen. His songs sing themselves –
whether he is mourning the Jacobite cause, laughing with Appie
McGie, waking 'the night wi' Annie O', or watching the lark mount
into the skies:

> Wild is thy lay and loud,
> Far in the downy cloud,
> Love gives it energy, love gave it birth.
> Where on thy dewy wing,
> Where art thou journeying?
>
> (p. 15)

It is fitting that Hogg's death, four years after his songs were collected, should have called from Wordsworth the most spontaneous of
all his later poems. His beautiful *Extempore effusion* links the Shepherd
with the Minstrel (died 1832), and goes on appropriately to become a
*Lament for the makers* in the manner of Dunbar:

> When first, descending from the moorlands,
> I saw the Stream of Yarrow glide
> Along a bare and open valley,
> The Ettrick Shepherd was my guide.
>
> When last along its banks I wandered,
> Through groves that had begun to shed
> Their golden leaves upon the pathways,
> My steps the Border-minstrel led:
>
> The mighty Minstel breathes no longer,
> Mid mouldering ruins low he lies;
> And death upon the braes of Yarrow,
> Has closed the Shepherd-poet's eyes.
>
> (ll. 1–12)

# 49

## PERCY BYSSHE SHELLEY

---

# The masque of anarchy
### 1832 (1819)

Leigh Hunt's publication of *The masque of anarchy* in 1832 brings together two highly important political events: the 1819 Massacre of
Peterloo, in which an orderly protest meeting in Manchester was dispersed by sabres and mounted troops, and the Reform Bill, which
headed off a still more impressive display of working-class solidarity.
'As I lay asleep in Italy', Shelley's poem opens beguilingly,

> There came a voice from over the sea,
> And with great power it forth led me
> To walk in the visions of Poesy.

We are wholly unprepared for the vision, or masquerade, that is to
come:

> I met Murder on the way –
> He had a mask like Castlereagh –
> Very smooth he look'd, yet grim;
> Seven bloodhounds followed him . . .
>
> (st. ii)

In prosaic truth, the 'voice from over the sea' that reached Shelley at
Livorno on 5 September 1819 consisted of a batch of English newspapers sent by Peacock in the days that followed the Massacre.

The meeting at St Peter's Fields had been long planned; the press was
there, and covered its violent outcome in detail. It was to have been a
peaceful display of strength. The crowd, put at sixty to a hundred
thousand, included many women and children. It was unarmed, but
carefully drilled; the different unions and contingents had marched to
the spot, with their banners demanding suffrage and an end to unem-
ployment. Henry 'Orator' Hunt (no relation to the brothers, John and

Leigh, of *The examiner*) was to have spoken, but was arrested almost at once on the orders of the local magistrates. The yeomanry sent in to make the arrest trod a child to death. Detachments of regular cavalry were called up, and in the scenes that followed ten more people were killed. Of the five to six hundred injured, 161 had sabre wounds, and more than a hundred were women. Much of the violence may have been due to panic, but some was clearly not. The *Times* reporter, whom Shelley would have read, witnessed a scene between 'two Yeomanry privates' and a known protester. 'There', said one,

'is that villain, Saxton; do you run him through the body.' 'No', replied the other, 'I had rather not – I leave it to you.' The man immediately made a lunge at Saxton.

Government instigation has never been proved. But the magistrates were congratulated at once by the Home Secretary, Sidmouth (featured by Shelley as Hypocrisy, riding on a crocodile) and the Prince Regent 'for their prompt, decisive, and efficient measures for the preservation of the public peace'.

England was close to revolution: Shelley in Italy was determined to play his part. 'These are', he wrote to Peacock, on 9 September, 'the distant thunders of the terrible storm which is approaching. The tyrants here, as in the French Revolution, have first shed blood.' The ninety-one stanzas of the *Masque* were written, and posted to Hunt for inclusion in *The examiner*, by 23 September – less than three weeks after news of the Massacre arrived. Hunt was afraid to publish, commenting a little disingenuously in 1832:

I thought that the public at large had not become sufficiently discerning to do justice to the sincerity and kind-heartedness of the spirit that walked in this flaming robe of verse. (p. v)

There would certainly have been a prosecution if *The masque* had appeared in 1819, but Shelley's poem (despite its 'flaming robe of verse') is not intended to provoke. Armed conflict must be prevented. Violence must not be met with violence. Law must be upheld. The people are to prevail through the rightness of their cause and the weight of numbers, exerted as a force of passive resistance.

*The masque* makes no direct reference to Peterloo (of three cabinet ministers named, only Sidmouth was personally responsible). Shelley's poem takes the form of a dream, the opening sequence revealing his anger in a surreal, nightmarish form of satire. It is not the Foreign Secretary, Castlereagh, himself whom the poet meets inconsequentially 'upon the way', but Murder, wearing a carnival-mask that looks like him. The seven countries with whom Castlereagh has leagued to delay abolition of the slave trade are transmuted by the dreaming mind into attendant bloodhounds, waiting for 'human hearts to chew'. Fraud, who comes next in the pageant, wears the ermined gown of Lord Chancellor Eldon, who refused Shelley custody of the children of his first marriage. Instead of having a single millstone tied about his neck, as in the Gospel, Eldon weeps the stones in a hail that is attractive and lethal:

> His big tears, for he wept well,
> Turned to mill-stones as they fell;
>
> And the little children, who
> Round his feet played to and fro,
> Thinking every tear a gem,
> Had their brains knocked out by them
> (sts. iv–v)

Still more bizarre, Hypocrisy can be at once 'clothed in the *bible*', and resemble Sidmouth on a crocodile (more tears implied). Shelley has created a world so strange, so full of destructive energy, that anything could be taken for granted – even the massacre of unarmed fellow-citizens.

Wearing a kingly crown, and seated on the white horse of apocalyptic Death, Anarchy sweeps through the English countryside,

> Trampling to a mire of blood
> The adoring multitude.
> (st. x)

The appalling circumstances of Peterloo are being woven into a poem that can talk about turning disaster to advantage. In a re-enactment of the massacre, Hope, daughter of palsied Time, lies down beneath the horses' feet,

> Expecting with a patient eye,
> Murder, Fraud, and Anarchy.
> (st. xxv)

Her rescue, and the death of Anarchy, might be described as supernatural if anything in the poem was anything else. In a work that depends upon personifications (whose name makes explicit their function), we are confronted by an unnamed and unnameable force, the product of a faith that Shelley never chose to define:

> With step as soft as wind it passed
> O'er the heads of men – so fast
> That they knew the presence there,
> And looked – and all was empty air.
>
> As flowers beneath the footstep waken,
> As stars from night's loose hair are shaken,
> As waves arise when loud winds call,
> Thoughts sprung where'er that step did fall.
>
> And the prostrate multitude
> Looked – and ankle deep in blood,
> Hope, that maiden most serene,
> Was walking with a quiet mien:
>
> And Anarchy, the ghastly birth,
> Lay dead earth upon the earth . . .
>
> (sts. xxx–xxxiii)

Christ-like, Hope makes the sacrifice, offering herself as a victim, and, in doing so, reversing the anarchic process of murder, fraud and hypocrisy. Rising, as from death, she is visible for a moment as an inspiration walking on the blood-stained earth, then fades from the poem, her role fulfilled. The 'words of joy and fear' that now 'arise' (as if from indignant earth herself) take the more positive form of exhortation. In effect they are promise, a covenant with the poor:

> 'Rise, like lions after slumber,
> In unvanquishable number,
> Shake your chains to earth like dew,
> Which in sleep had fall'n on you.'
>
> (st. xxxviii)

Confrontation such as that at St Peter's Fields is to be sought ('Let a great assembly be / Of the fearless, of the free'; st. lxv) so that the masses, following the example of Hope, may assert the power that is theirs. Shelley is remarkably explicit:

> 'And if then the tyrants dare,
> Let them ride among you there;
> Slash, and stab, and maim, and hew;
> What they like, that let them do.'
>
> (st. lxxxiv)

Finally *The masque* is a pageant, not of anarchy but of freedom and hopefulness.

Shelley's major works are powerful not least in the fact that no two are alike, but this must be among the oddest and greatest. Hunt's decision to publish *The masque* in 1832 offers an ironic comment which his Preface seems not to perceive. Reform did come, but not for the masses. Their numbers were to be neutralized as the 'tyrants' did a deal with the middle class. The new £10 franchise was nicely judged, buying supporters for the political establishment in sufficient proportion, yet excluding from the vote all but a tiny group (one in 150) of working men.

# 50

# HARTLEY COLERIDGE

## Poems
### 1833

Long time a child, and still a child, when years
Had painted manhood on my cheek, was I;
For yet I lived like one not born to die;
A thriftless prodigal of smiles and tears,
No hope I needed, and I knew no fears.
But sleep, though sweet, is only sleep, and waking,
I waked to sleep no more, at once o'ertaking
The vanguard of my age, with all arrears
Of duty on my back. Nor child, nor man,
Nor youth, nor sage, I find my head is grey,
For I have lost the race I never ran,
A rathe December blights my lagging May;
And still I am a child, tho' I be old,
Time is my debtor for my years untold.

(Sonnet ix, p. 9)

There are greater sonnets, but few more beautifully made. Hartley –
David Hartley Coleridge, to give him his full name – had been from
the first the subject of inspired poetry. *Frost at midnight* and *The
nightingale* celebrated his infancy, the Conclusion to *Christabel* Part
Two showed him already in 1801,

A little child, a limber elf,
Singing and dancing to himself . . .
(ll. 1–2)

In June 1802 his strange other-wordly quality called forth the most
enchanting of Wordsworth's lyrics, *To H.C., six years old*. That Hartley
the grown poet should speak the epilogue seems just. With elegance
and detachment, and quite without bitterness, he rounds off the myth
of himself.

Children of painters and musicians seem often to become painters and musicians; poet sons of poets are rare. Hartley was born in September 1796, just over a year before the writing of *Kubla Khan*. His father's expectations were daunting. 'In truth I have seen handsomer Babies', he wrote on 24 September 1796,

its name is DAVID HARTLEY COLERIDGE – I hope, that ere he be a man, if God destine him for continuance in this life, his head will be convinced of, and his heart saturated with, the truths so ably supported by that great master of Christian Philosophy.

Not only was Hartley to live up to the standards of his theologian namesake (for the time, Coleridge's mentor), he was to give back to his father the childhood he had lost, 'pent mid cloisters dim' in the City of London. '*Thou*, my babe', Coleridge wrote in *Frost at midnight*,

> Shalt wander, like a breeze,
> By lakes and sandy shores, beneath the crags
> Of ancient mountain, and beneath the clouds,
> Which image in their bulk both lakes and shores
> And mountain crags: so shalt thou see and hear
> The lovely shapes and sounds intelligible
> Of that eternal language, which thy God
> Utters, who from eternity doth teach
> Himself in all, and all things in himself.
> (1798, ll. 59–67)

Hartley quotes the lines himself in the notes to his Dedicatory Sonnet, adding ruefully: 'As far as regards the *habitats* of my childhood, these lines . . . were almost prophetic. But poets are *not* prophets' (p. 145).

Hartley gained, and gave, immense delight in his childhood at Keswick, beneath the mountain crags of Skiddaw. To Wordsworth, in *To H.C.*, it seemed that the 'eternal language' was his by right – naturally his:

> O THOU! whose fancies from afar are brought;
> Who of thy words dost make a mock apparel,
> And fittest to unutterable thought
> The breeze-like motion and the self-born carol . . .
> (ll. 1–4)

If *Frost at midnight* did not seem prophetic to the grown-up Hartley, he can hardly have been unaffected by Wordsworth's forebodings:

# Hartley Coleridge

O blessed Vision! happy Child!
Thou art so exquisitely wild,
I think of thee with many fears
For what may be thy lot in future years.

I thought of times when Pain might be thy guest,
Lord of thy house and hospitality . . .
                                    (*To H.C.*, ll. 11–16)

The 'happy child' grew up gentle, charming, weak, and only five-foot tall. He was learned, but lost his Oxford fellowship in 1820 for keeping bad company (failure to adjust himself to the sober ways of Oriel, where Keble and Thomas Arnold were among his colleagues). Returning to the Lake District in 1823, Hartley became a master at Mr Dawes's School in Ambleside, proving a good but frightened teacher:

Strange it may be, but I have an instinctive horror of big boys – perhaps derived from the persecution which I suffered from them when a little one. When I am unwell, which, I thank Heaven, is much seldomer than I have deserved, they are always at me in my dreams – hooting, pelting, spitting at me, stopping my ways . . . (*Memoir*, p. xcviii)

Though he loved from afar, and wrote one poem to 'a very pretty, but very little Lady' who might, one feels, have been suitable, Hartley never married. Publication of his *Poems* in 1833 was part of a larger scheme that involved spending a year in industrial Leeds, turning out lives of the 'Worthies' of Yorkshire (Andrew Marvell amongst them) at the rate of one a month:

I left the land where men with nature dwelling,
Know not how much they love her lovely forms . . .
Now, for the brook from moss-girt fountain welling,
I see the foul stream hot with sleepless trade,
For the slow creeping vapours of the morn,
Black hurrying smoke in opake mass up-borne,
O'er dinning engines hangs, a stifling shade . . .
                        (*From country to town*, p. 25)

There was to have been a second volume of the *Poems*, but the publisher went bankrupt. Hartley lost the only job that had ever suited his talents. The *Quarterly*, meanwhile, though grumbling at the writer's 'overweening worship of Wordsworth', came out in favour of the *Poems*: 'we shall expect more at his hands than from anyone who has made his first appearance subsequent to the death of Byron.' The promise was not to be fulfilled.

Back in the Lakes, Hartley continued to write, but never settled to anything for long. The Richardsons of Nab Cottage by Rydal Water (once the home of De Quincey's wife, Peggy Simpson) befriended him, very much as the Gillmans had befriended his father in Highgate. Until her death in 1845 his mother made arrangements that he should have lodging and clothes – and that he should not have money. Unlike the Wordsworths half a mile away at Rydal Mount, he was known to the whole community, cherished and protected, not as one of them, but as one who belonged. To the end of his life, Hartley wandered, sometimes drunk for days or weeks at a time, but always coming back to the Nab. In January 1849 he died. Wordsworth chose for him a place in Grasmere Churchyard beside his daughter, Dora, saying to the sexton as he did so:

'When I lifted up my eyes from my daughter's grave, he was standing there! Keep the ground for us – we are old people, and it cannot be for long.' (*Memoir*, p. clxxxvi)

Hartley was a link with Coleridge and the distant magical days of *Frost at midnight*. Wordsworth had known him for all but a few months of his fifty-one years. As the 'happy child' of *To H.C.*, he had created and peopled his own Gondal-world, Ejuxria, while round about him was being made some of the greatest English poetry. Such independence could hardly be maintained in his adult writing. A year younger than Keats, Hartley felt the influences that affected the second-generation Romantics, but experienced two of the most dominant in a uniquely personal way. Except in the pastoral *Leonard and Susan* (attacked as slavishly Wordsworthian by the *Quarterly*), he shows himself too good a poet to be guilty of pastiche. Coleridge – so often absent in his childhood – is a revered presence in the poems, never disabling or obstructive. For the most part Hartley is closer to Wordsworth than to his father, but he belongs to the later world of underlying Tennysonian sadness. He has extraordinary facility, and a quiet strength that is his own: 'For I have lost the race I never ran'.

# Index

# Index

# Index

Grammar School, 192; opium-dreams, 12, 191–5.
*Confessions of an English opium-eater*, 12, 191–5; *Suspiria de profundis*, 12, 193
Derwentwater, 16
Dickens, Charles, 61
Dissent in religion, 36; *see also* Dyer, Frend, Price, Priestley
Dove Cottage, *see* Grasmere
Drummond, William, 141, 143
Drury Lane, Theatre Royal, 69, 70, 71, 88, 95, 120, 136
Dryden, John, 126
du Fossé, 25
Dunbar, William, *Lament for the makers*, 202
Dyer, George, 4, 50–3; *Complaints of the poor people of England*, 4, 50–3
Dyer, John, *Grongar hill*, 20

Early death, 58, 59, 185
*Edinburgh review*, 2, 84, 146, 164, 176
Education, 35–8, 52
Eldon, John Scott, lord chancellor, 162, 205
English Revolution of 1688, 4, 33
*Englishman's magazine, The*, 186
Erskine, Thomas, 73
Euripides, 192, 193
*European magazine*, 20, 92
*Examirer, The*, 148, 165, 176, 204

Faust legend, 88, 190
Fox, Charles James, 29, 43, 176–7
France: constitution, 80; imperialism, 41, 106; invasion of Switzerland, 7, 105–6; National Assembly, 25–6, 39, 41, 62; threat of invasion by, 3, 116, 123; war with, 3, 6, 7, 20, 51, 56.
    French Revolution, 2, 3, 144; fall of the Bastille, 24, 54; Fête de la Fédération, 3, 24–5; radical attitudes towards, 3, 5, 6, 7, 24–7, 34, 41, 56, 105, 198; September massacres,

41, 62; the Terror, 4, 5, 6, 7, 25, 29, 34, 106
Freedom, ideas of, 4
Frend, William, 51, 73; *Address to the inhabitants of Cambridge*, 51; *Peace and union*, 51
Frere, John Hookham, 83
Fuseli, Henry, 92, 94

*Gentleman's magazine*, 189
George IV (as Prince of Wales and Prince Regent), 119, 145, 204
Gibbon, Edward, 141; *Decline and fall of the roman empire*, 169
Gifford, William, 197–8
Gilbert, William: *Fragment by a West Indian*, 79–80; *The hurricane*, 10, 79–82
Gilchrist, Alexander, 132
Gilpin, William, 8, 15, 48, 102, 116; Gilpin tint, 103, 104; *The highlands*, 103; *Observations on the river Wye* (*Wye tour*), 16, 48–9, 103; *Mountains and lakes of Cumberland and Westmoreland* (*Lakes tour*), 16, 47–8, 49, 103; *Three essays on picturesque beauty*, 103
Gillman, James and Anne, 211
Girondins, 4–5, 26, 62–3
Gisborne, John, 140
Gisborne (née Reveley), Maria, 92
God: in Blake, 133; in Coleridge, 74–5, 108, 111; in Mme Roland, 7, 65; in Shelley, 140–3; in Wollstonecraft, 9, 93; in Wordsworth, 112, 113
Godwin, William, 141, 196; rationalism, 6, 8–9, 32, 69–71, 73, 91–4, 140, 143; *Caleb Williams*, 69, 91, 98, 101; *Cursory strictures*, 91; *The enquirer*, 91; *Memoirs of the author of A vindication of the rights of woman*, 8–9, 37, 91–4; *Political justice*, 6, 32, 70, 91, 101, 143
Goethe, Johann Wolfgang von, 87–8; *Faust*, 88; *Sorrows of Werter*, 87

215

# Index

# Index

# Index

Nature: in Blake, 149–50; in Shelley, 169–70; in Wollstonecraft, 9, 93; in Wordsworth, 9, 16, 48, 55
Necessity, 100–1, 143, 197
Nether Stowey, Somerset, 8, 99
Newcastle, Margaret, duchess of, 197
*New monthly magazine*, 181, 196
*New Times*, 184
Newton, Isaac, 133
Newton, John Frank, 141
*Noctes Ambrosianae*, 200, 201–2
North, Christopher, *see* John Wilson

*Observer*, 73
Opie (née Anderson), Amelia, 92
Opium, 69; *see also* Coleridge; De Quincey
*Oxford herald*, 165

Paine, Thomas, 53, 63, 93, 141, 143; *The age of reason*, 143; *Rights of man*, 33, 162
*Pamphleteer*, 137
Pantheism, 9, 54–5, 93, 111, 173–4; *see also* Nature; Unitarian belief
Pantisocracy, 6, 72, 73, 101, 124, 161
Peacock, Thomas Love, 128, 167, 204
Peel, Robert, 43
Peterloo massacre, 5, 203–4
Picturesque, 8, 48–9, 60, 102; *see also* Gilpin; West
Pitt, William, earl of Chatham, 176
Pitt, William, the younger, 5, 29, 73, 162, 176–7
Plato, Platonism, 53, 129, 141, 142, 143
Pliny, 141
Plumptre, James, *The lakers*, 8, 102–4
Polidori, John William, *The vampyre*, 179–82
Poole, Charlotte, 72
Pope, Alexander, 113, 126, 145; *The dunciad*, 146
Poussin, Gaspard, 16
Price, Richard, 30, 33, 36, 43, 55

Price, Uvedale, *Essays on the picturesque*, 103
Priestley, Joseph, 36, 43, 51, 73, 74, 100–1, 123, 161, 173, 197; *Catalogue of books written by Dr Priestley*, 54; *Disquisitions on matter and spirit*, 54; *Experiments and observations on different kinds of air*, 54; *Farewell sermon* (*The present state of Europe compared with antient prophecies*), 54–7, 74; *History and present state of electricity*, 54; *History of the corruptions of Christianity*, 54; *Letters to the members of the New Jerusalem church*, 54–7
Prior, Matthew, 126

*Quarterly review*, 137, 160, 164, 197, 210, 211

Racedown, Dorset, 21
Radcliffe, Ann, *Mysteries of Udolpho*, 76, 87
Raphael, 132, 134
*Reflector, The*, 145
Reform Bill (1832), 2, 13, 203, 207
Rembrandt, 134, 135
Reveley, Maria, *see* Gisborne
Reynolds, John Hamilton, 164, 166
Richardson, Samuel, *Clarissa*, 130
Robespierre, François Maximilien Joseph de, 4–5, 25, 56, 62–4, 106
Robinson, Henry Crabb, 11, 60, 81, 131, 134
Robinson, Mary (Perdita): *All alone*, 121; *The haunted beach*, 120; *Lyrical tales*, 119–21; *Ode to the infant son of S. T. Coleridge*, 120; *The snow drop*, 120
Robinson, Robert, 50
Rogers, Samuel, 43–5, 46, 164; *Italy*, 43; *The pleasures of memory*, 10, 43–5, 46; *Table talk*, 44
Roland, Jean-Marie de la Platière, 4, 62–3

# Index

Roland, Mme (Jeanne-Marie Roland de la Platière), 4, 7, 25–6; *Appeal to impartial posterity*, 4, 7, 62–5
Rosa, Salvator, 16
Rossetti, Christina and Dante Gabriel, 181
Rousseau, Jean-Jacques, 4, 28, 30, 66, 67, 101, 141; *Confessions*, 30; *Eloisa (La nouvelle Héloïse)*, 4, 9, 30, 66, 116, 128–30, 169; *Émile*, 66; *Social contract*, 4
Rubens, 134, 135
Rydal, the Lower Fall, 48

St-Pierre, *see* Bernardin de St-Pierre
Sappho, 120
Satanic hero, 40, 98, 176
*Satirist*, 136
Schiavonetti, Louis, 132
Schiller, Friedrich: *The robbers*, 6, 39–42, 137; *Wallenstein*, 39
Scott, Walter, 10, 44, 76, 77, 113, 146, 171, 189, 196, 197, 200; death, 13, 202; *The chase* and *William and Helen*, 76–8; *Essay on imitations of the ancient ballad*, 77; *Lay of the last minstrel*, 44, 146; *The minstrelsy of the Scottish border*, 200
Shakespeare, William, 40, 70, 71, 113, 137, 141, 188
Sharpe, L., 59
Shelley, Mary Wollstonecraft, 92, 158; *Frankenstein*, 8, 90, 167, 179–180; *History of a six weeks' tour*, 9, 167–70
Shelley, Percy Bysshe, 2, 5–6, 43, 44, 128–9, 149, 164, 165, 176, 179, 185–6, 189; death, 3, 12, 140, 185. *Adonais*, 23, 185; *The Cenci*, 188; *The daemon of the world*, 140; *History of a six weeks' tour*, 9, 128–9, 167–70; *Hymn to intellectual beauty*, 129; *The masque of anarchy*, 5–6, 13, 203–7; *Mont Blanc*, 9, 10, 23, 167, 169–70; *The necessity of atheism*, 141; *Prometheus unbound*, 40, 140;

*Queen Mab*, 6, 20, 140–4; *Zastrozzi*, 179
Sheridan, Richard Brinsley, 136, 137
Sherwood, Neely and Jones, 161
Sidmouth, Henry Addington, viscount, 204, 205
Slave trade, 26, 73, 83, 205
Smith, William, 160, 162
Sophocles, *Oedipus rex*, 41
Southey, Robert, 9, 19, 56, 73, 74, 79, 83–6, 95, 99, 100, 109, 112, 113, 115, 116, 121, 146–7, 171, 176, 198; and the French Revolution, 3, 5. *Annual anthology* (ed.), 172; *Botany Bay eclogues*, 83, 113; *Donica*, 85, 121; *The idiot*, 112–13; *Inscription for Henry Marten*, 83–4; *Joan of Arc*, 55, 73, 173; *Letter to William Smith*, 162; *Mary*, 85, 121; *To Mary Wollstonecraft*, 83; *Omniana* (ed.), 153; *The pauper's funeral*, 83; *Poems* (1797), 5, 83–6, 121; *Poems on the slave trade*, 83; *Rudiger*, 85, 121; *The soldier's wife*, 83; *Thalaba*, 19, 146; *Wat Tyler*, 5, 9, 141, 160–3, 176, 178
Spenser, Edmund, 59, 113, 153; *The faerie queen*, 112
Spinoza, Baruch, 141
Spirit of the age, 8–9, 12, 42; *see also* Hazlitt, William
Spy Nozy episode, 123–4
Stanhope, Charles, third earl, 73
Stations, *see* West
Sterne, Laurence, 112, 152
Stevens, Wallace, 7
Stevenson, John, 127
Stoker, Bram, *Dracula*, 181
Stothard, Thomas, 35, 43, 131–5
Stuart, Daniel, 121
Susquehanna, *see* Pantisocracy
Swedenborg, Emanuel, and Swedenborgians, 55, 79–80

Talleyrand-Périgord, Charles-Maurice de, 43

219

# Index

# Index